Railroad Revitalization and Regulatory Reform

Railroad Revitalization and Regulatory Reform

Edited by Paul W. MacAvoy and John W. Snow

Ford Administration Papers on Regulatory Reform

American Enterprise Institute for Public Policy Research
Washington, D.C.

Paul W. MacAvoy is professor of economics at Yale University and an adjunct scholar at the American Enterprise Institute.

John W. Snow is a visiting fellow at the American Enterprise Institute.

Library of Congress Cataloging in Publication Data
Main entry under title:

Railroad revitalization and regulatory reform.

   (Ford Administration papers on regulatory reform) (AEI studies; 173)
   1.   Railroads and state—United States—
Addresses, essays, lectures.   2.   Railroad law—
United States—Addresses, essays, lectures.
I.   MacAvoy, Paul W.   II.   Snow, John W.   III.   Series.
IV.   Series: American Enterprise Institute for Public Policy
Research.   AEI studies; 173.
HE2757 1977.R34   385   77-14955
ISBN 0-8447-3273-7

AEI Studies 173

Printed in the United States of America

CONTENTS

FOREWORD

Early in 1975, I called for the initiation of a major effort aimed at regulatory reform. Members of my administration, and the Congress, were asked to formulate and accelerate programs to remove anti-competitive restrictions in price and entry regulation, to reduce the paper work and procedural burdens in the regulatory process and to revise procedures in health, safety and other social regulations to bring the costs of these controls in line with their social benefits.

My requests set in motion agency and department initiatives, and a number of studies, reorganization proposals, and legislative proposals were forthcoming last year. A number of these resulted in productive changes in transportation, retail trade, and safety regulations. Nevertheless, much remained to be done, in part because of the time required to complete the analysis and evaluation of ongoing regulations.

This volume provides one set of the analytical studies on regulatory reform that were still in process at the end of 1976. Necessarily, these studies would have undergone detailed evaluation in the agencies and the White House before becoming part of any final reform program. They do not necesarily represent my policy views at this time, but they do contribute to the analyses that must precede policy making. I look forward to the discussion that these papers will surely stimulate.

GERALD R. FORD

PREFACE

Railroads were the first industry in the United States to be brought under federal price controls. This occurred with the passage in 1887 of the Act to Regulate Commerce and the establishment of the Interstate Commerce Commission (ICC). Although this legislation has been amended many times, the public-utility-type regulation of the rail industry that was established at the turn of the century has extended to this day. The ICC has far-reaching jurisdiction over pricing, mergers, abandonments, and service in the industry.

Over the last fifteen years, there has been a great deal of criticism of the commission's regulation of the rail industry. Much of this criticism has come from the academic community. Many analysts of the industry have urged a relaxation of ICC controls, arguing that regulation was seriously eroding the basic economic health and performance of the industry.

In January 1974 the Department of Transportation submitted to the Congress a proposal, the Transportation Improvement Act (TIA), which sought to reform ICC regulation of the railroads. Although the bill received considerable attention in the Congress, it was not passed into law. In May 1975 the Ford administration transmitted to Congress its reform proposal, the Railroad Revitalization Act (RRA), which was designed to give railroads greater pricing freedom and more flexibility to adjust their plants to demand condition. The proposal also provided for financial assistance through loan guarantees to assist the railroads in making improvements in their facilities and to encourage rationalization of excess capacity in the industry. The regulatory reform provisions of the RRA drew heavily upon the concepts in the TIA, and much of the basic analysis undertaken in connection with the TIA was relied upon in developing the Ford administration's proposal. The RRA, however, went beyond the TIA and encompassed more extensive reforms.

Hearings were held in both the House and Senate on the issues raised by the RRA. During these congressional deliberations, the questions of regulatory reform, financial assistance, and restructuring were joined with the then-pressing issue of the financial collapse of the rail system in the northeastern United States. In February 1976 President Ford signed an omnibus rail bill, the Railroad Revitalization and Regulatory Reform Act of 1976 (4R Act), which dealt with all of these issues. Although this legislation fell short of the administration's objective, it did contain a number of "reform" provisions. In many cases, implementation of these provisions was left to the ICC, which was given broad discretion in administering them. The job of implementing the reform provisions is now under way at the ICC.

This volume presents a number of background analyses and other documents that underlie the development of the railroad reform proposals. The volume also presents papers that deal with the effort to implement the reform provisions in the 4R Act. Specifically, part one presents an overview of the problems in the rail industry and a discussion of the effect of regulation on the industry. It also discusses the need for corrective action to reform economic regulation of the industry and reviews the basic elements of the Ford administration's reform proposal. Part two deals with some of the basic issues that arose in connection with the debate over deregulation of the railroads. Part three deals with the problem of implementing the reform elements in the 4R Act.

The 4R Act contains the promise of a major reduction of economic regulation of the rail industry. It is still too early to determine with any certainty how significant the regulatory reform provisions of the act will be. Since the administration of the reform provisions has been left to the ICC, the extent of the reform ultimately achieved depends heavily upon the commission. The question arises: How well can such an agency go about self-reform? Or, put another way, can a regulatory agency effectively implement a basic reduction of its own powers? We hope that this volume will contribute to the continuing discussion of government regulation of industry and will further the effort to implement the 4R Act.

PAUL W. MACAVOY
Yale University

JOHN W. SNOW
American Enterprise Institute

November 1977

PART ONE

OVERVIEW OF RAIL INDUSTRY PROBLEMS

When President Ford took office in August 1974, one of the problems that he inherited was the virtual collapse of the entire rail system in the northeastern United States. Action had to be taken to solve that problem and to prevent its reoccurrence in other parts of the rail system. Moreover, early on in his administration, President Ford indicated that he wanted to take steps to reduce federal economic regulation that was unnecessary and harmful to the public interest. The Department of Transportation (DOT) quickly identified regulation of the rail industry as a prime candidate for reform. In 1974 the department had submitted legislation in the 93rd Congress to reduce regulation of the rail industry by the Interstate Commerce Commission (ICC). In the development of that legislation, DOT and others in the executive branch had undertaken extensive analysis both of the problems of the rail industry and of the impact of ICC regulation on the industry. They drew upon a number of important academic studies as well. These analyses and studies all pointed in the direction of less regulation. Thus, when the President sounded the call for regulatory reform, the department was ready and anxious to submit a new and strengthened proposal to the 94th Congress. The proposal, the Railroad Revitalization Act, was transmitted to Congress in May 1975.

In this part we present an overview of the rail industry's problems and an analysis of the effects of regulation on the industry. We also present a review of the Ford Administration's reform proposal. The first paper, drawn from the report of the Task Force on Railroad Productivity, reviews basic problems affecting the rail industry and discusses the direction for corrective action. The second paper reviews the reasons for the financial collapse of the railroads in the Northeast and suggests a number of actions to remedy the situation. This paper is drawn from a report by the Department of Transporta-

1

tion submitted to the Congress in March 1973. The next paper, taken from the Preliminary System Plan prepared by the United States Railroad Administration in February 1975, analyzes the fundamental nature of competition in this highly regulated industry. The fourth paper is drawn from a memorandum by Secretary of Transportation William T. Coleman, Jr., to President Ford setting forth the dimensions of the rail industry problem and calling for action to correct the problem. The final paper in this part, by John W. Snow, one of the editors, is a discussion of the reform proposal that the Ford administration proposed to the Congress—the Railroad Revitalization Act.

1

INTRODUCTION TO THE PROBLEM

Task Force on Railroad Productivity

Railroading is a troubled industry. Virtually every American suffers some consequence of the industry's afflictions. In the absence of traffic growth to offset gains in labor productivity, employment in the railroad industry has declined 61 percent in the past twenty-five years. The rate of return on the investment of Class I railroads in transportation property has averaged only 2.8 percent during the past decade. Unable to obtain the kind of service they need from railroads, shippers with a choice among transport modes have turned to trucks in increasing numbers. Shippers without a choice have suffered higher freight rates and in many instances poorer service as well. The railroads have petitioned for general rate increases in every year since 1967, and the general rate increases allowed by the Interstate Commerce Commission from 1967 through 1971 totaled more than 32 percent.[1] Consumers as well as shippers bear these higher costs of distribution!

To date, the rail crisis has been most acute in the Northeast, where the Penn Central and five other Class I railroads are in bankruptcy and loss of rail service in some areas of the region is threatened. The problems of the railroad industry, however, are by no means confined to the Northeast. Indeed, the Penn Central is in some ways only a more extreme manifestation of trends present throughout much of the industry.

This chapter is edited from the concluding chapter of *Improving Railroad Productivity*, a report prepared for the National Commission on Productivity and the Council of Economic Advisers, November 1973. The Task Force on Railroad Productivity had been established in June 1972 to analyze the problems affecting the rail industry and to recommend steps to improve the industry's performance.

[1] The consumer price index rose only 21.3 percent and the wholesale price index only 13.9 percent during the same period.

What actions, if any, can the federal government take to help the railroads regain their health? Before one can prescribe remedies, an accurate understanding of the problem and its causes is needed. It has been common practice among casual observers of the railroad problem to identify single causes and propose single cures. Railroad management, railroad labor, the Interstate Commerce Commission—all have been identified as "the devil" by various observers. Discriminatory property taxation, passenger train deficits, and even railroad technology itself have also been singled out as *the* cause at one time or another. Each analysis suggests its own cure: abolish the ICC, institute massive subsidies, abrogate agreements with labor about work rules, nationalize the railroads, and so forth. In fact, there is no single cause and no simple panacea for the ills of the industry.

Each of the above factors has contributed, however, to the present problem, and the diagnosis is incomplete without reference to all of them. Not only are there a multitude of causes, but the causes tend to be interconnected. To a large extent, regulatory practices, management practices, labor practices, railroad technology, and so on, are an accommodation to one another. With management and unions unable to agree on the sharing of labor productivity gains, work rules perpetuate jobs that innovation has rendered obsolete. Technology evolves along lines that are consonant with work rules, regulatory practices, and the organizational structure of the industry. Management regards work rules, regulatory practices, and technology as constraints within which it must work. Recognition of the interactive and mutually reinforcing character of the causes of the rail problem should spell the end of overly simple prescriptions—such as nationalization, deregulation, and massive subsidies—for solving the rail problem. Reform must be pursued on many fronts.

Only *fundamental* changes in the industry will restore the railroads to health. Sweeping changes in the U.S. economy have slowed the growth of aggregate intercity freight demand, and these changes, together with the rise of trucking and other transport modes, have profoundly altered the character of rail freight service that is demanded. The railroads have not adapted to these changes with sufficient alacrity. Various institutional arrangements inhibit this adaptation. The most important of these are politically motivated regulation, a Balkanized corporate structure, and counterproductive work rules.

The railroad industry is subject to detailed regulation pertaining to pricing, mergers, entry into trucking, and abandonment. The ICC, responding to political pressures, has used its regulatory powers to cross-subsidize low rates (in relation to cost) to small shippers, to shippers located along some lightly used branch lines, and to shippers of

4

some bulk commodities. Competition from trucks and unregulated carriers has made this policy of cross-subsidization unworkable, as these modes have diverted to themselves the very traffic that is supposed to "carry" the subsidized traffic, and they have forced down rates on this traffic. An unintended side effect of regulation, it is widely agreed, has been to stifle innovation in the railroad industry and, more subtly, to discourage managerial initiative. The cost to the consumer of various inefficiencies in surface freight transportation resulting from detailed regulation of this industry is estimated to be within the range of $4 billion to $10 billion per year.

The present fractured corporate structure of the rail industry severely handicaps railways in developing rail traffic and in handling rail shipments efficiently. Because the railroads must perform as an integrated system, strong and progressive railroads are dependent on weak and less responsive roads. Interrailroad differences and rivalries hinder the joint actions and joint decisions that are essential to the railways' performance as an integrated system. At the same time, competition among railroads is less effective because of the mutual interdependence of the competitors. Balkanization handicaps the railroads most in handling long, interregional shipments that must be interchanged between two or more railroads. Yet, the comparative advantage and greatest traffic potential of the railroads are in just this type of traffic. The formation of four to seven or so independent continental systems (north to south as well as east to west) through predominantly end-to-end mergers will help considerably in solving the industry's problems.[2] Freed of their previous level of dependence on the cooperation of other railroads, the executives of individual railroads will have the ability and incentive to manage effectively and to take promising initiatives in service, pricing, marketing, and technological innovation. Competition among these continental systems, in addition to intermodal competition, will further stimulate managements to be responsive to the needs of shippers. Indeed, the creation of four to seven independent continental systems by merger can actually enhance interrailroad competition.

Management and labor unions have had difficulties in agreeing on an appropriate sharing of the labor productivity gains that have resulted from technological innovation, merger, route abandonments, and reorganization of work. In general, labor unions have been put in the position of standing on job definitions known as work rules to protect workers from uncompensated loss of jobs. By inflating the perceived cost of labor, these work rules have induced management

[2] The dissolution of the Penn Central will probably be essential to the formation of these systems.

to minimize the use of labor whenever possible; for example, by substituting capital and purchased labor services for hired labor and by reducing train frequency to such a point that competitive, long-haul traffic is lost to trucking. Both the short-run and the long-run interests of labor and management would be better served by other ways of sharing productivity gains. Reform of the Railway Retirement System, necessitated by its prospective financial difficulties, offers one opportunity for the federal government to prompt such a solution.

Restrictive regulation, the Balkanized corporate structure, and counterproductive work rules have together discouraged and distorted technological progress in the rail industry. Railroad technology has not adapted to the changing intercity freight market and, in particular, does not permit the railroads to provide the higher standards of freight service that shippers of transport-competitive traffic are demanding. There are a number of innovations that will permit the railroads actually to improve the quality of rail service and to reduce costs simultaneously, thus yielding sizable gains in railroad productivity. The most important of these is "containerization of shipments,"[3] which promises to streamline railroad operations and the railroad network to the benefit of the railroads and shippers alike. Although piggyback traffic is growing year by year, the full potential of containerization is far from being reached. Revision of train schedules and operations and the implementation of a system for managing freight cars promise to improve the speed and dependability of delivery while improving car utilization.

What role has new capital to play in revitalizing the railroads? One of the more striking conclusions of this report is that the railroad problem is more a problem of productivity and of adaptation to changing markets than it is a purely financial problem. The railroad industry as a whole has had fairly good access to private capital, at least for rolling stock. The problem has not been the unavailability of capital so much as an inability to employ new funds profitably under present institutional constraints and with existing technology.

There have been frequent suggestions that federal subsidies or federally guaranteed loans are vital to the survival or recovery of the industry. Several reservations about such a policy might be noted. First, money, per se, does not always cure productivity and marketing problems. Second, the government should be cautious about investing in what may be obsolete technologies. Investments in rehabilitating light-density rail lines, constructing high-capacity automated classification yards, and adding to the fleet of conventional boxcars could ac-

---

[3] *Containerization* refers to both container-on-flatcar (COFC) and trailer-on-flatcar (TOFC), or piggyback, operations.

tually be counterproductive in the sense that such investments deepen the commitment of the industry to what may well be outmoded techniques and could thereby aggravate the problems of the industry. The low average and even marginal rates of return on recent investments in the railroad industry warn against further massive investment in some of the traditional ways of railroading. At any rate, federal funds probably ought not be employed for conventional freight cars for which the industry has fairly good access to private funds. Finally, the railroads have been paying out a comparatively large proportion of net income as dividends, substituting equipment debt for stockholder equity. An overly casual infusion of public funds could be used to substitute for private funds and could thereby end up purchasing the railroads for the taxpayer, that is, nationalization via the back door.

There are, however, several possibilities for which federal money might be used creatively and in return for a genuine social, political, or economic quid pro quo. For example, the federal government may find assisting in the refinancing of the Railroad Retirement System unavoidable; however, it might reasonably expect in return progress toward elimination of counterproductive work rules. The federal government might improve the financial health of the industry and facilitate containerization and the streamlining of rail service by purchasing railroad rights-of-way whose light traffic density justifies abandonment and whose value in other uses, public and private, often might be greater. The government can also stimulate innovations in the railroad industry by sponsoring research in appropriate areas.

The recommendations of this report cover complex and controversial subjects. They strike at the heart of labor-management bargaining, intraindustry and interindustry competition, and the use of scarce private and public investment funds. They even touch on delicate political relationships (for poor transportation service is and should be a political issue). The recommendations call for profound changes in the way corporate officials, labor union leaders, and government policy makers think about railroading and how they conduct their affairs.

This admixture of complexity and controversy means that implementation of the recommendations contained in the report will not be easily achieved. No one should expect that. The reward, however, can be an industry that is modern, competitive, lean, and specialized compared to the railroads of today. This revitalized railroad industry would differ not in physical appearance alone, but in the satisfaction it brings to employees, investors, shippers, and the public.

2

THE NORTHEAST PROBLEM

U.S. Department of Transportation

On February 9, 1973, Congress directed the secretary of transportation to provide, within forty-five days, a plan to deal with the problem of the railroads in the northeastern area of the country. This report is submitted in response to that request.

Before presenting our recommendations, a word of caution is in order. Forty-five days is a woefully brief time to deal thoroughly with problems that, in many ways, have been decades in the making. We have done our best to analyze the causes, to examine alternatives, and to outline what appears to us to be a workable plan of action. Obviously, other plans are possible and with further analysis improvements to this plan might be found. We believe, however, that our broad recommendations are sound and that they are in the overall national interest. We urge Congress to give them close consideration.

Key Conclusions

We arrived at eight key conclusions. First, the nation's private enterprise rail system is neither dead nor dying, even though it is suffering under many long-term burdens. Despite serious problems in the Northeast,[1] many rail companies are doing well and are showing signs of further gains. With prompt corrective action, the overall system

---

This chapter is edited from the study *Northeastern Railroad Problem: A Report to the Congress*, prepared by the U.S. Department of Transportation, March 26 1973. The report was submitted to Congress in response to section 2 of Senate Joint Resolution 59-2, enacted February 9, 1973. This resolution directed the secretary of transportation to provide within forty-five days "a full and comprehensive plan for the preservation of essential rail transportation services in the Northeast section of the Nation."

[1] The term *Northeast* refers to the area included within the Eastern Railroad District as defined by the ICC.

can be restored to its role as an efficient carrier of large quantities of freight, and it can provide rail systems for service by the National Railroad Passenger Corporation (Amtrak) as well.

Second, nationalization of the railroads is unnecessary and would solve little, although it might hide some of the short-term Northeast rail problems under the bed of the federal budget. Experiences elsewhere have made it abundantly clear that nationalization only means increasing subsidies and declining efficiency of resources, which our nation can ill afford. The largely state-owned rail systems of Japan, Great Britain, Germany, France, and Italy now report losses that in total exceed $2 billion per year. Moreover, we do not believe that partial or piecemeal nationalization, such as buying only the roadbeds of the bankrupt or ill carriers, is proper. It is difficult for the federal government to become a "limited partner" in a private enterprise operation, for one thing almost inevitably leads to another. Likewise, such piecemeal nationalization would weaken—and perhaps eventually destroy—the vigor of the private enterprise companies that would be forced to compete with this federally backed operation.

Third, without question we face a short-term rail crisis in the Northeast. Six of the rail carriers in this area are in bankruptcy, and the dominant one—the Penn Central—is on the verge of court-ordered liquidation in order to prevent further erosion of the creditors' estates. Correcting this short-term problem will require cooperative and public-spirited action by all parties involved—Congress, the administration, regulators, labor, creditors, shippers, and the courts. We believe that the problem can—and indeed must—be solved within the broad framework of the private sector. We are recommending such a plan of action.

Fourth, if there were a complete and abrupt shutdown of the Penn Central, the Northeast would, in the short-term, feel the impact quite significantly. Given the ability to make adjustments, however, other rail carriers and trucks would, in time, willingly step in and pick up most of the slack. The Penn Central, per se, is not essential, though much of the rail service provided over its main-line tracks is.

Fifth, although the Northeast has lost some of its rail freight business in recent years, the overall freight total remains quite large. The area is certainly large enough to support one or more new private sector rail systems that could be developed from the various systems owned by the six bankrupt carriers. Also, rail competition, which is clearly desirable, should be able to continue in high-density markets. Our studies suggest that, if permitted to emerge unencumbered from the tangled web that now embraces these carriers, a new entity (or entities) would generate sufficient profits and be able to raise sufficient cash to finance operations and expansions. In a word, quite clearly there is a healthy rail system trying to crawl out of the wreck in the Northeast. All of us working together can help it escape.

Sixth, the streamlining process will lead to a reduction in rail employees and to problems for some communities and some shippers. We recognize that plans concerning adequate job protection or compensation to the affected employees will need to be developed. These plans will require consultation with representatives of both management and employees, as well as with the trustees and creditors of the bankrupt estates. However, until we have a better understanding of the numbers involved and the extent of the dislocations, it is difficult to address these issues in specific terms. Likewise, special studies will be needed to determine the extent of the problems of communities and shippers, and how best to help them during the period of transition.

Seventh, the emergence of a healthy, streamlined rail system as a new ongoing company (or companies) would significantly add to the value of the total estates of the six bankrupt carriers. This added value, plus the proceeds from prompt liquidation of the remaining pieces (including sales to other railroads), should provide a sufficient total to permit the various claimants to work out equitable divisions of the values. Such incentives as special tax provisions and short-term suspensions of certain ICC regulations should encourage the parties to resolve their differences in a reasonable period of time. If the incentives to reach agreements are strong enough—and if the alternatives are sufficiently unpalatable—reasonable men should reach reasonable agreements. We believe that our plan provides for those incentives—that it helps to create the machinery and oil the gears. With the help of Congress, the private sector can make the machinery move.

Eighth, looking beyond the immediate problems of the Northeast, it is clear that significant changes are needed in the regulatory framework if rail systems throughout the nation are to avoid the problems of the Northeast and to become the effective private sector competitors they are capable of being. This report contains several specific recommendations for regulatory changes.

The Railroads in Perspective

From a meager start in about 1830, the nation's rail industry moved ahead rapidly following the Civil War. The decade of greatest expansion in railway trackage was the 1880s. By 1890, nearly two-thirds of the nation's railway mileage was in place. Railway mileage peaked in 1916 when there were 254,000 miles of railway in the United States.

As the industry matured, its overall growth rate slowed drastically and in the Northeast it has actually declined since 1947. The root of the decline lies in the railroads' changing economic and regulatory environment and in the industry's inability to adapt adequately to the changes.

As strong intermodal competition developed, the railroads' intercity freight and passenger markets suffered. The shifting from coal to oil, which is transported primarily by pipeline, was another blow to the railroads. Northeastern railroads in particular were hard hit following World War II by the relocation to the South and the West of industries dependent on heavy freight movements. The diminishing importance of agriculture, forestry, and mining in the Northeast and the shift to a post-industrial service-type economy also hurt. Figure 2-1 shows various indications of freight traffic trends since 1947.

One of the most important developments affecting the railroads, particularly in the Northeast, was the growth of the intercity trucking and barge industries. Before the advent of large, efficient trucks, the rails had laid thousands of miles of line and were serving virtually every economically important sector of the Northeast. But an extensive network of modern highways built in recent years has tied the big cities together and enabled the motor carriers to capture most of the short-haul and medium-haul nonbulk commodity traffic from the rails.

At the same time, motor carrier competition, with its constant threat of diverting traffic, has helped to place a ceiling on rail rates. Thus, even though the amount of freight traffic carried by the railroads has expanded as the economy has expanded, the average rail revenue per ton-mile in 1970 was 2 percent less than it was in 1958. The introduction in the late 1950s of piggyback service and of trilevel freight cars for transporting automobiles allowed the railroads to recover or retain some medium-haul traffic. It was not enough, however, to enable them to hold their own against the trucks.

Railroads have also suffered in recent years from government policies which have favored modes other than rail. This favored treatment has permitted these modes to improve their productivity and quality of service. In addition, many state and local governments have taxed railroads at a higher rate than other industries, and rails currently pay a higher proportion of their gross revenues in taxes than do motor carriers.

Since the railroad industry's costs are largely fixed, its financial performance is more closely tied to the cyclical ups and downs of the

Figure 2-1

GROSS NATIONAL PRODUCT AND INTERCITY FREIGHT
REVENUE TON-MILES (RTM) BY SELECTED MODE AND
RAILS BY DISTRICT, 1947–1972

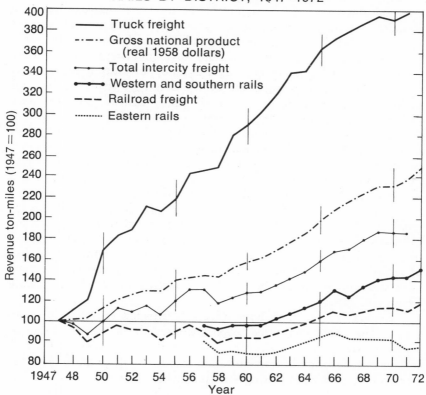

economy than other modes whose costs are more controllable. Because profits have not been adequate over these cycles, many railroads have not been able to survive some of the downturns. The industry's history is rife with bankruptcies. As one would expect, the largest number of bankruptcies resulted from the Great Depression. At one point in the 1930s, 33 percent of all railroad miles were in receivership. At the present time, 13 percent of all railroad mileage operated belongs to bankrupt railroads—virtually all located in the Northeast. However, the two situations are different. In the 1930s, the bankrupt railroads still had some earnings around which they could, and in fact did, reorganize. Today, the outlook is less favorable.

Unlike the case in other industries, bankrupt railroads have not

13

been allowed to reorganize and modernize their operations. Plant and equipment are not dismantled, nor are the land and other properties sold, which is the way other businesses that go through bankruptcy are liquidated. Despite the large number of miles of road in receivership, only an average 0.4 percent of the total road mileage has been abandoned annually since 1916, the peak year. Rail bankruptcies have not been treated as a sign that the industry had fundamental problems (such as overcapacity in a nongrowth industry) which needed correction. Nor have they been used as an opportunity to help correct the problems by allowing some of the bankrupt roads, or perhaps major parts of them, to go out of existence. Instead, railroads were deemed too important to the economy to be discarded. It was felt that the companies could be made viable simply by reducing their debt structure or by merging them with healthier roads. This patchwork policy has maintained essentially the same railroad network that was in place in 1920, a network that was geared to the environment and economy of the late nineteenth and the early twentieth centuries.

The gradual broadening of the Interstate Commerce Act to increase regulatory controls has had a similar restrictive impact on the railroads. The continuing decline of the railroads as an industry, the financial plight of the railroads in the Northeast, and the inflexibility of response to competitive conditions in the marketplace have, in part, been brought about by the regulatory restrictions of the Interstate Commerce Act.

Regulatory practices have adversely affected railroads in many ways. They have permitted, even encouraged, abuses of "value of service" pricing and freight car utilization in ways that have led to a serious misallocation of transportation resources. Regulatory practices have produced a rigid pricing structure which, for rails in particular, has prevented them from responding to the needs of a changing market. In addition, outmoded regulations have impeded efficiency within a given mode by restricting competition and by discouraging the abandonment of uneconomic branch lines.

The Nixon administration pointed out in its *Economic Report to the Congress* for three successive years (1970, 1971, and 1972) that economic and competitive conditions have changed considerably since regulation began in 1887, and that changes have not been adequately reflected in the regulations governing surface freight transportation. The Department of Transportation believes that regulatory reform is fundamental to any plan to restructure the railroads of the Northeast.

Before closing this brief historical overview, a comparison of experiences in the United States with railroads in other countries needs to be mentioned. The United States is one of the few countries in

Table 2-1

NATIONALIZED RAIL SYSTEM LOSSES, 1971

(millions of dollars)

Nation	1971	Route Miles
Britain	198	11,800
France	128	22,300
Germany	725	18,900
Italy	669	9,950
Japan	884	12,900

the world that has not nationalized its rail system. Without exception, nationalized carriers have found themselves increasingly involved in objectives other than providing efficient, low-cost rail service. Various data suggest that foreign rail labor costs and shipping costs are relatively higher than those of U.S. railroads and that overall operating losses are significantly higher. Table 2-1 shows published operating losses of nationalized rail systems in five major nations for 1971.

Since the railroads in this country historically have not operated with the same objectives as those of foreign nations, comparisons such as this are of limited value. Nevertheless, the general direction is indicative of a likely outcome of nationalization.

Causes of Present Problems. The causes of the nation's rail problems are both external and internal to the industry. The major external factors are: trends in intermodal competition, especially the relative competitive vigor of the trucking industry; financial vulnerability because of historic low profit rates; shifts in national transportation demand; unbalanced federal investment policies; and adverse regulatory policies. The main internal factors are: capital and operating difficulties, including complications brought about by mergers; inflexibility to change by both management and labor; and lack of technological, marketing, and pricing innovations.

Industry problems vary from region to region and from railroad to railroad. Most of the financially weak railroads are in the Northeast and, to a lesser degree, in the Midwest. On the other hand, in the West and the South traffic is growing steadily and most systems are reasonably healthy. Particular note should be made of the relative financial strength of such western and southern carriers as Union Pacific, Southern Pacific, Seaboard Coast Line, and Southern Railway. In addition, two eastern carriers—the Chesapeake and Ohio/Baltimore and Ohio and the Norfolk and Western—are relatively strong. (Table 2-2 gives recent selected financial data for these companies.)

Table 2-2
SELECTED FINANCIAL DATA FOR SIX RELATIVELY STRONG CARRIERS, 1971–1972
(millions of dollars)

	Union Pacific	Southern Pacific	Norfolk & Western	C&O/B&O (Consolidated)	Southern	Seaboard Coast Line
Revenue						
1971	691.5	1,028.7	727.6	1,025.0	423.3	530.2
1972	769.6	1,119.9	795.0	1,025.0	471.6	563.1
Net ordinary income						
1971	108.2	92.9	77.7	29.7	58.7	41.2
1972	122.9	93.0	89.8	60.0	59.6	50.7
Cash flow from operations (est.)[a]						
1971	168.7	162.5	139.5	95.8	90.1	71.0
1972	184.9	164.2	153.0	127.3	93.1	81.6
Shareholders' equity						
1971	1,416.8	1,493.8	1,173.4	1,060.2	734.7	923.3
1972	1,431.5	1,530.5	1,146.3	1,091.2	763.2	947.1
Total long-term debt						
1971	425.3	794.1	792.3	1,035.7	415.0	415.8
1972	453.8	834.6	763.5	971.8	424.2	396.0
Capital investments[b]						
1971	147.2	136.5	81.1	138.9	59.8	85.3
1972	108.6	171.9	68.0	61.2	62.8	65.1
Miles operated (1971)	9,474	13,525	7,611	11,477[c]	6,023	9,173

a Equals ordinary income plus depreciation.
b Gross expenditures for additions and betterments.
c Sum of C&O, B&O, and Western Maryland.

Nevertheless, taken as a whole, the railroad industry is not strong financially, as can be seen in Table 2-3, which shows net profits as a percentage of equity as compared with other transportation industries and all manufacturing industries. The recent drop to a zero earnings rate overall is, of course, because of the Northeast situation. Yet, even if this group is removed from the totals, we find that the rail industry in total has a rate of return below that needed to attract adequate capital for long-term growth.

Trends in intermodal competition. The growth of the intercity trucking industry over the past two decades and the increasing traffic in bulk commodities carried by barges and pipelines have taken their toll on the railroads. For example, the rail share of intercity freight ton-miles dropped from 54 percent in 1947 to 35 percent in 1970. Trucks increased their share from 5 percent to 16 percent, and pipelines from 10 percent to 21 percent, as shown in Table 2-4 and Figure 2-2.

During this same period, intercity passenger traffic showed an even sharper shift away from rail, with air capturing the bulk of the for-hire intercity passenger market. In 1950, automobiles and buses accounted for 91 percent of the intercity passenger-mile total, rail 7 percent, and air 2 percent. In 1970, automobiles and buses had 89 percent of the total, rail 1 percent, and air 10 percent.

Financial vulnerability because of historically low profit rates. Railroads and some other regulated industries, which historically have been thought to be low risk, typically have low rates of return. The railroads' financial vulnerability because of low profit rates has resulted in a downward trend that is for some, at least, feeding on itself. Once an industry's profit rate falls near zero, its weaker members find that increasingly they are unable to survive the normal swings in economic activity.

The financial failure (or near failure) of the weaker companies has affected the healthier ones in at least two ways. It has cut into their ability to serve existing business and reduced their prospects for attracting new business. This is because the railroads are a national system and must rely on their interconnections to complete most of their freight business and to generate adequate new traffic.

Shifts in national transportation demand. Railroads are extremely vulnerable to both short-term and long-term changes in the national economy. Much of the growth of the U.S. economy in recent years has taken place in the services, finance, trade, and government sectors. By contrast, the bulk commodity sectors such as agriculture, forestry, and mining that rails have historically served have not par-

Table 2-3

RETURN ON EQUITY OF REGULATED CARRIERS AND ALL MANUFACTURING INDUSTRIES, 1960–1971

(percent)

Year	All Manufacturing	Rail	Truck	Bus	Water Carrier	Pipeline
1960	9.2	2.6	4.9	11.0	5.7	15.7
1961	8.9	2.2	10.2	11.3	6.1	16.3
1962	9.8	3.3	12.4	11.0	7.7	17.6
1963	10.3	3.7	12.1	12.3	9.5	16.0
1964	11.6	4.0	13.6	12.1	13.4	16.0
1965	13.0	4.6	15.7	18.2	11.9	16.3
1966	13.4	5.0	14.5	15.3	12.5	16.5
1967	11.7	1.8	9.2	11.6	12.2	17.7
1968	12.1	3.1	12.9	14.4	11.0	16.2
1969	11.5	2.6	9.8	15.2	8.9	15.6
1970	9.3	0.4	6.7	13.4	10.5	17.1
1971	9.2	0.0	16.2	15.8	9.6	16.7

Source: Interstate Commerce Commission, *Annual Report to Congress* for the years 1960–1971; *Economic Report of the President* for the years 1960–1971.

Figure 2-2

VOLUME OF U.S. INTERCITY FREIGHT BY MODE, 1929–1970

(trillions of ton-miles)

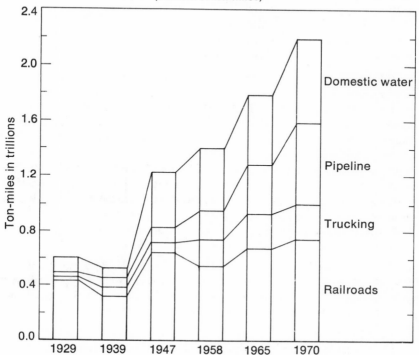

Table 2-4

INTERCITY SURFACE FREIGHT TON-MILES BY MODE, 1947–1970

(percent of total)

Year	Rail	Truck	Domestic Water	Pipelines
1947	54	5	31	10
1958	39	13	32	16
1965	39	14	28	19
1970	35	16	28	21

ticipated equally in that growth.[2] Thus, despite good growth potential in transportation, the base traffic which could generally only be handled by rail has declined. The remaining markets are highly competitive and much higher risk.

As a result, without the stability of a growing base market, railroads have become especially vulnerable to rising money costs and to rising average costs of labor and materials.

Unbalanced federal policies. Major federal transportation policies of the post-World War II period have been unbalanced in favor of the competing modes. This may have been inadvertent, but the negative impact upon the railroads has been serious. Federal funds (many of which are backed by user taxes) have helped build the Interstate Highway System, provided for improved inland waterways, built the Saint Lawrence Seaway, and helped finance a national system of airports and airways. As a result, competing modes have been able to operate on smaller amounts of capital and have been better able to survive economic ups and downs in ways that railroads cannot. Further, these investments have allowed other modes to improve their productivity and quality of service.

Adverse regulatory policies. Federal and state regulatory policies have made it difficult for the railroads to adapt to changing economic and competitive conditions. The Interstate Commerce Act seems especially in need of modification and incorporation of regulatory relief in the following areas:

1. Abandonment: Lengthy procedures often prevent or unnecessarily hinder a railroad's efforts to abandon branch or other lines that can no longer cover even variable costs. Hearings, briefs, rebuttals, and other procedures may delay abandonments for years—all the while forcing the railroad to provide the service at a loss.

2. Rate making: The present procedures are time consuming and inflexible; they discourage innovation and encourage preservation of the status quo. Some of the rates are discriminatory in that they force one class of service to subsidize another (for example, perishables and freight on light-density lines are subsidized by other freight). Also, some bulk commodities apparently are carried below the carriers' variable costs.

3. Rate bureau activities: Certain rate bureau procedures tend to perpetuate historic distortions in rate structures, and they limit flexibility to adjust rates to cope with competition from other modes.

---

[2] The growing export market for agricultural commodities should help improve rail's long-term prospects.

20

4. Merger proceedings: Protracted hearings and court reviews may take so long that expected merger benefits can be dissipated well before the actual merger is permitted.

5. Joint usage: Regulatory procedures inhibit joint usage and joint control of common trackage, causing inefficient service and expensive operating practices.

Another problem is that some states continue to permit the taxation of railroad assets at higher rates than other commercial assets. This is done either by overassessing rail assets relative to other assets or by imposing higher tax rates.

Capital and operating difficulties. The nation's rail system also has problems in raising money and in operating efficiently.

1. Capital: Because of poor earnings, poor prospects, high debt ratios, and the reality of several large bankruptcies, railroads face a limited and high-cost capital market. The lack of capital has impeded modernization of plant and equipment and caused right-of-way maintenance to be neglected. It also may have caused an overuse of high-cost, indirect financing through leasing.

2. Management: Viewed broadly, there is evidence that rail management has been relatively inflexible to change and less innovative than management in other major industries. It is not altogether clear whether this problem is a cause of or a response to the railroad industry's declining fortunes and the restrictive regulatory and unbalanced federal financing environment in which it operates. It does seem clear, however, that a relaxation of some regulatory restrictions under which rail management must operate would contribute towards a long-term solution of this problem.

3. Labor: For a number of reasons, labor-management relations in the rail industry must be improved. There are situations in which operating procedures have not been modified to meet changing market needs. Since labor costs represent more than one-half of the industry's total expenses, a flexible, long-term relationship is an essential element in assuring the future viability of the industry.

4. Rail networks: Most freight shipments require interconnections with one or more other rail companies. Virtually all rail networks and branch lines were in place fifty to sixty years ago. Mergers and abandonments have been difficult and tedious, leaving the nation's rail system with uneconomic trackage and excessive overhead. In addition, interconnecting terminals are generally outdated and inefficient, and they have not been relocated with shifts in demand centers. Serv-

Figure 2-3

ANNUAL GROWTH RATE IN REVENUE TON-MILES
OF CLASS I RAILROADS
OVER VARIOUS TIME PERIODS

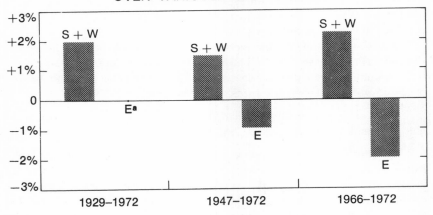

a No change from 1929 to 1972 for railroads in the eastern district.
Note: E: eastern district railroads; S + W: southern district plus western district railroads.

ice offered by the financially weak railroads adversely affects the capability of the strong railroads to deliver. Further complications and inefficiencies come from lack of any coordinated means of programming the nationwide movement of freight cars from one system to another, and from legal restraints on joint control or even cooperation with competing modes, such as intermodal piggyback, rail-truck, and containerized systems to serve branch-line areas.

Special circumstances affecting railroads in the Northeast. The railroads in the Northeast have experienced the problems described above to a significantly greater extent than those in other sections of the nation. By any measure, these railroads as a whole are in worse financial shape than those in other areas. Profits are lower, labor costs are higher, investment needs are greater, and utilization of manpower and investment resources is less efficient. As can be seen in Figure 2-3, the volume of freight ton-miles moved by railroads in the eastern district has declined over the past several years, while that moved by railroads in the southern and western districts has increased. Also, improvements in capital and employee productivity of the eastern roads have failed to match similar improvements of the southern and western roads.

Economic growth in the Northeast has shifted more sharply than in other regions away from bulk commodities and toward industries and services that require little freight movement. Also, environmental restraints have seriously cut the demand for high-sulfur coal, traditionally a major source of rail revenue in the Northeast.

Because of the nation's historical beginnings along the East Coast, the northeastern railroads are more complex, more outdated, and more in need of rationalization than those in any other section of the country. In addition, the area's greater demands for commuter service intensify public and political pressures for action. Unfortunately, the regulatory framework—especially the Interstate Commerce Act—has made needed changes most difficult to realize. Freight revenues of the northeastern railroads are inadequate (because of either regulatory restrictions or competition from other modes), and capital for modernization is largely unavailable.

A measure of the extent of the "blind alley" that the northeastern railroads find themselves in can be seen in Table 2-5, which shows that about 50 percent of the rail system in the Northeast (measured in miles) is in bankruptcy.

Developments accelerating the Penn Central's failure. Penn Central is the dominant carrier in an area where rail systems are most in need of change and flexibility, but Penn Central is among the systems that are least able to meet these challenges. In addition, the Penn Central situation has been aggravated by the following factors:

(1) The merger between the Pennsylvania Railroad and the New York Central Railroad was a "last resort" response to trends that probably should have been faced years earlier. Numerous other regional mergers finally forced these two giants to realize that there were few potential partners left. During the five years of the merger's gestation (1962–1967), excessive management effort was required to keep the merger plan intact and to participate in seemingly endless regulatory and court reviews.

(2) Penn Central's management paid a dear price for final approvals, especially in its obligations to try to save the New Haven Railroad and in labor agreements.

(3) Once merged, Penn Central represented both the best and the worst aspects of the northeastern rail system, but its management did not move ahead to develop the railroad's potential and make needed changes.

A rough measure of the extent to which Penn Central is burdened with excessive operating costs can be seen in the data in Table

23

Table 2-5

STATUS OF EASTERN DISTRICT RAILROADS, REVENUES AND MILES OF ROAD, 1971

	Revenues (millions of dollars)		Miles of Road Operated	
Bankrupt railroads				
Boston & Maine	77		1,497	
Central of New Jersey	52		591	
Erie Lackawanna	269		2,979	
Lehigh Valley	45		926	
Penn Central	1,775	(38.2%)	19,864	(36.9%)
Reading	113		1,172	
	2,331	(50.1%)	27,029	(50.3%)
Other eastern district railroads				
Ann Arbor	11		300	
Grand Trunk Western	85		946	
Delaware & Hudson	45		718	
Maine Central	29		908	
Western Maryland	51		862	
Pittsburgh and Lake Erie	37		211	
Baltimore & Ohio	496		5,543	
Chesapeake & Ohio	455		5,048	
Norfolk & Western	728		7,619	
	1,937	(41.7%)	22,155	(41.1%)
Other eastern railroads	382	(8.2%)	4,601	(8.6%)
Total eastern district	4,650	(100%)	53,785	(100%)
Total U.S.	12,689		210,197	

Note: Figures in parentheses are percentages of eastern district totals.
Source: Interstate Commerce Commission, *Transport Statistics*, 1971.

2-6, which ranks net ton-miles of freight moved per employee for the nation's major railroads. Although there are many variables in comparing the number of employees to the ton-miles of freight moved, the overall pattern appears significant.

To bring the Penn Central ratio from its bottom position up to the average of all eleven carriers—that is, between 1.4 million and 1.5 million ton-miles per employee—would require either a very sharp jump in freight ton-miles, or a sharp reduction in the number of employees, or perhaps some of each.

Table 2-6

TON-MILE/EMPLOYEE RATIO FOR MAJOR RAILROADS, 1970

(ton-miles in millions)

Carrier	Net Ton-Miles per Employee
Southern	2.0
Missouri Pacific	1.8
Southern Pacific	1.7
Union Pacific	1.6
Norfolk & Western	1.6
Illinois Central	1.5
Seaboard Coast Line	1.4
Burlington Northern	1.4
C&O/B&O	1.3
Erie Lackawanna	1.1
Penn Central	0.9

Note: Excluding employees operating passenger service.

Rail passenger service in the Northeast. For the most part, the financial burden of unprofitable rail passenger service is no longer a major factor contributing to the financial problems of the northeastern railroads because of the creation of Amtrak and the gradual takeover of the main commuter rail services by metropolitan transit authorities. Most intercity rail passenger service in the United States was taken over by the Amtrak in 1971. The existing agreements between Amtrak and the railroads require continuation of such service. States and localities have taken the lead in preserving commuter services in the Northeast, and they are now moving into direct lease or ownership of plant and equipment. It appears that, under this type of agreement, the railroads will in time receive proper compensation for maintenance of track and other operational service.

Rail's Role in the Economy. Despite problems such as described above, railroads still must be recognized as the nation's most important intercity freight carrier. And, because of the many interrelationships between transportation and production, it is obvious that rail's importance extends deep into the nation's economic system. Tables 2-7 and 2-8 give some highlights of the role of railroads in the economy. Of particular significance are the data in Table 2-8 which show the several basic industries for which rail hauls 50 percent or more of the ton-miles.

Table 2-7
SELECTED RAIL INDUSTRY STATISTICS, 1970

Value added by the rail industry	$8.7 billion
Percentage of transportation value added	9.4
Percentage of GNP (= sum of all value added)	0.9
Gross output of rail industry	$11.9 billion
Freight	$11.5 billion
Passenger	$0.440 billion
Percentage of transportation gross revenue	6.6
Rail employment	636,000
Percentage of transportation employment	7.4
Percentage of total national employment	0.7
Employee compensation as percentage of rail value added	72
Employee compensation as percentage of rail gross revenue	51
Estimated value of rail capital stock	$37 billion
Plant	$21 billion
Equipment	$16 billion
Rough estimate of value of land in rail transportation	$4 billion

Table 2-8
MOVEMENT OF SELECTED COMMODITIES BY RAIL, 1970

Commodity	Percent Ton-Miles by Rail
Paper and products	82
Coal mining	79
Ordnance	78
Nonferrous metals	75
Lumber and products	72
Stone, clay, and glass products	66
Furniture	63
Chemicals	63
Motor vehicles	59
Agriculture	58
Food and drugs	58
Farm-construction machinery	53
Iron and steel	50

The major bankrupt railroads in the Northeast are the Penn Central, the Erie Lackawanna, the Boston & Maine, the Central of New Jersey, the Lehigh Valley, and the Reading. These six railroads together represent an important rail network moving about 45 percent of the freight in the Northeast. Their service area includes nineteen states and the District of Columbia and stretches from Maine to Missouri. More than 75 percent of all rail freight service in Connecticut, Rhode Island, New Hampshire, Massachusetts, New York, eastern Pennsylvania, New Jersey, and Delaware is now provided by the bankrupt roads. These roads also dominate rail service in major areas of Ohio, Indiana, Michigan, Maryland, and western Pennsylvania. Table 2-9 summarizes the important characteristics of the six bankrupt railroads.

The Proposed Plan

The Department of Transportation will submit legislation to authorize the implementation of the plan proposed below. The key steps are as follows:

Core Rail Service. Using projections of freight and passenger traffic, the Department of Transportation would identify "core rail service" for the Northeast, based on the concept of long-term economic efficiency in the use of transportation resources. The department's review would take into account potential intermodal connections and substitutions, and it would serve as a guide for the long-term restructuring of the existing rail system.

The core would be identified in terms of areas that should be served and connected by rail service; it would not deal with specific rail networks.

During a ninety-day period following enactment of enabling legislation, the secretary would prepare a report on the core, which would be made available for public comment. The secretary would then make a final identification of the core, and his decision would not be subject to judicial review.

Formation of a New For-Profit Corporation. After core rail service has been identified, a way is needed to ensure that the rail system in the Northeast would, as a minimum, provide such service. Because of the fragmented and competitive nature of many of the present bankrupt estates, we think it unlikely that the estates, working separately, could agree on an acceptable plan to reduce excess facilities

Table 2-9

CHARACTERISTICS OF THE SIX BANKRUPT RAILROADS IN THE NORTHEAST, 1971
(money amounts in millions of dollars)

	Freight		Passenger Revenues	Total Railroad Operating Revenues[a]	Net Railroad Operating Income (loss)[b]	Net Ordinary Income (loss)[c]	Miles of road[d]	Employees (average number)
	Revenue ton-miles (billions)	Revenues						
Penn Central	79.09	1,534	95	1,775	(180)	(285)	19,864	88,518
Erie Lackawanna	13.79	240	11	269	9	(1)	2,979	12,811
Reading	3.61	93	9	113	(6)	(12)	1,172	6,271
Boston & Maine	2.61	65	6	77	(2)	(6)	1,497	3,597
Lehigh Valley	2.48	44	0	45	(6)	(8)	926	2,527
Central of New Jersey	1.21	38	4	52	(1)	(6)	591	2,567
Total six bankrupt railroads	102.78	2,014	125	2,331	(186)	(318)	27,029	116,291
All eastern district	225.30	4,131	212	4,650	(32)	(250)	53,785	222,540
U.S. Class I railroads	739.40	11,786	294	12,689	695	347	210,197	544,369
Six bankrupt railroads as percent of U.S. total	13.9%	17.1%	42.5%	18.4%	(26.8%)	(91.6%)	12.9%	21.4%

a Includes revenues for freight, passengers, mail, express, and incidentals.
b This is essentially the profits from operating the railroad before considering how the railroad is financed. It is the remainder of railroad operating revenues after deducting operating expenses, taxes, and rents for equipment and joint facilities, but before adding nonoperating income and deducting fixed charges such as interest on debt and rents for leased lines.
c Net income (profits) of the company after taking into account income from nonrailroad operations, rentals for leased lines, interest, and other deductions, but before extraordinary and prior-period items.
d Represents the aggregate length of roadway operated, but does not include the mileage of yard track or sidings.

Source: Interstate Commerce Commission, *Transport Statistics, 1971*; all figures exclude Amtrak.

and to share those facilities which remain. Consequently, we propose that a new, private, for-profit corporation be chartered and charged with the job of selecting certain assets from among the estates on the basis of the core identified by the secretary.

Termination of service. Once final core rail service is identified, bankrupt railroads should be permitted to terminate rail service (but not abandon track) in those areas not included in the core. This termination of service should occur within a specific time period and without ICC approval. A procedure should also be established whereby states and local communities, other viable railroads, shippers, and others would be afforded the opportunity to provide for the continuation of service not included in the core. They could acquire the necessary assets of the bankrupt estates by purchase or lease and then could either operate the service themselves or negotiate a contract whereby the new corporation or operating entities would operate the service. The bankrupts would, however, have to continue to provide a minimum level of maintenance of those rights-of-way over which service has been discontinued until actual abandonment is achieved.

Responsibilities of the new corporations. The enabling legislation would authorize the establishment of the new corporation, with the board of incorporators to be appointed by the President. The initial purpose of the corporation would be to design one or more rail systems in the Northeast based upon providing the core rail service identified by the secretary. After appropriate study and analysis, the board would:
  (1) design one or more rail systems based on the core;
  (2) select for such a system(s) certain rail lines, facilities, and equipment presently operated by the bankrupts, and possibly others; and
  (3) obtain rights of first refusal and agreements that such properties as selected above are available for purchase.
In designing the system(s) and allocating the elements, the board would apply as its criteria:
  (1) the economic viability of each element of the system(s), and
  (2) the continuation of rail service competition in high-density markets to the greatest extent feasible.
Following a review by the secretary of the board's specific proposals to assure that they are reasonably consistent with core rail service, the board would take steps to acquire the facilities and equipment through negotiations with the bankrupt estates and others. Because the "going-concern value" of the acquired assets should exceed their uncertain value under protracted, piecemeal liquidation, we be-

lieve that the trustees would find it in their best interests to work out equitable agreements with the board within specific time limits. If more than one new system has been approved, the board would establish such additional corporations as are required and assign the properties acquired to the appropriate corporations.

Within a specified time after the secretary's approval of the board's proposals, the bankrupts would be able, without ICC approval, to terminate service not included in the board's final approved proposals or not acquired by others, and to abandon such rights-of-way. At this point, additional facilities could be added to the system if those states, localities, or shippers that want them are willing to subsidize fully any deficits involved. Also, depending upon the actions of the board with regard to operating rail passenger service, possible separate arrangements might have to be made with Amtrak and transit authorities to continue passenger service they consider necessary. Properties of the bankrupt railroads not acquired by a new corporation could then be liquidated by the bankrupt estates.

The actions of the board of incorporators and the secretary's approval would not be reviewable in any court.

Valuing the corporation and the distribution of assets. The stock of the new corporation(s) would be placed in escrow until it could be allocated equitably to the bankrupt estates. One possibilitiy would be to prorate the stock on the basis of assets contributed to the corporation. The stock could then be distributed to the bankrupt estates pursuant to the allocation procedure, and each new corporation would become an independent operating entity.

The establishment and operation of the streamlined system(s) would be timed to occur within one year of the date of enactment of enabling legislation.

Transition. The period of transition, as the Northeast rail systems are streamlined and returned to a viable place in the private sector, will inevitably cause strains and dislocations. Three areas require particular consideration:

(1) the impact on labor;
(2) the impact on rail carriers as they shift from today's overbuilt structure to the new streamlined structure; and
(3) the impact on those state and local communities and shippers who will be required to deal with changing types and costs of freight service.

Proper and equitable handling of the various problems will require further analysis and planning. In this report we can only suggest some tentative approaches.

Labor. The six bankrupt railroads in the Northeast employed approximately 116,000 persons in 1971. (Table 2-10 shows the breakdown of this total by railroad and by general classification of employees.) Specific plans must be developed, in consultation with management and employee representatives, as well as with the trustees and creditors of the bankrupt estates, to provide adequate job protection or compensation to affected employees. Such plans can, of course, only be developed following an understanding of the numbers involved and the extent of dislocations.

Those employees of the bankrupts who are hired by a new entity would be guaranteed appropriate job protection in their agreements with the new corporation. Some of the employees of the bankrupts may also be hired by nonbankrupt railroads that acquire parts of the bankrupts' systems or by other rail freight and passenger systems. Those employees would also be guaranteed appropriate employment and labor protection rights.

With respect to the labor protection rights of other employees, some form of appropriate compensation will have to be found. It is recognized that labor may seek a share of the estates. The cash required for any payments from the estates could come from receipts from early liquidation of assets or from advanced borrowing against the liquidation.[3] If additional cash were needed to finance such compensation, a loan secured by the stock in the new corporation would be a further possibility. If the various regulatory and other changes outlined in this plan are forthcoming, we believe that this stock would constitute ample security for such a loan.

Rail carriers. Until new operating entities take over rail service from the bankrupt railroads in the Northeast, most existing service would be continued by the bankrupt railroads. Based on current experience, these operations will produce a continuing cash loss for these railroads. We believe that the courts and creditors would permit these cash losses provided that they can reasonably expect a higher liquidation value in the future.

A key issue is the constitutional right of the creditors to prevent the continued erosion of the estates' assets. Certainly, if there were no end in sight, cessation of operations and prompt liquidation would be the proper course of action. However, with evidence that this plan

---

[3] Such lump-sum payments may be eligible for tax treatment that recognizes the special nature of the payments.

Table 2-10

EMPLOYMENT BY CLASSIFICATION AT SIX BANKRUPT NORTHEASTERN RAILROADS, 1971

Occupational Group	Penn Central	Reading	Central of New Jersey	Lehigh Valley	Boston & Maine	Erie Lackawanna	Total
Executives, officials, et cetera	1,634	143	82	63	76	294	2,292
Professional, clerical, et cetera	17,327	1,542	593	575	799	2,501	23,337
Maintenance of way	10,382	756	331	433	540	1,682	14,124
Maintenance of equipment	21,295	1,474	534	469	715	2,689	27,176
Transportation (yard)	1,644	115	68	53	61	182	2,123
Transportation (train & engine)	29,411	1,820	724	795	1,141	4,380	38,271
Transportation (other than yard and T&E)	6,825	421	232	139	265	1,083	8,965
Total	88,518	6,271	2,564	2,527	3,597	12,811	116,288

Source: Interstate Commerce Commission, *Transport Statistics*, 1971.

would be implemented, it seems reasonable to expect the courts to permit further limited losses during the transition period.

Another area of consideration is the need for start-up financing for the new corporation or other entities which will operate the re-structured system. Financing will be required for initial working capital, deferred maintenance, and capital for equipment, facilities, and possibly some new connecting track. An analysis of these requirements, viewed in the context of the viable system which will emerge, leads us to believe that the private capital market will meet these needs. It would appear, however, to be proper to allow the new corporation to be able to use the tax losses of the bankrupt railroads. This action would help generate extra cash during the critical early years and would provide an incentive for immediate efficiency.

Communities and shippers. Once the core and additional service areas that are to be retained have been identified, the problem of communities and shippers who are affected by abandonments can be better understood. These groups, together with governmental agencies, can then determine the appropriate action to deal with these problems.

An important objective will be to provide the affected communities and shippers sufficient lead time to make plans for obtaining an alternative means of transportation or new markets. Even with the substantial abandonment of light-density branch lines, we would expect rail service to continue to be available close to most of these areas. In addition, shippers would have access to trucking service and rail terminals. Also, states and local communities will be given the opportunity to ensure the continuation of rail service if they find it necessary and are willing to subsidize the deficits fully.

Although Congress asked that the department consider alternatives for those areas which might not have future rail service, it is not possible to make specific recommendations until the core is identified and the board of incorporators takes action.

Regulatory Revisions. In addition to the near-term problem of the Northeast railroads, we must also address the problem of outmoded and excessively restrictive regulatory procedures which affect the entire industry. Railroads are no longer the monopoly they were when most of the regulations were developed, and appropriate changes are long overdue. The proposed changes, which will shortly be submitted in detailed legislative proposals, are as follows:

Liberalize rail abandonment procedures. Existing regulatory procedure tends to discourage rail abandonments. Abandonment cases often entail protracted hearings and too often offer a railroad only the prospect of expense and delay. In addition, the standards for the adjudication of these cases lead to uncertainty and prevent the early settlement of issues. As a result, despite the availability to shippers of highway and, in some cases, water and pipeline networks, light-density lines continue to operate long after they should have been abandoned.

It is necessary to make changes to the abandonment process in order to speed up the cases and provide appropriate standards for their resolution. To accomplish this, it is proposed that the ICC be required to permit the abandonment of a service where it can be shown that continued operation would not provide sufficient revenues to cover the long-run variable costs of operating the line. The proposed new procedure would provide for rapid investigation by the commission and quick disposition of any contested abandonment.

Make rate making more flexible. The current regulatory pricing system severely limits the scope of an individual carrier's freedom to innovate in pricing its service and often produces rates that do not meet the costs of the service. The economic consequences on the railroads have been serious. In addition to losses incurred from underpricing some services, some overpriced rail service has resulted from "across the board" percentage increases. This rigidity in the rate structure is discouraging experimentation with service innovations, and it delays the introduction of innovations because of the time and the cost of litigation.

We recommend regulatory changes to permit individual rail carriers to increase or decrease their rates and to improve the range of service offered without undue ICC delay. To eliminate rates below variable costs and to provide for flexibility in the rate-making process, we propose two basic revisions:

(1) that rail carriers be required to raise all below-cost rates to the variable costs level; and

(2) that where any new rate is a reduction from the current rate it shall go into effect as long as the new rate is above variable costs.

To allow railroads additional flexibility in introducing new rates and new service, it will also be proposed that the ICC be required to rule promptly on such proposals. Should the commission fail to act promptly, the rates or service would go into effect.

Eliminate subsidization of government service at the expense of others. Federal, state, and local governments are currently permitted to negotiate rates with carriers. These rates may be below rates which nongovernment shippers are required to pay and thus may unfairly require other shippers to subsidize government shipments. To correct this situation, it is proposed that federal, state, and local governments be required to pay the same rates as other shippers.

Restrict certain practices of rate bureaus. Concerted action by carriers subject to the Interstate Commerce Act is now exempt from prosecution under antitrust legislation. Under the carrier agreements permitted by the ICC, the rate bureaus or carrier associations make decisions for the carriers on the rates each shall charge, whether these rates are for a single line or whether they are joint rates involving two or more carriers.

Rates set in the context of agreements between carriers tend to ignore an individual carrier's cost and are based on the average costs of all carriers who are parties to the rate. Such rate agreements maintain the historic distortion in the rate structure, channel traffic away from its direct routing, and restrict rate-making flexibility in intermodal competition.

It is proposed that antitrust immunity no longer be extended to rail carrier agreements for rates applicable to the traffic of a single rail carrier, nor to any agreement which allows a rail carrier to participate in discussions or to vote on joint or through rates applicable to a joint movement in which that carrier is not involved. Rail rate associations would be required to allow individual members independent action, and the associations would not be permitted to protest or seek the suspension of rates. They would be required to dispose of any joint rate proposals filed within 120 days and to publish their votes.

Provide procedures to expedite mergers and other consolidations. Excessive duplication of facilities is a major problem of the rail industry. Efforts to reduce excess capacity by mergers are often long delayed by protracted ICC hearings (in one case, at least, ten years). Joint usage of facilities, another possible solution to the problem of excess capacity, has been used only moderately. Such arrangements should be encouraged. Current law also raises artificial barriers to intermodal ownership, thereby limiting arrangements to provide greater efficiency in transportation operations.

It is proposed that a twelve-month time limit be imposed upon ICC deliberations on applications for mergers and other consolidations, after which cases would be transferred directly to the federal courts. It is also proposed that the ICC be required to grant any application for the joint use of facilities which the petitioner can demonstrate to be in the public interest. New applications of common carriers to engage in intermodal operations should be encouraged by simplifying procedures and removing other restrictions on intermodal operations.

Permit easy entry of motor and water carriers to fill gaps created by liberalized rail abandonments. Means must be provided to ensure that shippers have an effective and efficient transportation alternative when low-density rail service is abandoned. Current standards require a finding of an immediate and urgent need for new services before ICC approval can be obtained. This standard could be too restrictive if liberalized rail abandonment procedures are adopted. It is proposed that the ICC be required, upon application by a motor or water carrier or by a railroad seeking to operate truck or barge service, to authorize immediate and permanent service in markets abandoned by rail carrier service.

Amend section 77 of the Bankruptcy Act to give courts adequate authority to act promptly and rationally to solve railroad bankruptcies. Statutory provisions dealing with bankrupt railroads are out of date. Geared to the problems of the Great Depression, they are designed primarily to deal with a railroad suffering from too great a debt structure. But, as the current Penn Central situation demonstrates, they are generally inadequate to deal with a debtor railroad which is unable to generate sufficient earnings to stop losses, or to provide an adequate basis for a plan of reorganization in the time frame demanded by the constitutional rights of its creditors.

In order to provide for reshaping a debtor railroad's organization, the proposed amendments would require trustees, with court approval, to abandon uneconomical lines and, if necessary, to raise rail rates to cover variable costs. Mergers and consolidations with another railroad would be effected without ICC approval, while providing for the job protection or compensation of affected employees.

Eliminate discriminatory state and local taxation of rail assets. Discriminatory taxation by many state and local governments contributes to the financial problems of the railroads. These jurisdictions should be prohibited from continuing discriminatory practices in assessing railroad property and establishing tax rates for such property.

Eliminate delays in state approval of intrastate rates that coordinate with changes in interstate rates. Action should be taken to alleviate the problem of time lags between federal and state action to change rail rates. Because of the substantial amount of intrastate traffic, these time lags deprive rail carriers of a significant amount of needed revenue.

3

INTERMODAL AND
INTRAMODAL COMPETITION

United States Railway Association

Competition among firms in the same industry and market is an important feature of public policy toward business in the United States. Competition, an underlying premise of the private enterprise system, is protected and encouraged by antitrust laws and numerous pieces of special legislation. Even in highly regulated industries like railroading, competition is prized as a means of controlling abusive business behavior because it is automatic, penetrating, and persistent. Shippers and consumers generally value competition among suppliers as the best guarantor of reasonable prices and as the best mechanism for assuring good service, technological progress, and efficient management. Those who advocate less public regulation of quasi-public utilities like railroading—in order to give industry greater flexibility in pricing and services—place heavy reliance on the self-regulating character of competition. Without a healthy and balanced competitive system, the public will demand more, not less, regulation.

On the other hand, with respect to industries that have some, if not all, of the characteristics of public utilities, competition may be more valuable in theory than in fact. Head-to-head competition of rival firms may be valuable to shippers by lowering their rates, but other less direct forms of competition may be equally valuable over the long run. Indirect forms of competition may be sufficient to bring

This chapter is edited from chapter 8 of United States Railway Association, *Preliminary System Plan for Restructuring Railroads in the Northeast and Midwest Region Pursuant to the Regional Rail Reorganization Act of 1973* (Washington, D.C., February 26, 1975). The USRA was established by the Regional Rail Reorganization Act of 1973 for the purpose of planning and organizing the Consolidated Rail Corporation (ConRail). The USRA published its Preliminary System Plan for future rail service in February 1975. Following evaluation of that plan by the Rail Services Planning Office of the ICC in April 1975, USRA's Final System Plan was submitted to Congress on July 26, 1975.

about improved cost performance and innovations in services. In areas of great excess trackage, as in the Granger states, excessive competition has been known to result in less frequent service, poorer utilization of plant and equipment, higher unit costs, and higher charges to the shipper than otherwise would have been required. Too much competition may be one of the causes of financial instability and bankruptcy of some railroad carriers. Hence, excessive competition is no more a friend of the shipper than inadequate competition.

The Regional Rail Reorganization Act of 1973 gives prominence to the goal of maintaining and enhancing effective competition in the Northeast and Midwest (the region). Section 202(b)(2) states that "in addition to its duties and responsibilities under other provisions of this Act, the [U.S. Railway] Association shall . . . prepare an economic and operational study and analysis of . . . the competitive or other effects [of the Final System Plan] on profitable railroads." In section 206(a)(5) the act provides that: "the Final System Plan shall be formulated in such a way as to effectuate [among other goals] . . . the retention and promotion of competition in the provision of rail and other transportation services in the Region."

Competition is a goal of the act that may conflict with other goals. For example, section 202(b)(5) requires the association to consider methods of achieving economies through consolidations and pooling arrangements, and section 206(b) mandates consideration of ways to achieve rationalization of rail services and the rail service system in the region.

Competition Defined

It is a basic tenet of economics that a purely competitive market economy will produce the best allocation of social resources. Proper resource allocation enables production of a given bundle of goods and services at the lowest possible cost or, as a corollary, assures that the mix of goods and services produced by the economy best satisfies consumers for any given level of expenditure.

Thus, pure competition produces the condition of maximum social welfare: All goods and services are produced in the proper amount, all "inherent advantages" are fully exploited, all economic resources and factors are most efficiently used, prices in the market are reasonably low (given the size of the market and available technology), and undue concentrations of economic power do not accumulate.

The Definition of Markets. The economist's model of pure competition seldom is realized in actual business practice. Nevertheless,

American public policy toward business places great stock in maintenance of competition; but, how much competition and what kind? Statutory boundaries of anticompetitive behavior are found in the antitrust laws and transportation statutes,[1] but seventy-five years of antitrust case law and regulatory rulings have failed to provide a precise definition of the lawful minimum of competition.

To get at the question of how much competition should exist (or, conversely, the degree of "monopoly power" which should be allowed), it is necessary to define the market in which competition is supposed to exist. Economists measure the degree of monopoly power in a market by "cross-elasticities of demand," or the degree to which one product can be substituted for another. Antitrust law comes at this by attempting to define "relevant markets"—the range of substitutable products that the law will not allow to be monopolized. Unfortunately, the definition of "relevant markets" cannot be determined any more precisely than "adequate competition"; indeed, the two concepts are fully interdependent.

The transportation industries pose difficult problems of market definition because of the point-to-point character of traffic movements and the high degree to which modes can be substituted for each other. For example, if a shipper wants to move steel from Pittsburgh to St. Louis, it will be significant that the Penn Central, the Chessie System, and the Norfolk & Western all provide single-line service. The shipper is well situated with respect to intramodal competition, but intermodal competition also may be a factor in this market. Steel is a valuable commodity and earlier delivery may save the shipper some distribution expenses; trucking firms could haul the steel to St. Louis in competition with the railroads, probably with faster delivery. Also, steel products are heavy, and inland waterway carriers might be able to move the steel at rates low enough to cover the time-related costs of (presumed) slower delivery by barge. For this point-to-point movement, there is high cross-elasticity among rail, truck, and barge service or, in other words, intermodal competition is highly effective.

Workable Competition. Because pure competition rarely exists, economists and antitrust lawyers have arrived at the notion of "workable competition." This concept strikes a balance between theory and pragmatism—between pure competition, which relies on large num-

---

[1] Two sources on statutory and regulatory standards for competition in the transportation industries are Alfred E. Kahn, *The Economics of Regulation: Principles and Institutions* (New York: John Wiley and Sons, 1971); and Michael Conant, *Railroad Mergers and Abandonments* (Berkeley: University of California Press, 1964).

bers of sellers to prevent monopoly control of prices and service levels, and the undeniable fact that total market demand places a limit on the number of sellers of a size large enough to take advantage of production economies.

"Workable competition" is best achieved when a market has the largest number of firms which can exist in an industry, without any firm being too small to reap all of the economies which might come from being big—such as specialization, research work, volume purchases, advertising advantages, and the like. Each firm in an industry should be large enough to achieve these economies; if a firm is larger than the threshold size, however, the total number of firms is reduced unnecessarily.

In railroading, economies resulting from dense traffic flows are likely to be so great that only one firm can be of optimal size in many point-to-point markets. Two firms of optimal scale may be able to co-exist in larger markets. In general, two railroad firms in a large freight market will produce a "workable" level of intramodal competition.

For smaller city-pairs, only one rail carrier is practicable, but that does not mean that no competition exists or that shippers are at the mercy of the railroads; there are several avenues of escape. First, there is intermodal competition. Second, there is the option to route traffic to other rail carriers at intermediate junctions (called short-hauling). Third, the shipper over time may relocate or revise production and distribution strategies. Fourth, a multiplant firm can threaten to reallocate production toward other existing plant locations.

Public economic regulation of an industry substitutes for market competition under the antitrust laws. So long as there is regulation, the number of competitors in "relevant markets" is not so important as it is under market competition. If a policy choice were made to lessen public regulation of rates, however, the number of effective competitors in each market could not be ignored.

In sum, "workable competition" is a practical balance between pure competition of large numbers of sellers and no competition or monopoly. "Workable competition" produces acceptable results; that is, prices close to production costs, good service to customers, efficient management, and technological progress at reasonable costs.

Competition versus Competitors. In our complex industrial society, individual people as consumers rarely participate directly in freight transport decisions. Shippers and receivers serve as intermediaries for consumers, paying the freight bill as part of the final production costs of goods and services purchased by consumers. To the extent that there are benefits of competition, those benefits are received indirectly by consumers and directly by shippers or receivers. In defining types or levels of competition, therefore, it makes sense to view competition as it is perceived by shippers and receivers—the directly participating beneficiaries.

A contrary view often is presented by rail industry representatives who, in a merger case, for example, typically are more interested in impact on *competitors* than impact on *competition*. Their argument is that there can be no competition without healthy firms to compete. That is so, but when public policy has sought to protect *competitors*, it often has done so at the expense of consumers, who may be made to pay higher rates to keep inefficient firms in business. If, instead, the competitive forces were permitted full rein, efficient firms would survive and inefficient firms would fail. Public policy must intervene, of course, to prevent predatory competition and its excesses.

The U.S. Railway Association believes that protection of competition comes before protection of competitors. USRA cannot neglect competitive impacts on rail carriers in the Northeast and Midwest, but where the interests of these carriers may conflict with the interests of creating the best long-run solution for consumers generally, the latter course must be favored. A most serious policy problem exists if, in mapping a competitive industry structure, potential competitors refuse to engage in territorial extensions designed to bring about an acceptable level of competition. In that case, absence of willing competitors becomes an immediate problem which must be solved in the interests of competition generally.

Intramodal (Rail–Rail) Competition

Efficiency of railroad service in the Northeast and Midwest is affected considerably by the nature and extent of competition between railroads. Resolution of this complex subject was a key part of the association's deliberations in preparing the Preliminary System Plan. Few areas have evoked such differences of expert opinion, and it has been impossible to reconcile these differences with statistical or other factual findings.

Some observers believe rail–rail competition is costly to provide in the region because it necessarily implies retention of duplicate and underutilized facilities. Others believe that the goal of preserving rail–rail competition is consistent with creating a financially sound rail system in the region. This latter group believes that whenever a choice between one larger firm and two smaller firms serving the same markets is to be made, the more competitive solution (two firms) also

41

results in establishment of firms of more efficient size. According to this view, the two competitive firms will be managed better, and will be more aggressive and more progressive than a single larger firm. As a result, they will provide better service at lower rates, over time, than will the larger firm. These two conflicting viewpoints are summarized in Table 3-1.

The association has made special studies of the kind and level of competition in the region, has made preliminary investigations of economies of scale and economies of density in railroads, has reviewed the report of the secretary of transportation[2] and the testimony of witnesses before the Rail Services Planning Office of the Interstate Commerce Commission, and has solicited expert opinion from key economists, transportation consultants, and rail shippers. The viewpoints expressed and the analytic results reported in these sources amount to a near-unanimous rejection of anticompetitive solutions in major markets.

USRA's approach to the resolution of the issue of the proper level of rail–rail competition was to define types of competitive service which might be created or maintained, then to determine which areas of the region should be served by each type of competition. USRA determined that the proper *amount* of competition cannot be resolved without reference to multiple *types* of competition. The various types of rail–rail competition are defined and analyzed in the preceding section. The association's basic plan for competitive service in the region is described in chapter 3 of the Preliminary System Plan.

The general policy adopted by USRA is that effective rail–rail competition must be provided in key markets, including markets presently dominated by bankrupt carriers. Rail competition need not be sustained, however, in markets where traffic volumes are such that rail efficiency would be impaired significantly by duplication of facilities and services. Given a choice between two or three railroads, each providing an inadequate level of service, and a single carrier providing a high quality of service, the single carrier choice is preferred.

Determinations of traffic levels adequate to sustain competitive rail services can be made only by consideration of the specifics of each market. Withdrawal of services must be considered on a case-by-case basis. Because of the way the main-line rail networks have developed, for example, it may be relatively inexpensive to maintain two-carrier service to one particular traffic generating area, while elsewhere two

[2] *Northeastern Railroad Problem: A Report to the Congress*, submitted by the secretary of transportation in response to Senate Joint Resolution 59-2, U.S. Department of Transportation, March 26, 1973. The report is included in the present volume as chapter 2.

Table 3-1

CONFLICTING VIEWPOINTS ON INTRAMODAL
RAIL COMPETITION

For Emphasizing Competition

1. Firms of small or moderate size are equally or more efficient than the largest firms.
2. Economies of density can be achieved through creating proper route structures and expanding joint operations.
3. Rails already have lost almost all divertible traffic to other modes, so only rail–rail competition is effective.
4. A larger number of competitive firms keeps open a larger number of future restructuring options and avoids putting all the eggs in one basket.
5. Good service to shippers derives from aggressive competition of more than one firm for a given amount of business.
6. Competitive firms will be financially sound if underlying conditions are adequate, because competition provides incentives to good management and firm size is at optimal scale.

For Deemphasizing Competition

1. Larger firms are at least potentially more efficient than smaller firms, especially if the latest managerial techniques are employed.
2. Economies of density are best achieved by consolidating freight flows over the minimum number of firms.
3. Rail–rail competition was beneficial in the past but is largely non-existent or irrelevant today because firms in other modes, not other rail carriers, set cost and service standards.
4. A smaller number of firms enables concentration of scarce managerial talent and focusing of federal assistance funds in limited areas.
5. Good service to shippers derives from concentration of traffic flows, enabling more frequent schedules, run-through trains, better plant, et cetera.
6. Financial viability is a function of minimum plant duplication and avoidance of "destructive" competition—which undermines the rate level.

carriers could not split the same amount of traffic and earn the same aggregate amount of profit. Most important, when considering how to continue competition in markets which otherwise would be monopolized, it is essential to find a carrier *willing* to provide competition.

Finally, continuation of rail–rail competition in the region is not necessarily incompatible with increased rail efficiency or reduction of duplicative facilities and services. Opportunities for coordination of services between carriers enable achievement of economies of density without reducing service to a single-carrier monopoly.

The association, like the U.S. Department of Transportation in its report of February 1, 1974,[3] has rejected the extremes of monopoly rail service in the region and an industry organization of many small firms. The institutions recommended in the association's Preliminary System Plan are of manageable size. No part of the region generating large amounts of traffic is left without rail–rail competition in the general vicinity. The association has given substantial credence to the argument that concentration of traffic flows is an important source of economies and can result in better service to shippers in the aggregate. Further, USRA tentatively has concluded that, while economies traceable to large corporate size are not obvious in this industry, economies of density are important.

Existing and Proposed Levels of Rail–Rail Competition. The USRA staff has analyzed the market share of dominant railroads in counties served by candidates for consolidation. Table 3-2 shows the distribution of 171 counties by the share of the rail market of the dominant railroad, both at present and for one proposed configuration of consolidated roads. At present, the 171 counties examined in Table 3-2 are distributed fairly evenly across the three classifications tabled. In 62 of the counties, no railroad possesses a dominant traffic share, defined as 70 percent of carloads generated. Complete monopoly positions in railroad traffic exist in 51 counties. The association's proposed three-carrier system results in an increase in traffic dominance by individual railroads. The number of counties with no dominant railroad drops to 42, while the number monopolized by one railroad rises to 74.

The lower half of Table 3-2 shows the percentage of carloads generated in various dominance classifications. The proportion of carloads in areas with 100 percent dominance rises from 8 percent at present to 17 percent under this configuration, while traffic in counties with no dominant carrier falls from 64 percent to 51 percent. It should be noted, however, that for this example more than half the carloads generated still would be served in competitive markets, and by no means would all the monopolized markets be under the influence of the consolidated network of railroads.

A more direct measure of the degree of competition between railroads is the availability of multiple-line service and reciprocal-switch-

[3] Secretary of Transportation, *Rail Service in the Midwest and Northeast Region*, 2 vols., U.S. Department of Transportation, February 1, 1974.

Table 3-2

MARKET SHARE OF DOMINANT RAILROAD IN
171 COUNTIES EAST OF OHIO, AT PRESENT AND FOR
THE PROPOSED THREE-CARRIER SYSTEM

	Less than 70 Percent	70 to 99 Percent	100 Percent
Number of counties			
Present	62	58	51
Three-carrier system	42	55	74
Percentage of total carloads			
Present	64	28	8
Three-carrier system	51	32	17

Notes: This covers the eastern portion of the region only, that is, east of the Ohio/Pennsylvania border, with a small number of counties excluded where no service exists by the five candidates for consolidation. Carloads refers to carloads originated or terminated. Dominant railroad refers to the railroad with the highest carloads generated in the county; shares less than 70 percent were not considered dominant and were consolidated into one grouping. Three-carrier system is a proposed alternative involving consolidation of five carriers plus two systems of solvents.

Source: U.S. Railroad Association staff analysis.

ing agreements to individual customers versus service by a single line. Table 3-3 shows the number of customers with service in these three classifications for selected areas of Pennsylvania and northern New Jersey. Very few customers—only 24 of 2,669—have direct connections to more than one railroad, and only another 150 customers are covered by reciprocal-switching agreements whereby one railroad will pick up cars to exchange with a second carrier (usually) for a small fee. Fully 2,495 of the 2,669 customers have only single-line service, indicating that direct rail-to-rail competition at the shipper's location is very rare, even in highly developed industrial areas such as these.

The Problem of Competitive Service to Small Shippers. Small shippers suffer several disadvantages relative to large shippers;[4] these disadvantages are clearest in the area of service quality. Small shippers generally are harder to serve per unit of work and have less leverage over carriers than large shippers do. Understandably, therefore, small shippers may place a premium on competition, hoping that the rivalry of carriers will produce benefits that they cannot exact from a single

---

[4] A small shipper is defined as one who generates small volumes of carload traffic, as distinct from a shipper (large or small) of small parcels.

Table 3-3

NUMBER OF CUSTOMERS SERVED BY RAILROADS IN THE PHILADELPHIA AND NORTHERN NEW JERSEY AREAS, DISTINGUISHING SINGLE-LINE SERVICE, MULTIPLE-LINE SERVICE, AND RECIPROCAL-SWITCHING SERVICE

Railroad(s)	Stations								Total
	Philadelphia	Newark	Harrison	Elizabeth[a]	Jersey City	Bayonne	Perth Amboy	Allentown, Bethlehem, Easton	
Single-line service									
B&O	40	...	...	...	...	...	...	...	40
EL	...	57	22	...	36	...	...	...	115
PC	859	241	23	155	65	11	6	...	1,360
CNJ	...	119	...	99	...	53	9	...	280
RDG	563	...	...	...	...	...	...	15	578
LV	...	30	...	...	...	...	23	69	122
Subtotal	1,462	447	45	254	101	64	38	84	2,495
Multiple-line service (direct connection)									
PC-RDG	12	...	...	...	...	...	...	...	12
RDG-LV	...	...	...	...	...	...	...	2	2
PC-CNJ	...	...	...	...	...	1	...	...	1
PC-EL	...	...	...	...	1	...	...	...	1
CNJ-LV	...	3	...	...	1	2	1	...	7
LV-EL	...	...	...	...	...	...	...	1	1
Subtotal	12	3	0	0	2	3	1	3	24

Multiple-line service
(reciprocal switching)

PC-RDG	..	..	..	..	..	..	..	..	..
PC-LV	..	25	..	..	42	..	5	1	73
PC-CNJ	..	..	..	..	50	..	8	..	58
PC-EL	..	..	..	..	..	..	..	..	..
RDG-LV	..	..	..	..	..	..	..	18	18
LV-EL	..	..	..	..	..	..	..	1	1
Subtotal	0	25	0	0	92	0	13	20	150
Grand total	1,474	475	45	254	195	67	52	107	2,669

[a] Includes Port Newark.

Note: B&O = Baltimore and Ohio; EL = Erie Lackawana; PC = Penn Central; CNJ = Central Railroad of New Jersey; RDG = Reading; LV = Lehigh Valley.

47

carrier or hope to obtain by regulation alone. The large shipper, which on the surface has the most to gain from competition, may be less vociferous on the subject than the small shipper, because the large shipper can exact through leverage ("monopoly power" in the economist's jargon) what the small shipper can get only through competition or very extensive and careful public regulation. The irony is that service to large shippers may be sufficient in volume to warrant competition, whereas competition for the small shipper is uneconomic under any definition.

There are three ways small shippers can partially overcome their competitive disadvantages. First, a small shipper can join with other small shippers in an association, which then has sufficient total volume to achieve the advantages possessed by large shippers. For example such an association can provide research services on available rates—a function that a single small shipper might not be able to afford. Shipper associations also enable consolidation of shipments to achieve more favorable multiple-car rates. Second, a small shipper can locate in a market area with one or more large shippers. Proximity to major points of traffic generation may result in improved service and even more favorable rates. Third, the small shipper can seek effective regulation, pursuing the rights and remedies that the applicable law and regulations afford.

Shippers' Views. In order to learn more about how shippers view the advantages of competition, USRA asked one of its consultants[5] to gather a group of knowledgeable shipper representatives to discuss these issues. A few of the findings are pertinent.

Shippers believe that the "personality" of the individual railroad is a significant factor in the treatment of its customers—both large and small. Some small railroads consider every account of major significance to them, are generally successful at maintaining good communications with their customers through personal contacts, and achieve efficient operation in all aspects of their business over which they have control.

One shipper complained of the arrogance of a carrier that assumed its traffic to be in bondage by reason of plant locations. This carrier refused to discuss the possibility of a rate adjustment until the shipper had entered into serious negotiations with a motor carrier. A shipper noted that large firms frequently experience the same kinds of

---

[5] Simat, Hellieson and Eichner, Inc.

problems with railroad service that smaller companies do, particularly where decentralized facilities of major firms include individual plants which account for small volumes of freight traffic. This would seem to imply that location (a factor affecting rail operating costs) is more important than leverage.

The larger and more sophisticated shippers seem to rely on splitting traffic between competing carriers in order to obtain improved railroad performance. To split their traffic, some shippers have elaborate "report card" rating systems. Obviously large shippers are better placed to engage in this practice than are small shippers.

The shippers agreed that traffic splitting was an extensive practice that could work both for and against the shipper and the railroad. Splitting could produce better service and reward the carrier for improved service; it also could make the railroads more responsive to shipper interests. On the other hand, traffic splitting can result in lower volume and thus higher cost to both carriers, which makes each such carrier less efficient.

Traffic splitting can be used to good effect because larger shippers often feel that they know rail costs better than the railroad carriers themselves. Large shippers seem to want railroads to cover costs of all shipments and make a fair return, but they also want favorable rates for volume shipments.

These shippers sought competition among railroads and between other modes because it promotes good performance in service, cost levels, technical and marketing innovation, and management. Rail–rail and intermodal competition was important to companies when deciding on plant location and marketing strategies. The shipper conference concluded, however, that effective competition did not require door-to-door duplication of competing facilities; if a railroad becomes indifferent to service, these shippers contended, that railroad will be punished by systematic short-hauling to other carriers. But once again, it is the large shipper that holds this trump card.

Shippers are fearful of finding themselves with no rail service if they should happen to be on the line of a single rail carrier which fails. Thus, rail–rail competition is sought actively by companies in making decisions about plant location, in setting marketing strategies, and in making production decisions, because it ensures service continuity as well as a routing option and rate leverage. Users of rail transportation generally presume that rail–rail competition is essential to them, and that the burden of proof should fall on parties advocating lessened competition rather than on those urging retention of competition.

Intermodal Competition

Intermodal competition serves many of the classic economic values achieved by intramodal (rail–rail) competition. To the extent that rail–rail competition is considered to be inadequate in the region or to the extent that it might be reduced by consolidation, intermodal competition must be relied upon to pick up the slack.

Intermodal competition establishes an effective ceiling on rail rates and a floor under rail service quality. The marketability of railroad services is sharply constrained by intermodal competition, since no shipper will pay a higher rate if comparable service is available elsewhere at the same or lower charge. Shippers may be willing to pay more for better service, and trucking companies can provide high quality service at costs competitive with rail over a wide range of commodities and distances. Barge lines transport bulk commodities between points on the inland waterway system at rates substantially

Table 3-4

MODAL SHARE OF INTERCITY FREIGHT TRAFFIC IN THE UNITED STATES, 1929–1973

(billions of net ton-miles)

Year	Railroad		Motor Carrier[a]		Inland Waterway System	
	Ton-Miles	Percent of Total	Ton-Miles	Percent of Total	Ton-Miles	Percent of Total
1929	454.8	74.9	19.7	3.3	8.7	1.4
1939	338.8	62.4	52.8	9.7	19.9	3.7
1942	645.4	69.5	59.9	6.5	26.4	2.8
1947	664.5	65.3	102.1	10.0	34.5	3.4
1952	623.4	54.5	194.6	17.0	63.8	5.6
1957	626.2	46.9	254.2	19.0	114.6	8.6
1962	600.0	43.8	309.0	22.5	133.0	9.7
1967	731.2	41.4	388.5	22.0	174.0	9.9
1970	771.0	39.8	412.0	21.3	204.0	10.6
1971	746.0	38.2	445.0	22.7	210.0	10.7
1972	784.3	37.8	470.0	22.6	229.8	11.1
1973[b]	860.0	38.7	510.0	23.0	237.0	10.7

a Includes both for-hire and private carriers.
b Preliminary figures.

Source: American Trucking Associations, *American Trucking Trends,* 1973; American Waterway Operators, *Inland Waterborne Commerce Statistics*; Association of American Railroads, *Yearbook of Railroad Facts,* 1974 edition, and

lower than railroads can charge. Pipelines have captured nearly all of the market in long-distance transport of petroleum and petroleum products and threaten to take away coal traffic if slurry pipeline technology improves in the future. Mine-mouth power generation already has made inroads into the traditional rail business of coal transport. Great Lakes shipping has lost traffic to other modes, but still carries traffic which might have gone by rail. Table 3-4 shows the change in shares of the transport market realized by each of the major modes over the last half century.

There are two conflicting viewpoints from which to discuss intermodal competition. The first is the broad policy issue of whether intermodal competition is effective in keeping transportation rates close to costs and ensuring good service to shippers in the absence of sufficient traffic density to warrant rail–rail competition. The second viewpoint emphasizes the marketing and financial outlook for railroad traffic and

Table 3-4 (Continued)

MODAL SHARE OF INTERCITY FREIGHT TRAFFIC IN THE UNITED STATES, 1929–1973
(billions of net ton-miles)

Great Lakes		Pipeline		Air Cargo			Real GNP
Ton-Miles	Percent of Total	Ton-Miles	Percent of Total	Ton-Miles	Percent of Total	Total	(billions of 1958 dollars)
97.3	16.0	26.9	4.4	0.003	—	607.4	203.6
76.3	14.0	55.6	10.2	0.012	—	543.5	209.4
122.2	13.1	75.1	8.1	0.034	—	929.0	297.8
112.2	11.0	105.2	10.3	0.16	0.01	1,018.7	309.9
104.5	9.1	157.5	13.8	0.41	0.03	1,144.3	395.1
117.3	8.8	222.7	16.7	0.57	0.05	1,335.6	452.5
90.0	6.6	238.0	17.3	1.30	0.09	1,371.0	529.8
107.0	6.1	361.0	20.5	2.59	0.15	1,765.0	675.2
114.0	5.9	431.0	22.3	3.30	0.17	1,935.9	722.5
105.0	5.4	448.0	22.9	3.50	0.18	1,954.0	746.3
108.9	5.2	480.0	23.1	3.70	0.18	2,076.7	792.7
114.0	5.1	495.0	22.3	4.20	0.20	2,220.2	839.2

Railroad Transportation: A Statistical Record 1921–1959, December 1960; Interstate Commerce Commission, Intercity Ton-Miles 1939–1959, April 1961; Transportation Association of America, Transportation Facts and Trends, 10th ed., July 1973.

revenues; such prospects are highly dependent on the effectiveness of competition from other modes of transport.

Effects of Intermodal Competition on Railroad Rate Levels. Intermodal competition tends to result in lower freight rates. One piece of evidence is that rail average revenues per ton-mile (adjusted for inflation) are declining, yet the railroads are not winning but losing percentage shares of total traffic to other modes.

Motor carriers in particular have taken the more attractive traffic from the railroads, leaving the railroads with the so-called rail-bound commodities such as coal, grain, fertilizer, and other bulk commodities. Rails have lowered rates on even these commodities in an effort to prevent further erosion. As a result, total tonnage originated has been at a fairly constant level over the postwar period, but average revenue per ton-mile in constant dollars has declined. These relationships are shown in Figure 3-1. To reemphasize, declining average revenue per ton-mile is the result both of changes in the mix of rail traffic and of decreases in rates on many bulk commodities kept by rail.[6]

Economist Ann F. Friedlaender offers another piece of evidence on the efficacy of intermodal competition. In *The Dilemma of Freight Transport Regulation,*[7] Friedlaender gives examples from congressional testimony in which rail rates were 55 percent lower in the presence of water competition for numerous commodity classes than would be experienced in the absence of competition. These data are several years old, but the point remains valid. One extreme example involved aluminum billets from Riverdale, Iowa, to points in Arkansas (rail only) and Texas (rail and water). Although the Texas destination was 94 percent farther than the Arkansas destination, the water-competitive rail rate was only 40 percent as large as the noncompetitive destination rate.

More recent evidence of the influence of competition in holding down the level of rates was made available to a USRA consultant by the U.S. Army Corps of Engineers, which is conducting an analysis of the extent to which waterway operations in the Southwest have served to hold down rail rate levels. Table 3-5 shows rail rates for selected iron and steel commodities in 1972 before and after the opening of

---

[6] Between 1953 and 1966, rail average revenue per ton-mile decreased in absolute terms (current dollars). Since 1966, the rate level has increased gradually in current dollars but is hardly changed in constant dollars. For example, the 1973 average was 29 percent above the level prevailing in 1966. Even more striking, the 1973 average was only 12 percent above the 1959 level.

[7] Ann F. Friedlaender, *The Dilemma of Freight Transport Regulation* (Washington, D.C.: The Brookings Institution, 1969).

Figure 3-1

U.S. CLASS I RAIL CARRIERS' TRENDS OF ORIGINATED TONNAGE, MARKET SHARE, AND REVENUE PER TON-MILE IN CONSTANT DOLLARS, 1945–1973

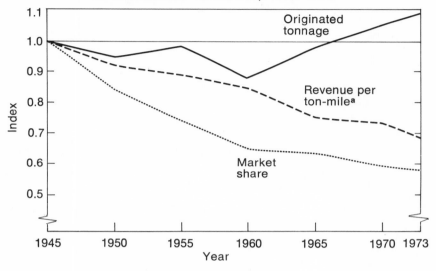

a Deflated with the 1967 wholesale price index.

Source: Association of American Railroads, *Facts and Figures*; Transportation Association of America, *Transportation Facts and Trends*.

waterway service competitive with railroads. Average reductions in the range of 15 percent to 20 percent were the rule.

Cost Advantages: Different Modes and Markets. Railroads function in the middle of a spectrum of transport costs. The lower end of the spectrum is inhabited by pipelines and waterway carriers. These modes are capable of accommodating shippers with cost structures lower than the rails and with different, generally slower, service characteristics because of limited route structure and commodity capability. At the higher end of the spectrum is the motor carrier. Trucks generally charge rates higher than rail rates but offer faster point-to-point speeds, smaller loadings, some improvement in shipment loss and damage, and route flexibility.

Alexander Morton has shown that major portions of present rail traffic are susceptible to diversion by motor carriers. Trucks are especially strong competitors for manufactures. Morton concluded that competition between the modes exists across a broad front of traffic.

Table 3-5

SELECTED RAILROAD RATE REDUCTIONS RESULTING FROM NEW WATERWAY COMPETITION, 1972

Commodity	Origin-Destination	Rate in Cents/Hundredweight		Percent Reduction
		Before competition	After competition	
Iron rods	Birmingham, Ala.–Fort Smith, Ark.	90	72	20.0
Steel bars	Minnequa, Colo.–Tulsa, Okla.	95	76	20.0
Steel plate	Elk Grove Village, Ill.–Jacksonville, Ark.	97	77	20.6
Steel sheets	Allenport, Pa.–Tulsa, Okla.	143	121	15.4
Rough iron castings	Wheeling, W.Va.–Tulsa, Okla.	139	115	17.3
Coiled sheet steel	Chicago, Ill.–Fort Smith, Ark.	105	85	19.0
Steel plate	Wheeling, W.Va.–Little Rock, Ark.	125	103	17.6
Hot rolled sheets	Youngstown, Ohio–Tulsa, Okla.	141	118	16.3
Coiled sheet steel	Pittsburgh, Pa.–Tulsa, Okla.	143	121	15.4
Steel sheets	Cleveland, Ohio–Tulsa, Okla.	133	110	17.3
Coiled sheet steel	Vicksburg, Miss.–Tulsa, Okla.	82	67	18.3
Steel shapes, unfinished	Lone Star, Tex.–North Little Rock, Ark.	48	40	16.7
Steel sheets	Shreveport, La.–Little Rock, Ark.	46	37	19.6
Coiled sheet steel	Dallas, Tex.–Fort Smith, Ark.	57	45	21.1

54

Steel plate	New Orleans, La.–Fort Smith, Ark.	91	74	18.7
Steel beams	Birmingham, Ala.–Little Rock, Ark.	67	60	10.4
Steel beams	Birmingham, Ala.–Fort Smith, Ark.	90	76	15.6
Steel angles	Minnequa, Colo.–Muskogee, Okla.	100	83	17.0
Steel beams	Kansas City, Mo.–Fort Smith, Ark.	58	50	13.8
Steel plate	Crescentville, Pa.–Tulsa, Okla.	181	152	16.0
Steel rods	Tulsa, Okla.–Chicago, Ill.	105	101	3.8
Coiled sheet steel	Milwaukee, Wis.–Little Rock, Ark.	105	89	15.2
Coiled sheet steel	Pittsburgh, Pa.–Fort Smith, Ark.	141	121	14.2
Steel bars	Atlanta, Ga.–Tulsa, Okla.	123	103	16.3
Steel rebar	Sand Springs, Okla.–New Orleans, La.	68	61	10.3
Steel shapes	Chicago, Ill.–Tulsa, Okla.	105	70	66.7

Note: Selected commodities are a representative sample of many railroad commodities susceptible to intermodal competition from barge lines.

Source: Sample made available to USRA consultant Simat, Hellieson and Eichner in worksheet form by U.S. Army, Corps of Engineers, Southwestern Division, Dallas, Texas.

Either mode can divert substantial amounts of manufacturing traffic from the other.[8]

Morton's study found motor common carrier rates averaged only 18 percent more than rail rates on shipments of manufactures of equal weight and length of haul; such shipments accounted for 30 percent to 35 percent of highway ton-miles. The study concluded that about 40 percent of manufacturing tonnage is subject to effective intermodal competition between regulated motor carriers and railroads, and that is a lower bound.

A study by the Association of American Railroads (AAR) compared truck costs with a sample of rail rates for certain commodity groups. On canned goods moving between 1,100 and 1,500 miles, the rail rates were 2.6 to 2.7 cents per ton-mile; the private truck costs were 2.4 cents per ton-mile with a 25 percent empty backhaul.[9] On steel moving distances of 900 to 1,050 miles, rail rates were 2.8 to 3.1 cents per ton-mile. This compares with the cost of an "owner-operator" truck of 2.3 cents with a 25 percent empty backhaul and 3.2 cents with a 75 percent empty backhaul. In all cases, the motor carrier costs would have been still lower if they had been computed at the 80,000-pound minimum weight limit recently authorized by Congress.

Competitive Advantages and Alternative Modes. This section describes various characteristics of the three modes most competitive with rail: trucking, water transport, and pipelines. Table 3-6 displays market shares by mode for fourteen key commodities. This list excludes pipelines, which specialize and predominate in the transport of petroleum and natural gas products.

Trucking. Motor carriers can be classified on many bases, among them the three operating characteristics—size, service area, and service type. Their size can range from the individual owner-operator to the large well-known interstate common carriers. Their service area can range from a single small municipality to all of the United States. The type of service can range from carriers of special commodities, such as cement or steel, to common carriers of general commodities.

The motor carrier industry can be divided further on the basis of economic regulation—exempt, contract, and common carriage. Car-

[8] Alexander L. Morton, "Intermodel Competition for the Intercity Transport of Manufactures," *Land Economics*, vol. 48 (November 1972).

[9] Association of American Railroads, Staff Studies Group, various memoranda, including: 74-9 (June 21, 1974), 74-19 (October 22, 1974), 74-19 addendum (October 31, 1974), 75-3 (January 20, 1975), and 75-3 addendum (February 7, 1975).

Table 3-6

MARKET SHARES BY MODE OF DOMESTIC INTERCITY FREIGHT TONNAGE FOR FOURTEEN COMMODITIES, 1970

(percent)

Commodity	Railroads	Private and For-hire Trucking	Water
Agriculture	34.8	56.6	8.3
Iron ore	52.6	7.3	39.9
Coal	78.0	9.1	12.9
Food and drugs	33.4	62.8	3.6
Textiles	6.7	92.4	0.1
Lumber	46.9	18.5	34.5
Paper products	56.6	39.1	4.1
Chemicals	43.1	44.0	12.7
Stone, clay, glass	36.0	62.3	1.6
Iron and steel	36.6	53.1	10.1
Nonferrous metals	45.2	49.3	5.3
Fabricated metal products	22.9	75.8	0.8
Motor vehicles	32.5	65.6	1.6
Scrap	82.6	5.5	12.0

Source: U.S. Department of Transportation, *Transportation Projections 1970–80*, July 1971.

riage exempt from ICC regulation accounts for up to 60 percent of the ton-miles moving in interstate commerce. Exempt carriers are not constrained by rate or other economic regulation when carrying raw agricultural commodities, livestock, fish, newspapers, goods moving to and from agricultural cooperatives, and certain other miscellaneous cargoes, or when operating within a single locality.

Private and contract carriage also do not fall under ICC regulation. Private carriage, another category of exempt motor carriage, involves the operation of a truck fleet by firms for the movement of their own raw materials and products. Contract carriers operate under contract to one or more persons or firms to supply the exclusive use of vehicles or services to meet the purchaser's particular needs. They fulfill many of the same functions and often replace private carriage. In 1970 almost half of all intercity freight ton-miles moved by non-regulated for-hire carriers or by private carriers transporting their own goods. Out of a total U.S. truck fleet of 21 million vehicles in 1972, the combination tractor-trailer units were the most competitive with railroads. There are about 1 million of these units, approximately 4.7 percent of all trucks, and more than half are in private fleets.

Common carriers engaged in interstate or foreign commerce are required to serve all shippers, under rules and regulations set by the Interstate Commerce Commission. The ICC grants to common carriers operating rights which may specify the routes, terminals, and commodities allowed to each carrier. The regulated segment of the industry handled less than one-third of the ton-miles of intercity truck transport in 1970.

Exempt and irregular-route common contract carriers typically haul full truckload traffic, while regular-route common carriers usually handle less-than-truckload (LTL) traffic as well. The nonregulated and private carriers provide the strongest competition for the railroads.

There are approximately twenty-five thousand owner-operators of trucks which haul both exempt and regulated commodities. Nearly half of these operators achieve 125,000 miles per power unit per year, compared with regulated carriers which average approximately 65,000 miles per year. Owner-operators who maintain no terminals, carry no insurance, and avoid other services have costs generally below those of large motor carrier companies.

New and improved highways provide shorter, faster routes between significant market areas, contributing to better use of equipment and lower direct operating costs. Urban feeder highways are being improved along with the interstate highway program. These urban feeder changes will hold down truckers' pickup and delivery costs even more. In addition, dedicated rights-of-way for trucks and buses are a distinct possibility in the future.

The cost to the rail industry for the maintenance of its right-of-way and the interest charges it carries to own and upgrade that right-of-way have more than doubled over the last two decades and may double again within the next decade. If rail traffic volume cannot be increased sharply, rail unit costs will continue to rise rapidly, and the rail industry will become even less competitive for traffic which can be accommodated by trucks.

The rail industry will be affected competitively by other changes in the efficiency of motor carriers. Technical improvements in truck engine performance, streamlining, and the use of radial tires will result in lower operating costs for motor carriers. But most important, potential legal changes which would permit higher operating weights would reduce truck costs and weaken the competitive position of the rail industry wherever both modes can handle the same products.

Water carriers. The second major mode which competes with the railways is the water carrier. Approximately 80 percent of the tonnage handled by this mode moves through mid-America and along the Gulf intercoastal system. Federal funds have been spent for the direct benefit of the inland waterway system, including several billion dollars since the turn of the century. Locks and dams were built, sharp river bends minimized, and channels dredged. In addition, major improvements, expected to cost several billion dollars, are currently under way within the region.

Technological improvements such as improved hull designs, more powerful towboats, and better navigational aids also are taking place. Operators are experimenting with thirty-barge tows on the upper Mississippi system. On the Great Lakes system, bigger ships are being introduced, and the navigation season is being extended. There are reasonable prospects that year-round operation will be possible in the future.

Barge lines and railroads compete primarily on the basis of price. Given expected improvements in lock size and channel depth as a result of direct federal expenditures and the expected growth of tow sizes, water carrier costs may be reduced by up to 25 percent.[10] Partly because of this form of federal support, it is significantly less costly to ship by water if shipments are in very large volumes and are between points on or very close to the waterways.

Diversion of freight from rail to water is a response to changes in rates, and the potential for greater diversion has required lower water-competitive rates to retain certain rail movements. The financial condition of rail carriers in the region, therefore, is affected by the generally low level of their own water-competitive rates, and further competitive pressures seem certain.

Furthermore, declining barge transportation costs induce industry to relocate along the waterways and away from railroads. This has been particularly true of large manufacturing plants such as chemical and sugar refineries which are bulk shippers well served by water carriers.

Pipelines. The pipeline mode, ideally suited to moving large volumes of liquid or gas, has exhibited rapid growth. Today there are 220,000 miles of oil pipelines and 250,000 miles of gas pipelines in the United States.

Although there are no slurry pipelines at present within the region, interest has been shown in transporting solids, particularly coal,

---

[10] Reebie Associates, *Freight Transportation: Future Modal Competitiveness*, study performed for the United States Railway Association, February 1975.

by this mode. Large deposits of coal, combined with adequate water supply, suggests that this mode may increase in importance as a competitive force. Pipeline advantages are minimal environmental impact, reduced energy requirements, low unit-operating expenses, and high reliability.

Regulation. Many economists and others believe ICC regulation has inhibited the railroads from adjusting their rates to reflect cost or service advantages and has thus hindered their ability to compete effectively with the other modes of transportation. Recent proposed legislation would allow railroads to lower their rates so long as variable costs are covered. In years past, the ICC has at times protected water and motor carriers through "umbrella" rate making and has refused to allow railroads to take advantage of lower variable unit costs by reducing rates, even when long-term variable costs indicated that rail was the more efficient mode.

As mentioned above, common carriers operate under a mandate to maintain proper standards of service (price, quality, frequency, and so forth), while the franchises (that is, restrictions on further entry) are supposed to help assure adequate profits and industry stability. Regulation (affecting, as it does, price competition and service competition between railroads and other modes of transportation) often is thought to thwart realization of the broad goals of common carriage—thus continuing the misallocation of transport resources.

The ICC's early disinclination to approve rate-cutting efforts by the railroads aimed at winning traffic back from the trucks has contributed to the present financial plight of the railroads. It then was believed that the trucks probably would match the railroads' rate reductions and would continue to compete with the rails at the reduced rate levels by cutting back services or forcing rate increases to smaller shippers and areas of lesser traffic volume. If the trucks successfully lowered their rates to meet rail rate reductions, the rails would have lost revenue on this competitive traffic; then the rails might try to compensate by increasing rates on routes not subject to competition. "As a result, the Commission often found such proposed rate changes, either truck or rail, to be destructively competitive and in violation of national policy."[11]

Common carriage has declined during the postwar years, led by the decline in railroads—the principal totally regulated surface mode.[12]

---

[11] Robert A. Nelson and William R. Greiner, "The Relevance of the Common Carrier under Modern Economic Conditions," in *Transportation Economics* (Washington, D.C.: National Bureau of Economic Research, 1965), p. 369.

[12] The *ASTRO Report* noted that "an estimated 75 percent of today's rail

At the same time, the combination of advantages inherent in trucking and frequently restrictive conditions on motor common carriers (routes, commodities, and backhaul operations) has contributed to the rapid growth of private, contract, and exempt motor carriage markets. As a result, the regulated motor carriers' share of the trucking market has declined relative to private and contract truckers and motor carriage of exempt commodities.

Moreover, regulation has tended to aggravate the misallocation of transportation resources. Exempt and private truckers are free from economic regulation, but they are not allowed to carry payloads of regulated commodities when returning from their destinations. Common carriers may be hampered by restrictions limiting what they can handle and similarly may experience empty backhauls. These factors have increased highway congestion and energy use.

Conclusion

There is a delicate balance between the perceived costs of transport service provided by rail and by competitive modes. This balance shifts with the type of commodities transported, length of haul, and the climate created by public policy. Intermodal competition is an adequate substitute for rail–rail competition in many markets. As transport technologies and public policies change, the number and character of markets competitive between rail carriers and other modes also changes. In general, the trucking mode is becoming competitive with rail for more and more types of shipments. If this trend continues, there will be less need for rail–rail competition as a guarantor against monopolistic abuses, because trucking alternatives will be readily available. Increasing intermodal competition also hurts railroads' financial condition, leaving the rail industry less able to suggest multiple-carrier service between any two market areas, at the same time that the need for rail–rail competition has diminished.

Intermodal competition may not be capable of producing some of the benefits associated with rail–rail competition that were discussed in the first section of this chapter. Those benefits probably can be derived from indirect rail–rail competition, however, as well as from direct competition. If that is the case, as it probably is, the steadily advancing efficacy of intermodal competition will reduce the benefits of having multiple railroads exist in the same markets. These

traffic could move without such regulation on at least one other mode." See America's Sound Transportation Review Organization, *The American Railroad Industry: A Prospectus* (Washington, D.C., 1970).

developments will strengthen the tentative conclusion that indirect rail–rail competition fulfills the act's competitive mandate in most markets.

Much of the high-rated traffic, the "cream" that the trucks and the rails have squabbled about, has been skimmed from the common carrier system altogether. The ICC must attempt to balance the competing interests of various regulated modes while recognizing the increasing competitive pressure from unregulated carriage, an effort which offers no hope for an easy solution. If such a balance cannot be achieved, with respect to both market access and rate levels, the ultimate responsibility for supporting the common carrier system will shift from the private consumer to the public taxpayer, and control of that system will shift from private enterprise to government.

4

TIME FOR CORRECTIVE ACTION

William T. Coleman, Jr.

Mr. President, as your principal advisor on transportation matters, I feel compelled to convey to you my sense of the desperate plight of the nation's railroads. The state of the rail industry today not only endangers any prospect of economic growth in this country but also imperils our important national objective of energy independence. There is a growing mood in Congress that the only answer to the crisis of the railroads is some form of nationalization. I believe that a private sector solution is possible—if we move quickly. There is an urgent need for action. Therefore, I respectfully urge you to undertake a dramatic, coordinated program to revitalize the nation's private enterprise railroad system.

The Importance of the Railroad Industry

For more than a century, the railroads have been the backbone of this nation's transportation system. Even after years of decline, railroads still carry 38 percent of all freight (in ton-miles), easily exceeding the 23 percent transported by motor carrier and the 16 percent moved via inland waterway. Railroads carry 70 percent of the automobiles produced in this country, 66 percent of the food, 78 percent of the lumber and wood, 60 percent of the chemicals, 60 percent of the primary metal products, and 71 percent of the pulp and paper. If the nation is to realize its economic growth potential during the remainder of the twentieth century, the railroads must be in a condition to move significantly increased freight volumes quickly and safely.

This chapter is edited from a memorandum entitled "The Crisis of the Nation's Railroads," prepared for President Gerald R. Ford by Secretary of Transportation William T. Coleman, Jr., April 11, 1975.

Moreover, a healthy railroad industry is crucial to the energy needs of this country. The railroads must play the predominant role in supplying the nation with coal during the remainder of this century. The railroad industry transports 70 percent of the coal produced in this country, a task involving approximately 81 percent of its main-line network. Your Project Independence, to make the nation self-sufficient in energy, envisions a doubling of domestic coal production by 1985. To meet this goal, railroads will be required to double their coal-carrying capacity. Actual ton-miles of coal carried by rail, however, must triple because of changes in origin from eastern coal to low-sulphur western coal. This would necessitate coal shipments over 90 percent of the railroad main-line network. Greatly improved railroad service is, therefore, essential to the development and use of coal for energy. In addition, rail transportation is the most energy efficient of all the modes, both freight and passenger. With regard to freight transportation, our research indicates that railways are significantly more energy efficient than trucks, their ubiquitous competitor, or airlines, and slightly more efficient than even barge movement. As for passenger service, our research indicates that railroads, when properly utilized, are substantially more energy efficient than either automobiles or airlines in moving passengers and are approached in efficiency only by intercity bus. In summation, a healthy, progressive, strengthened railroad system is absolutely essential to our national objective of energy independence.

The Problem Facing the Railroad Industry

Given the paramount importance of the railways in both the past and the future of this country, the dilapidated state of the railroad industry is alarming. The facts are startling. Over one-half of the present rail track in the country is unfit for high-speed operations. It is not uncommon for train operations on main-line tracks to be limited to speeds of ten to twenty miles per hour. Accidents and derailments have nearly doubled since 1967. Because of outdated equipment and methods and the resultant inefficiency, a typical freight car moves loaded only twenty-three days a year. It is becoming increasingly apparent that the rail industry, as presently constituted, will be manifestly unable either to support the traffic our economy generates or to meet the challenge of increased coal carriage which energy independence demands.

For many years now the income generated by the American railroads has been insufficient to meet the requirements of plant maintenance and rehabilitation and, with rates of return of 3 percent or less, funds from outside sources are virtually unavailable. The deferred maintenance in the industry is now estimated to range as high as $7.5 billion. Although the problems of railroads are most severe in the Northeast and Midwest (where eight carriers are bankrupt), numerous other railroads, especially the so-called Granger roads that operate in the Plains states, are in precarious financial condition. The massive problems of the railroad industry are most recently aggravated by the largest quarterly deficit in rail history. Today the United States is confronted with the grim reality that a major breakdown of our rail freight system is a distinct possibility.

It is important that the underlying causes of the railroad problem be clearly understood. A great deal of the discussion on this subject is focused on the poor condition of main-line track and on the bankruptcies. These are symptoms but they are not the underlying causes of railroad difficulty. The principal factors underlying railroad difficulty are: (1) redundant facilities and excess competition; (2) outmoded regulation; (3) archaic work rules; (4) lack of capital to finance rehabilitation; and (5) preferential treatment of other modes.

Perhaps the principal factor underlying railroad problems is the redundancy of plant and the excess competition that exists within the industry. This is especially true in the Northeast and Midwest and, as a result, these are the areas where railroad problems are the worst. There are simply more facilities of all types—yards, main-line tracks, and branch lines—than are required to provide economical and efficient service. In many instances, two or more railroads compete for traffic sufficient only for the survival of one carrier.

Second, slow and cumbersome regulatory procedures impede responses to competition and changes in market conditions and at times result in traffic being handled at noncompensatory rates. These procedures also have created a serious impediment to needed restructuring. Regulation that was necessary when it was enacted decades ago is simply unresponsive to today's needs. This inflexibility stemming from Interstate Commerce Commission procedures and rules is a major deterrent to railroad efficiency and viability. For instance, after twelve years, the attempt to restructure the Rock Island Railroad through merger with other carriers is still incomplete.

Third, the existing work rules in the industry are a major obstacle to achievement of economic potential in the railroad system. Archaic arrangements regarding both the size of the crews that man trains and crew payment weigh heavily upon the industry and severely limit productivity.

Fourth, lack of capital and the resultant deferred maintenance has caused widespread deterioration of main-line track and other parts of the railroads' physical plant. Clearly, there is a need to rehabilitate the essential portions of the industry's physical plant—but that rehabilitation will be effective in revitalizing the railroads only if the burdens of redundant facilities, regulatory constraints, and costly work rules are also alleviated.

Finally, there has been, over the years, preferential treatment of the other transportation modes by the federal government. Only the railroads (with the exception of the pipeline companies) own their own rights-of-way and have to carry the fixed charges of ownership and maintenance of this extensive plant.

The Congressional Reaction

There is a great deal of pressure building in Congress for a solution to the railroad problem, and there is growing feeling on the Hill that the only answer lies in some form of nationalization. Faced with the prospect of continuing crises and the necessity of providing more and more federal money, there is an understandable desire to ensure that the American public receives something in return for its heavy investment. In the absence of a constructive alternative, Congress may indeed turn to nationalization. Senators Vance Hartke (Democrat, Indiana) and Lowell P. Weicker, Jr. (Republican, Connecticut), have introduced legislation to nationalize the railroad rights-of-way, as has Senator Hubert H. Humphrey (Democrat, Minnesota). Congressman Brock Adams (Democrat, Washington), a leading spokesman on rail matters in the House, has publicly stated that serious consideration should be given to such a proposal. Privately, many other congressmen and senators are saying that the only solution to rail industry problems lies in nationalization. In any event, Congress has already seized upon the obvious problem of deteriorating track and roadbed as an interim means of improving the railroad situation. Senator Jennings Randolph (Democrat, West Virginia) intends to introduce a bill to provide for a $1 billion program for upgrading rail rights-of-way. Congressman Henry John Heinz III (Republican, Pennsylvania) and Senator James L. Buckley (Conservative-Republican, New York) have each introduced separate bills to spend $2.5 billion and $2.0 billion, respectively, to upgrade deteriorating trackage through employment programs.

It is highly unfortunate that some of the solutions receiving serious consideration in Congress are excessively expensive, inappropriate responses to the real problem, and bad for the country. The congressional proposal of nationalization of the industry, or, at least, of the rights-of-way, would mean not only an injection of unnecessary federal control into another area of our national life but also unnecessary rehabilitation and maintenance expenditures on excess railroad plant. Total physical rehabilitation of the existing rail system is not only prohibitively expensive but also undesirable. What is needed is a major rationalization of the rail facilities of the country and an elimination of redundant capacity through mergers and joint use of facilities. Only the components of a rationalized rail plant should be rehabilitated. Moreover, rehabilitation of track will be of little benefit to the railroads or to the nation unless the other difficulties of the railroads can be overcome as well. A track rehabilitation program should only be commenced as a part of a broader program to overcome other industry problems such as regulatory restraints and work rules.

A Program to Rebuild the Railroad Industry

The Department of Transportation has a comprehensive program which I believe will assure the United States of a viable private enterprise rail system capable of meeting the commerce and energy needs of this country. The program involves: (1) a consolidation and streamlining of the national rail system utilizing financial incentives and relief from impediments to rail mergers and joint use of facilities; (2) removal of a number of outmoded and inequitable regulations on railroads; (3) as an important first step to nationwide rail consolidation, the forging of a successful conclusion to the current rail restructuring process in the Northeast in a form consistent with the national program of consolidation; (4) measures to reduce preferential treatment of competing modes; and (5) recognition of the indispensability of rail passenger service in certain corridors and the public (and congressional) demand for such service in other areas.

Implementation of the Program

The cost of rehabilitating even the streamlined rail plant that I have proposed will be high. On the other hand, I am keenly aware, Mr. President, of your dedication to fiscal responsibility. Therefore, the Department of Transportation has already developed two concrete legislative proposals which will not only take great strides in furthering the program I have outlined but also be consonant with your opposition to any new spending programs.

First, we have prepared a bill called the Railroad Revitalization Act of 1975 to provide $2 billion in loan guarantees to railroads to finance the rationalization and streamlining facilities. The $2 billion in the bill is already a part of your budget proposals, and the proposal is awaiting White House approval. As a condition of receiving assistance, the secretary of transportation will be able to require railroads to enter into agreements for the joint use of tracks, terminals, and other facilities and to enter into agreements for mergers to rationalize further the rail system. The proposed bill also provides significant regulatory reform by amending the Interstate Commerce Act to permit increased pricing flexibility, to expedite rate-making procedures, to outlaw anticompetitive rate bureau practices, and to improve the procedures for dealing with intrastate rates.

Second, I have proposed a $1.2 billion Emergency Railroad Rehabilitation Program to attack forthwith the accelerating deterioration of the railroad physical plant. The proposal carries with it significant immediate benefits for employment in the country. The money for this bill could, as one alternative, come from rescinding $1.2 billion of the $9.1 billion for highways currently being impounded. As a result, it would not increase federal funding authorizations but rather would reallocate funds from lower priority to higher priority transportation programs. I believe that public reaction, except for the die-hard supporters of expanded highway programs, will be positive. This proposal also is awaiting White House approval. The primary emphasis of the proposal is to rehabilitate and maintain main-line routes and major terminals that will be included in any restructured and streamlined railroad system. This legislation will significantly assist the nation's energy goals by giving priority to those projects which will aid in the movement of coal.

The financial assistance provided through the proposed Rail Revitalization and Energy Transportation Act and the Emergency Railroad Rehabilitation Program, coupled with the regulatory reform contained in the former, will provide the *foundation* for a viable private enterprise railroad industry. Moreover, these two legislative proposals will announce the administration's determination to deal with urgent national problems even while simultaneously maintaining a commitment to fiscal responsibility. At the least, the Emergency Railroad Rehabilitation option of using highway money would put pressure on Congress to consider trade-offs rather than add-ons to the budget as the means for financing the railroad programs it is considering.

In conclusion, Mr. President, I believe that the two legislative proposals I have outlined are important initial steps in constructing a comprehensive program to save the American railroads.

5

THE FORD ADMINISTRATION'S PROPOSAL FOR RAIL REGULATORY REFORM

John W. Snow

Few economic issues have captured the attention of Washington more than economic regulatory reform. The Ford administration has made modernization of government regulation a high priority. The President's *Economic Report to Congress* in 1975 devoted an entire chapter to regulatory reform. In April, speaking to a White House Conference on Domestic and Economic Affairs held in New Hampshire, the President announced that he would send to Congress a comprehensive legislative package to revitalize many aspects of federal economic regulation. Much of this attention is focused on intercity freight transportation, one of the most highly regulated domestic industries. Calling competition "the key to productive innovation," President Ford stated that "forthcoming legislation will contain proposals designed to allow railroads, airlines, and trucking firms to lower their rates, while increasing competition, which will also result in a more efficient use of energy and savings to the consumer." The administration's railroad regulatory reform bill will be sent to Congress in the very near term and will be followed shortly thereafter by legislation dealing with motor carrier regulatory reform and airline regulatory reform. The basic thrust of these proposals will be to place greater reliance on competitive market forces in transportation.

There is a growing recognition that the regulatory system is amiss and in need of basic change. The failures of the present regulatory system and the inherent unresponsiveness of regulations to changing market conditions are increasingly evident. The corrective

This chapter is edited from a paper that was initially prepared for the National Conference on Surface Freight Transportation sponsored by the Public Interest Economics Foundation and the Urban Environment Conference in early May of 1975, several days before the Ford administration submitted the Railroad Revitalization Act to the Congress.

is to allow the dynamics of market forces to operate in transportation.

The failure of the current system of transport regulation is most apparent in the case of the railroad industry. Both the financial condition and the operating condition of the railroad industry today bear witness to this fact. Many railroads are in bankruptcy and the rate of return for the industry in general is anemic. As a whole, the railroad industry cannot generate sufficient earnings to make needed improvements in track, roadbed, and facilities, while funds from outside sources increasingly are not available for these purposes. As a consequence, a substantial part of the total rail industry in the United States is in a state of deterioration. The railroad industry's share of total intercity freight ton-miles and the average revenue per ton-mile have declined over a long period of time. The industry, furthermore, is burdened by many miles of uneconomic lines which are a financial drain and add substantially to operating costs. At the same time, parts of the railroad system are operating at or close to capacity, and these segments must be upgraded and expanded if the industry is to make its full contribution to the national transportation system.

In short, the railroads are in a vicious cycle. Low earnings rob them of the ability to make improvements in plant which are needed to reduce costs and improve service. The inability to reduce costs and improve service hampers the competitive position of railroads and adversely affects their net income—so the cycle is repeated. If we are to revitalize the railroad industry and achieve the full measure of benefits which healthy, progressive railroads can offer, it is essential to break this cycle.

A major cause (but certainly not the only cause) of the railroad industry's problems is an outmoded and excessively restrictive federal regulatory policy. Existing regulatory policy has seriously hampered the railroads' ability to adapt to changing economic and competitive conditions in the transportation industry. It has discouraged abandonment of uneconomic rail lines and has hindered the industry in introducing new services, responding to competitive conditions, and attracting additional traffic in areas where railroads have a competitive advantage.

The basic regulatory policy towards the railroad industry has changed very little since 1887 when the Interstate Commerce Act was adopted and the Interstate Commerce Commission was formed. In the intervening period, the competitive position of the railroad industry has changed dramatically with the rise of alternative modes of transportation—pipelines, trucks, barges, and aircraft. Whatever monopoly position railroads may have enjoyed in 1887, today railroads face intense competition from other modes of transportation.

This is clearly revealed by the railroads' loss of total intercity market shares to the other regulated modes. While the basic competitive conditions in transportation have changed dramatically, federal regulatory policy towards the railroad industry has not.

The time has come when we must substantially modify the present overly restrictive federal regulatory policy toward the railroad industry if we are to continue to have a viable rail system in the United States. We are at the crossroads. We can continue on the path which we have been on for the past fifty years or more and watch continual decline of our national rail system. This course will entail further decline in the quality of service to shippers, further loss of market shares, further plant deterioration, and the spread of bankruptcies throughout the system. At the end of that road lies nationalization. On the other hand, we can seize the opportunity to change the regulatory system, remove obsolete rules, and place greater reliance on the competitive market system. If we are to have the benefits of a viable, progressive, private-sector system, we must remove the restraints which prevent the rail system from adjusting to changing economic conditions and which sap its competitive vitality. By giving the rail managers pricing freedom, the ability to innovate new services, and the ability to adjust capacity to demand, we will create the essential conditions for a healthy, progressive, private-sector rail system. I am confident that, if the constraints of the present overly restrictive federal regulatory system are removed, we can avoid the specter of nationalization and we will witness the revitalization of this important industry.

The basic goal of the administration's forthcoming rail bill will be to improve the regulatory climate under which railroads operate and to encourage restructuring and revitalization of the nation's rail system. The bill also will provide financial assistance to modernize the rail plant and to encourage the long-term rationalization of the rail system. A major regulatory reform objective of the bill is to improve the rate-making system—in fact, improvements in rate making are at the heart of the regulatory reform in the bill. At the heart of the rail industry's problem is the inability of the railroads to adjust their prices and test their markets by experimenting with new prices and services.

Improvements in Rate Making

The current system of regulating rates severely limits an individual railroad's freedom to establish rates and innovative services. As a consequence, the system has created serious rigidity and distortions in railroad service and rate structures. This rigidity has hindered the introduction of new services and prevented railroads from responding effectively to the needs of the changing transportation market. It has also interfered with the establishment of cost-related rates and has prevented railroads from offering shippers the lower rates that would attract traffic from relatively less efficient modes.

Efficient allocation of transportation resources requires that carriers have wide latitude to set rates to reflect their costs. Available evidence indicates that some railroad rates are far above the true economic costs of providing service, while other rates do not even cover variable costs. As a result, some shippers subsidize other shippers and there is misallocation of traffic among the modes. Railroads should be able to attract additional traffic by reducing rates on overpriced rail service. By raising rates on traffic moving below variable costs, a significant financial drain on rails will be removed. The net result will be a healthier, stronger rail industry and a better, more efficient use of scarce transportation resources.

A basic thrust of the bill is to place greater reliance on competitive forces in rate making, while preserving appropriate regulatory supervision for the protection of shippers and carriers. Giving greater latitude to individual carriers to set rates will result in improved service, a more economical distribution of traffic among the modes, and a lower and more equitable overall freight bill. To provide for greater rate flexibility and to expedite the hearing process, the bill would set a definite time limit for completing rate-increase hearings at the ICC, establish a "no-suspend zone" in which carriers could introduce nondiscriminatory rate changes without fear of suspension by the commission, and provide that rates which are compensatory could not be attacked as being too low.

The no-suspend zone is a particularly important feature of the bill. It provides that increases or decreases could not be suspended pending investigation for being too high or too low. Increases or decreases could still be suspended for violating sections 2, 3, or 4 of the Interstate Commerce Act, which are the basic sections prohibiting discrimination and prejudice toward either an individual shipper or a community. The no-suspend zone would be phased in over a three-year period (7 percent in the first year, 12 percent in the second year, 15 percent in the third year, and thereafter 15 percent for increases, with no limit for decreases). The no-suspend zone will allow carriers to respond rapidly to market conditions and it will also improve the ICC's rate-deliberation process. Today, rate cases are often decided in a world of suppositions and "maybe's." When rate proposals are suspended by the ICC, the hearing on the lawfulness of the rate is without the benefit of "real world" experience regarding the effect of the rate. By allowing rates within the zone to go into effect before the hearing, the no-suspend provision will make concrete evidence available in the proceeding.

The present regulatory process has also resulted in the rates of one mode being held up by the ICC to protect another mode; this causes a waste of resources, adversely affects the financial condition of the more efficient mode, and increases the total cost to shippers and ultimately to consumers. Section 15(a) of the Interstate Commerce Act was amended by the Congress in 1958 in order to allow carriers greater rate-making freedom to meet the competition of carriers of other modes. Although the amendment was a step in the right direction, the full benefits of greater intermodal competition have not been realized because the ICC has interpreted the amendment in such a way as to prevent genuine cost efficiencies from being reflected in the marketplace. The bill directly addresses this problem by prohibiting the ICC from holding the rates of a carrier of one mode up to a particular level for the purpose of protecting the traffic of a carrier of another mode. The bill also provides that a railroad rate which equals or exceeds variable costs cannot be found to be unjust or unreasonable on the basis that it is too low. This provision will lead to greater flexibility in transportation rate making. The net result will be a more efficient transportation system in which rates are allowed to play the critically important function of allocating scarce resources to the most efficient use.

The time, expense, delay, and uncertainty associated with the regulatory process have also discouraged experimentation and have impeded the introduction of service innovations. The bill addresses the problem by providing that, where a tariff proposed by a railroad would require a total capital investment of $1 million or more by the carrier or by a shipper, a receiver, or some other interested party, the ICC must determine, within 180 days from the date the carrier files a notice of intention to publish the tariff, whether the proposed tariff would be lawful. This procedure would also protect those rates from being attacked for three years, thus giving a carrier the security necessary to undertake major investments.

Another vice of the present regulatory system is the fact that rates on a significant volume of traffic appear to have been held below cost. It is estimated that about 10 percent of all rail revenue is derived from traffic that does not cover the variable costs of the service. The bill confronts this problem in two ways. First, it would prohibit the commission—following an appropriate complaint—from approving rate decreases which lower the rate to a noncompensatory level. Second, with respect to existing noncompensatory rates, the bill would prohibit the commission from disapproving any increase which brings a noncompensatory rate to a compensatory level. These provisions will provide a significant source of additional revenue to the railroads and will ease the burden on those shippers who have been making up the difference. Correcting this practice will reduce the misallocation and waste of resources within both the transportation industry and the economy at large.

Restriction of Anticompetitive Practices of Rate Bureaus

If the benefits of rate flexibility contemplated under the administration's proposed bill are to be fully realized, it is essential that the collective rate-making practices of the industry be altered. Collective rate making must be strictly limited to those conditions and situations where it is required to promote orderly and efficient transport service. Under the present section 5(a) of the Interstate Commerce Act, the carriers subject to the commission's jurisdictions are permitted to act collectively in establishing rates and charges for transportation services. Such concerted action, when taken pursuant to an agreement approved by the ICC, is immune from the antitrust laws which apply to the mainstream of U.S. business. Rate bureaus or carrier associations have been established pursuant to carrier agreements approved by the ICC. These rate bureaus are the vehicles through which carriers make decisions regarding the rates of the member lines.

Although rate bureaus provide a number of valuable services to their members and to the shipping public, they also dampen competitive forces in the rate-making process and discourage pricing flexibility and service innovation. As a consequence, they have interfered with the establishment of rates based on the costs of the most efficient carrier and have provided a mechanism through which carriers seek to and do set and hold rates above a competitive level.

The associations provide a number of administrative services to carrier members, such as arranging for and facilitating the interchange of traffic moving over the lines of two or more carriers, publishing rates, and collecting statistics on traffic movements, rates charged, and related costs. The bill would not affect these administrative activities. Rather, it is addressed only to those activities of the rate bureaus which interfere with efficient allocation of resources.

The bill prohibits railroad rate bureaus from voting on single-line movements and limits consideration of joint-line rates to those railroads that will participate in the joint movement. The bill also prohibits rail rate bureaus from taking any action to suspend or protest rates. Thus, on single-line rates individual railroads will have complete freedom to propose rates based on the cost of the most direct routing, while on joint rates the influence of carriers not participating in the joint movement will be reduced.

The bill also requires all rate bureaus to dispose of proposed rate changes within 120 days from the time they are filed. It requires all rate bureaus to maintain and make available for public inspection the records of the votes of members. These provisions are designed to bring about speedier treatment by the rate bureaus of proposed rate changes and to encourage greater initiative by individual carriers in making rate changes.

Although some antitrust immunity is retained for joint rates, the proposed legislative change with respect to single-line rate agreements would exert a competitive influence upon joint rates because the territories of carriers overlap and single-line rates are often competitive with joint-line rates.

Taken together, the rate bureau changes and the rate-making changes should lead to a significant improvement in the pricing of rail services. Good pricing is essential to efficient resource allocation, and the plain fact is that the pricing mechanism in the railroad industry has been operating very badly. There cannot be any meaningful regulatory reform without the kind of far-reaching and fundamental change in the pricing system that I have discussed.

Financial Assistance through Loan Guarantees

An efficient, financially sound rail system is a great national asset. The railroad system in the United States is experiencing severe financial difficulties. Modernization of both the regulatory system and the physical plant is essential to the long-term viability of the nation's railroads. The rate-making and related regulatory improvements proposed in the administration's bill are a vital first step. There remains the task of rationalizing and upgrading the facilities and equipment necessary to provide efficient rail transportation service.

The bill would provide up to $2 billion in federal loan guarantee authority to finance improvements in rail plant facilities, track, terminals, and rolling stock. Loans guaranteed by the secretary of transportation could be financed through the Federal Financing Bank at interest rates below those available in the private market. Also, the provision is written in broad terms to allow financing with deferral of interest and principal payments. The conditions to the guarantee would assure that the capital improvement would make a significant contribution to the overall efficiency of rail operations. Thus, the loan guarantee provisions of the bill are designed to encourage needed long-term restructuring of the existing rail system.

Restructuring the System

One of the most significant and far-reaching problems in the rail industry is chronic excess capacity. The substantial excess capacity which characterizes the rail industry today has come about because the industry has not been able to adjust capacity to demand. This inability contributed enormously to the rail crisis in the Northeast. Unless this problem is dealt with, it will be a source of continuing crises in the rail industry. There are essentially two avenues through which carriers can adjust capacity to demand—abandonments and mergers—and both routes have been badly constrained by the Interstate Commerce Commission's regulatory practices. In order to encourage needed rationalization of the rail system, the administration's bill would authorize the secretary of transportation to make the granting of loan guarantees contingent upon an agreement among applicants or other railroads to restructure their facilities. Such restructuring could include merger, consolidation, sale or acquisition of assets, or joint use of facilities. Such agreements would be voluntary and the secretary could not require a railroad to enter into such an agreement except as a condition for loan guarantee. The essential purpose of this provision is to improve the efficiency of the nation's railroads by eliminating duplicative and excessive facilities.

In its interpretation of section 5 of the Interstate Commerce Act, the ICC has hindered this needed restructuring by failing to reach a decision about proposed agreements within a reasonable length of time and by dissipating the benefits of proposed agreements by imposing third-party conditions on such agreements. This bill will remedy these two defects by providing a new hearing procedure and a new definition of "public interest" in those cases where restructuring accompanies financial assistance.

Essentially, the bill calls for a two-part procedure. Agreements will first be considered by the secretary in a public proceeding similar to that used in rule making. Notice of the agreement will be given to the public, and comments may be made in writing or in an informal oral hearing. The secretary may then initially approve the agreement which contains the restructuring terms if it is in the public interest and certify the agreement to the ICC. The ICC will then have six months to decide whether the agreement is in the public interest. The "public interest" is defined in the bill to mean that (1) the efficiency gains of the transaction substantially outweigh any adverse effects on competition, and (2) there are no substantially less anticompetitive alternatives to the transaction. Unless the ICC specifically finds, by "clear and convincing evidence," that the proposed agreement is not in the public interest, it must approve the agreement. In addition to its concern for the preservation of competition, the bill makes specific provision for the rights of labor and shippers. If the ICC should fail to act within the specified time, it must certify the proceeding back to the secretary, and the secretary—with the concurrence of the attorney general—must, on the basis of the ICC proceedings and his own information and data, approve, modify, or reject the proposed agreement in accordance with the public interest standard. The final decisions of both the secretary and the ICC can be appealed to the U.S. Court of Appeals for the District of Columbia.

Since the Transportation Act of 1920, Congress has recognized the need in the railroad industry for corporate simplification and restructuring in order to achieve an integrated national transportation system. However, the result of the past twenty years of merger activity has been to create regional railroads. Interregional shipments are still at the mercy of the interlining procedure which creates a number of distortions and inefficiencies in rail operations. End-to-end mergers offer an opportunity to redress this problem and realize a number of other advantages. Such interregional mergers can promote both rail and intermodal competition. Rail competition could be fostered both regionally, as the dominant regional road is forced to compete with a transnational road, and nationally, as a number of transnational systems are developed. The ability of the roads to develop new markets, emphasize competitive strengths, and effectuate cost savings could be greatly enhanced. With this could come a variety of innovations, such as piggybacking and containerization, which should improve both competitive conditions and coordination with other modes. The bill should contribute enormously to restructuring and integration of the rail system and lay the basis for further legislative change to attain these objectives.

Taken together the various elements of the bill provide the basis for arresting the long-term decline of the railroad industry and setting the industry in a new direction—a direction which will keep the railroads in the private sector and enable them to make their full contribution to the commerce of the country.

PART TWO

BASIC ISSUES IN THE RAIL DEREGULATION DEBATE

In the course of congressional consideration of the administration's reform proposals, a number of basic issues arose and were the subject of serious debate. Speaking broadly, the Railroad Revitalization Act was designed to achieve four major objectives: (1) allow the industry to have greater pricing freedom; (2) enhance the industry's ability to introduce new services; (3) expedite and improve the abandonment process; and (4) expedite the merger process to bring about needed restructuring in the industry. Adoption of the administration's proposals would have significantly altered the ICC's responsibilities and changed the nature of regulation. Existing regulations had created a considerable number of interest groups—shippers, communities, railroads, competitive transportation modes, and railroad employees. There were some within each group who thought that they would be adversely affected by the proposed changes. In this part we review a number of questions that arose in connection with this debate.

The first paper is drawn from the set of answers prepared by the Department of Transportation in response to questions raised by the Senate Commerce Committee about the effects of the reform proposals. This reading treats a variety of issues, particularly pricing and abandonments. One of the more controversial issues in the debate concerned the appropriate cost standards for railroad pricing. The administration's proposal would have permitted the railroads to reduce rates free of ICC interference as long as the rates did not fall below variable costs. The second paper is drawn from studies on this issue prepared for DOT by two economists, Stephen Sobotka and Thomas Domencich.

The next two readings deal with another controversial issue—the possibility that, if railroads were given pricing flexibility, they would engage in predatory competition against other modes. The barge industry vigorously opposed allowing railroads the freedom to reduce rates unless the barge lines were given assurance that they would be protected against "predatory pricing" by the railroads. The barge industry drafted an amendment to the administration's bill in order to accomplish this objective. The Department of Transportation then commissioned several analyses both of the issue and of the barge industry's proposed amendment. Two of these analyses are presented here: an economic analysis by P. David Qualls, an economist at the University of Maryland, and a legal analysis by Glen E. Weston, a professor at the George Washington University Law School.

The proposal to liberalize abandonment procedures sparked another heated debate. The final paper in this part is a review of the potential for rail abandonments outside of the Northeast and an assessment of their likely impact. The paper is drawn from a report prepared by the Department of Transportation to fulfill a requirement set by Congress in the Railroad Revitalization and Regulatory Reform Act. Although this report was thus submitted after the final passage of the 4R Act, it drew heavily upon work which had been undertaken prior to passage.

6
QUESTIONS ON LIKELY
EFFECTS OF REFORM

U.S. Department of Transportation Staff

In preparing for its evaluation of proposals for reforming regulation of freight transportation, the Senate Commerce Committee in 1975 requested the assistance of the Department of Transportation in developing information on government regulation of carrier activities. Specifically, the committee called for answers to seventy-six questions which related to proposed reforms and their effect on the transportation industries. The most important and comprehensive of these questions and the department's answers are provided here. They indicate the expectations regarding the results of reform.

General Results

QUESTION: How will the legislative proposal improve the quality of railroad service? Do you think that quality of service is an important issue? Should quality of service be tied to rate adjustments? How can this be done? What studies has the department done on this subject?

ANSWER: Yes, we do believe that quality of service is an important issue. The various provisions of the proposed bill are mutually reinforcing in bringing about more efficient and better service. The rate-making changes will enable railroads to adjust their prices to reflect new service innovations. This should encourage service innovations. As discussed in detail in the analysis of the need for the bill, the provisions of the bill dealing with financial assistance and the develop-

This chapter is edited from responses by the U.S. Department of Transportation to a series of questions submitted by the Senate Commerce Committee in connection with its consideration of the Ford administration's railroad reform proposal, the Railroad Revitalization Act, in 1975.

ment of a control system for rolling stock will result in a substantial improvement in the quality of service. The abandonment provisions will allow for the necessary pruning of the rail plant so that railroads can concentrate on providing that kind of service for which rails are best suited.

The variable-costs standard will put an end to the existing cross-subsidization which is a heavy financial drain on the industry and which causes rates on other commodities to be higher than would otherwise be the case. Such pricing also leads to diversion of the higher rate commodities to other modes of transportation, thus further weakening the financial condition of the railroad industry. This, in turn, limits the ability of the railroads to make improvements in plant which are essential to upgrading service.

In essence, the bill is designed to break a vicious cycle in which regulatory resistance and outmoded regulatory policy has brought the industry to a position where its earnings are low and inadequate and its plant is in a badly deteriorated state. We believe that the bill will break this cycle by removing the regulatory resistance and enabling the railroads to compete more effectively, while providing the railroads with the financial assistance needed to upgrade their plant. The consequence of breaking the cycle will be to reverse the forces of deterioration and decline in the railroad industry and to revitalize the industry.

The whole thrust of the bill is to improve service. Quality of service should be tied to rate adjustments. Thus, higher quality of service should be permitted to command a higher rate that is based upon the higher costs which the service entails. Similarly, lower quality service should be permitted to carry a lower rate that reflects the lower costs involved in providing such lower service. Relying on market forces in transportation will tend to produce this kind of result in which high quality service carries a higher price, reflecting its higher costs, while lower quality service carries a lower price, reflecting its lower cost. An efficient transportation system should produce both high quality service at high cost for some shippers and lower quality service at reduced cost for shippers who prefer the cost savings to the high quality service.

One example of this situation would be seasonal and nonseasonal pricing. Shippers during the peak season would pay a premium price reflecting the higher cost for providing service during the peak season. Shippers willing to ship during the off-peak season would obtain a lower rate reflecting the reduced cost of providing service during the off-peak season. The department has done extensive studies on this subject, particularly with respect to air transportation. We now have under way a research project designed to identify the benefits of seasonal pricing in the railroad transportation field.

QUESTION: What would you expect to be the results of enactment of the proposed bill? For example, in what areas of the country would you anticipate significantly increased applications for abandonment of lines? Will rates go up or down? How fast? On what commodities?

ANSWER: The impact of the rate-making proposals will vary from commodity to commodity and probably from region to region. We anticipate that some rates will rise and others will fall. The significant thing about the rate changes, however, is that they will be related to market forces. Thus, although it is not possible to determine with any degree of certainty which rates will rise and which rates will fall, we can be confident that the resulting rates will be more closely related to costs and will encourage a more efficient division of traffic among the carriers and among the modes than is now the case. The likely candidates for rate reductions will be those commodities which have a relatively elastic demand and which have been held at artificially high levels because of the regulatory system and the effect it has had upon rail management's willingness and ability to initiate lower rates.

The provision of the bill requiring rates to be raised to the level of variable costs will undoubtedly result in an increase in some rates. Likely candidates for increases are commodities which have been held at artificially lower levels because of the regulatory system and the effect the system has had on management's willingness and ability to initiate rate increases. However, because of the substantial amount of actual and potential intermodal competition, we do not believe that this proposal will result in rail rates that are in any way monopolistic. There are few, if any, commodities for which substitute forms of transportation would not become economically attractive to shippers if railroads were to raise rates within a fairly narrow range.

By providing rail management with increased pricing flexibility, the bill encourages railroads to give greater attention to pricing and to use pricing policies more intelligently and more effectively. In addition, by providing for the development of a new system of cost accounting and revenue accounting, the bill will substantially increase the knowledge about the costs and revenues associated with the movement of different commodities and will thus encourage intelligent and rational pricing.

With respect to abandonments, the majority of the affected rail mileage will be concentrated in the Midwest and Northeast sections of the country where rail capacity is seriously in excess. The report of the secretary of transportation entitled *Rail Service in the Midwest and Northeast Region,* released on February 1, 1974, indicates the potential dimensions of future abandonment activity. Generally, bankrupt carriers in the Northeast and Midwest will be able to use the abandonment procedures provided in the Regional Rail Reorganization Act of 1972. Other carriers, however, will have to rely upon the present provisions of the Interstate Commerce Act, unless the provisions of the proposed bill with respect to abandonment are enacted.

QUESTION: If the proposed legislation is to result in the kinds of savings that the Department of Transportation predicts, there would seem to be a possibility of significant short-term economic and social dislocation resulting from the adjustment of rates. What dislocations do you anticipate?

ANSWER: We would not expect any severe economic or social dislocations, even though savings may be substantial. The first rough estimates of savings are given in Table 6-1. Although these figures may be inaccurate, they give the impression that changes will be positive, not disruptive. Of course, shippers in particular localities or those using particular carriers will have to pay more, or transfer their traffic to other modes, or reduce the total movement of certain commodities.

Nationwide, the most important commodities for which the rates are below variable costs are primary forest products, crushed and broken stone, miscellaneous mixed shipments, and fresh vegetables, fruits, and tree nuts. Among other commodities moving below variable costs in or between various territories, grain mill products and gravel account for much of the flow. The rates at which these commodities move are generally 80 to 100 percent of system-wide variable costs, with a very few as low as perhaps 25 percent. It is probable that variable costs for some of these specific movements for individual carriers are lower than system-wide variable costs, thus reducing the size of the rate increase needed to comply with the rate provisions of the proposed bill.

The Effect on Abandonments

QUESTION: The proposed bill provides for a strict economic standard as the basis of abandonment decisions by the ICC. What is the justification for the abandonment criterion employed in the proposed legislation? Is this standard adequate to compensate for the full range of what has been conceived of as public convenience and necessity?

Table 6-1

ANNUAL SAVINGS TO THE RAILROAD INDUSTRY
RESULTING FROM ENACTMENT OF THE REFORM BILL
(millions of dollars)

From increasing all rates to variable costs	$150

Not all rates would be raised to variable costs as defined by Form A for railroad costing. Railroads feel that some rates not meeting variable costs as defined by this formula are compensatory. Some rates are held below variable costs by shipper pressure as a condition of securing other, more profitable traffic from the shipper.

From permitting the Interstate Commerce Commission to raise intrastate rail rates to interstate levels	$50

There is no available precise estimate of the level of difference between intrastate and interstate rates. This savings from bringing intrastate levels up to interstate levels is a very rough estimate.

From rate flexibility within the range of 7 percent the first year, 12 percent the second year, and 15 percent the third year	$250

The savings should be annual and should average $250 million, although it will be lower for the first few years. The effect can be expected to be cumulative.

From reduction in costs because of regulatory lag	$250

The savings would depend on the number of rate increases suspended under sections 2, 3, or 4 of the Interstate Commerce Act, and the average length of time suspension under the new rules. General increases are largely a function of the rate of price inflation. The more general the inflation, the greater the savings resulting from the reduced time lag associated with general increase requests.

From downward price flexibility	$50

Currently, the value of downward price flexibility is minimal because of the high rate of inflation. This estimate is indicative of the savings under normal (noninflationary) conditions. It results from being able to lower rates to meet competition.

From discriminatory state taxation	$55

This represents the amount of reduction in state taxes that would occur if states were required to impose tax

Table 6-1 (Continued)

rates on railroads no higher than those imposed on other businesses.

From interest rate guarantee $50

This figure is based on the assumption that the guarantee will lower the cost of borrowing to finance investment in right-of-way by about 1.5 percent. In addition, the guarantee will reduce uncertainty and permit loans to railroads that, because of capital market imperfections, could not otherwise secure them.

From railroad restructuring $130 to $1,300

The loan guarantees are to be granted on the condition that the railroads will be restructured. The saving expected from such restructuring is hard to estimate. If it results in a 1 percent reduction in railroad costs, the saving is $130 million. If the reduction in railroad costs is 10 percent, then the savings would amount to $1.3 billion.

ANSWER: The basic justification for the standard employed in the proposed bill is the need to reduce significant excess capacity in the railroad industry. Reduction of excess capacity, particularly light-density branch-line trackage, is essential to improving the industry's financial condition. It is notable that the railroads in the greatest financial difficulty all have a substantial amount of branch line relative to main line, whereas the railroads in the strongest financial position have relatively little branch-line trackage.

By reducing uneconomic light-density lines, the railroad industry could lower per-unit operating costs and substantially improve its financial condition. In 1971 the railroad industry was operating approximately 205,000 route miles of line. Of this total, approximately 21,000 miles were light-density branch lines for which the carriers incurred operating losses. These 21,000 miles of line accounted for less than 1 percent of total rail freight. The Federal Railroad Administration estimates that the railroad industry would be able to save between $29 million and $42 million annually on a nationwide basis by discontinuing service over these uneconomic lines. The railroads in the Northeast would be able to save on the order of $15 million to $22 million annually. In addition to these savings, the salvage value of these rights-of-way would return approximately $105 million to the railroad industry on a nationwide basis and $56 million to the railroads in the northeastern part of the country. Moreover, the continued operation of these lines would require considerable expenditures for rehabilitation, which would be saved if these uneconomic lines were abandoned.

The detrimental effects resulting from the operation of uneconomic lines are not limited to the railroad industry. Rather, their continued operation causes a basic misallocation of transportation resources. It appears clear that motor carriers are better suited to handle much of the short-haul traffic which presently moves on low-density rail branch lines, whereas railroads have a comparative advantage in long-haul markets. Thus, the abandonment of uneconomic branch lines would enable railroads to concentrate their efforts on providing those services in which they have a relative advantage and would provide a further opportunity for trucking service to develop in markets where it has a relative advantage. The net result would be more efficient use of transportation resources.

The standard proposed in the administration's bill—that is, revenue versus cost—is different from the "public convenience and necessity" standard. This new standard is designed to eliminate certain lines that would not be eliminated under the old standard. On the other hand, the provisions of the act also provide a process whereby the full range of what has been conceived of as public convenience and necessity can be properly treated. First, shippers and communities have the option to subsidize those operations which, although uneconomical to a rail carrier and to the efficient allocation of transportation resources, are beneficial to a specific community or to specific shippers. Second, motor carriers would be permitted to provide substitute service along routes over which rail service is abandoned.

QUESTION: How many miles of track have the railroads sought to abandon over the past ten years? How many miles of track have been authorized for abandonment? What has been the average length of time taken to dispose of these cases?

ANSWER: In 1920, the ICC was given authority to control both the abandonment and the construction of rail lines. Since that time, the approach to abandonments has been largely piecemeal, with the average application involving a line sixteen miles long and the vast majority of these applications involving very low density lines serving lightly populated areas. Further, abandonment activity has been cyclical in nature. Until 1927, the country enjoyed general prosperity, the railroads realized satisfactory profit levels, highway competition was just beginning to be felt, and there was some unfamiliarity with abandonment regulation. During this period, there was little abandonment activity.

Between 1928 and 1941, the combined effects of competition from automobiles and motor carriers and the Great Depression gave rise to a high level of abandonment activity. However, the tremendous surge of rail freight and passenger traffic during World War II and the Korean War greatly reduced the abandonment activity between 1942 and 1953. Another contributing factor to the reduction of abandonments during this period was the impact of a U.S. Supreme Court decision which upheld the right of the ICC to impose employee-protection conditions in abandonment authorizations.

After 1954, the impact of competition from automobiles and trucks again began to take its toll on rail traffic. This impact was heightened by the construction of the Interstate Highway System which began in 1956, the introduction of jet aircraft in 1959, and several periods of economic recession. The result was an upward trend in abandonment activity. Since 1969, the financial distress of a number of railroads and the inadequate earnings of most rail carriers have given rise to a substantial increase in both the number and the scope of abandonment applications.

Figure 6-1 summarizes the trends in abandonment applications filed by the railroads with the commission between 1920 and 1970. The cycles in activity are clearly indicated. Table 6-2 summarizes the number of abandonment applications and the mileage involved for each ten-year period from 1920 through 1969.

During the period 1960–1972 there were 1,224 abandonment applications filed with the commission. These applications involved a total of 19,767 miles (an average of 16 miles an application). Of these applications, 83 percent were approved, 2 percent were denied, 6 percent were dismissed, and 9 percent were not acted on. The applications that were approved involved 13,958 miles or 70 percent of the mileage petitioned for abandonment. The difference between 83 percent of the applications approved and 70 percent of the mileage approved indicates that proposals involving shorter lines are approved more readily than are proposals involving longer lines.

Finally, the data show that, although 13,958 miles of railroad were authorized for abandonment between 1964 and 1972, the net reduction in rail mileage was only 8,603. This was the result of several factors. First, 1,502 miles of railroad were authorized for construction. Second, changes in management policy and court actions resulted in continued operation of some of the rail mileage. Third, some of the lines or portions of lines were taken over by other railroads or were assumed by new operating entities.

90

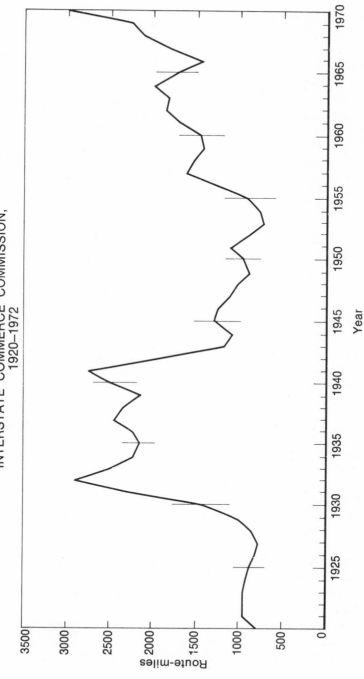

Figure 6-1

RAILROAD ROUTE-MILES PER YEAR REPRESENTED BY
ABANDONMENT APPLICATIONS FILED WITH THE
INTERSTATE COMMERCE COMMISSION,
1920–1972

Table 6-2

NUMBER OF ABANDONMENT APPLICATIONS FILED BY U.S. RAILROADS WITH THE INTERSTATE COMMERCE COMMISSION, 1920–1970

Decade	Number of Applications Filed	Mileage Sought to Be Abandoned	Average Number of Miles Per Application
1920–1929	464	8,192	17.7
1930–1939	1,184	21,260	17.9
1940–1949	1,014	15,989	15.7
1950–1959	758	10,631	14.1
1960–1969	1,053	17,483	16.6
Totals	4,473	73,555	16.5

Source: Data supplied by the Interstate Commerce Commission.

The Effects on Rate-Making Practices

QUESTION: The proposed changes in rate-making standards and procedures are apparently designed to give the railroads pricing freedom. However, the railroads have the freedom at least to initiate pricing innovations now. To what extent have they done so? Where they have done so, to what extent have their proposed actions been thwarted by the ICC? What is in your legislation that would induce the carriers to do more?

ANSWER: The proposed changes in the rate-making standards and procedures *are* designed to give the railroads greater pricing freedom. Although it is true that the railroads already do have the freedom at least to initiate pricing innovations, it is our view that the resistance to pricing innovations which railroads encounter through the regulatory system discourages the initiation of such new rates and new services. Where railroads have sought to initiate pricing innovations, as in the "Big John" case or the "unit train" case,[1] they have encountered substantial regulatory resistance. The cost, uncertainty, and delay associated with establishing new rates and new services certainly discourage innovation.

Our legislation would induce or encourage the carriers to introduce innovations because it changes the existing regulatory system. The commission would have to make a finding of unlawfulness in

[1] "Big John" refers to 100-ton aluminum hopper cars for carrying grain. See below, p. 98 for a discussion of the "Big John" and "unit train" cases.

connection with a proposed innovation requiring a capital investment of at least $1,000,000 within 180 days. If the commission fails to make this finding within 180 days, the rate becomes effective and cannot thereafter be challenged for a period of five years, except on the grounds that it is noncompensatory. Thus, the bill reduces the cost, uncertainty, and delay associated with service innovations. Beyond this, the bill seeks to provide a new climate in which, to a much larger degree, the forces of the marketplace will be substituted for the judgment of the commission regarding rates. Thus, the bill changes the substantive law of rate making by providing that a compensatory rate may not be found to be unlawful on the grounds that it was too low.

The bill also changes the rule of rate making in connection with intermodal competition. It also modifies the suspension provisions of the Interstate Commerce Act and provides for greater flexibility.

Taken together, these provisions will create a new regulatory climate and will encourage management to initiate new services and new rates.

QUESTION: The proposed legislation will prevent rate bureaus from challenging rate proposals of individual carriers unless the rate is below variable costs. What is the main reason for challenges by rate bureaus now? Precisely how would this proposal change the present situation?

ANSWER: Generally, the rate bureaus challenge a rate on the basis that it is unreasonably low. The agreements between the carriers tend to be based on the average costs of all the carriers—not on the costs of the most efficient carrier. Thus, the bureau will challenge the rate proposed independently by the efficient carrier. Moreover, the bureau attempts to maintain the present market share of its members and will challenge any rate that disrupts the shares.

Section 5(a)(6) of the Interstate Commerce Act provides that any carrier member of a rate association may take independent action; however, such action may be preceded by the review process of the rate bureau, and this may substantially delay the introduction of the new rate. In addition, independent action always faces the threat of suspension as well as costly and time-consuming litigation before the commission. Although some of the major independent actions are eventually sustained by the commission, extensive procedural activities have to be endured, including the preparation of detailed cost studies, which often cover a large range of commodities. The burdens of such procedural actions can deter all but the largest carriers and limit independent action to those cases involving large volumes of traffic and revenues.

Essentially, the proposed bill will, in certain instances, prohibit the rate bureaus from challenging a rate and, in other instances, will significantly restrict their opportunity for challenges. The proposed bill prohibits railroad rate bureaus from voting on single-line movements and limits consideration of joint-line rates to those railroads which actually participate in the joint movement, except with respect to scale or group rates. The proposed bill also prohibits rail rate bureaus from taking any action to suspend rates established by independent action, while prohibiting rate bureaus of other modes of freight transportation from protesting a rate filed by independent action unless the protest is supported by facts showing that the rate appears to be less than the variable costs of rendering that service. Thus, on single-line rates individual railroads will have complete freedom to propose rates based on the cost of the most direct routing, while on joint rates the influence of carriers not participating in the joint movement will be reduced. Scale rates—that is, rates established in terms of cents per hundred pounds for specified distances—are excepted from this provision because these rates are designed for large interregional or intraregional flows where traffic tends to move over all carriers.

The bill requires all rate bureaus to dispose of proposed rate changes within 120 days from the time a rate change is proposed to the bureau. In addition, the bill requires all rate bureaus to maintain and make available for public inspection records of the votes of members. These provisions are designed to reform internal procedures of bureaus, to bring about faster treatment by rate bureaus of proposed rate changes, and to encourage greater initiative by individual carriers in making rate changes.

Although the antitrust immunity with respect to joint rates is retained, the proposed legislative change with respect to single-line rate agreements would exert a competitive influence upon joint rates because the territories of carriers overlap and single-line rates are often competitive with joint-line rates. It should also be noted that the commission retains its present authority to approve all rate bureau agreements and to impose such additional limitations and conditions on the activities of rate bureaus as it believes are reasonable and necessary.

QUESTION: How would the provisions of the bill change the steps through which proposals for rate changes must now travel—starting with the rate bureaus? Please prepare a comparative analysis showing present and proposed procedures and evaluate the desirability of the differences.

ANSWER: The proposed bill makes a number of changes in the existing law with respect to rate making and rate bureaus which will affect the steps through which rate proposals travel. Various provisions in the proposed bill change the substantive law of rate making, while other provisions deal essentially with the procedural law affecting rate changes. The rate bureau provisions affect matters which the rate bureaus may lawfully consider and actions which the rate bureaus may lawfully take.

Under the bill, railroad rate bureaus may not consider single-line rates or joint-line rates except where the carriers physically participate in the traffic. Today, of course, rate bureaus do consider single-line and joint-line rates. Thus, enactment of the bill would mean that rate changes involving single-line movements or joint-line movements for carriers not participating in those movements would fall completely outside of the activity of the rate bureaus. Thus, one "step"—consideration of the proposal by the rate bureaus—through which such rate changes travel today would be eliminated under the bill.

Under the act today, before a rate can go into effect, it must be filed with the commission, normally with notice that it will go into effect in thirty days, although procedures exist for a shorter notice period. The commission may suspend the rate proposal on its own motion or in response to protests within the thirty-day period and may conduct an investigation into its lawfulness. Alternatively, the commission may allow the full increase to go into effect, or it may allow a portion of the increase to go into effect and investigate the remaining portion of the increase. If the commission suspends the rate or a portion of it and has not issued an order within seven months the rate may go into effect, subject to the final order of the commission. Today, a proposed rate change may be suspended on the grounds that the rate is too high or too low or that it violates sections 2, 3, or 4 of the Interstate Commerce Act. The proposed bill makes the following significant changes in the existing procedure:

(1) Whereas today the commission may suspend a rate on its own motion, the proposed bill provides, in effect, that a rate change may not be suspended unless it is protested by a shipper. However, as is the case today, any rate proposal may be investigated by the commission.

(2) Whereas today the commission can suspend a rate change on the ground that the rate is too high or too low, the proposed bill essentially removes this ground for suspension, except where the rate change exceeds the class rate.

95

(3) Whereas today the provision for escrow starts at the end of the seven-month period, under the proposed bill it would start at the time the rate increase is not suspended or the rate decrease is suspended.

In addition, the proposed bill provides a new procedure with respect to establishing a rate for a new service involving a capital investment of $1,000,000 or more. Under the proposed bill, where the carrier notifies the commission that it intends to institute such a service, the commission is required to determine within 180 days whether the proposed rate is lawful or unlawful. At present, there is no such requirement in the act for a speedy final determination of the lawfulness of rates for new services involving substantial capital investment. This provision should speed up consideration by the commission of the lawfulness of the rates on new services involving a substantial capital investment.

The provisions of the proposed bill with respect to suspension of rate changes and establishment of a new service involving a capital investment of $1,000,000 or more are essentially procedural in nature. The proposed bill also affects the substantive law with respect to the lawfulness of rates. Thus, the bill provides that "a rate that is compensatory may not be found to be unjust or unreasonable on the basis that it is too low." Moreover, the bill provides that "in a proceeding involving competition between carriers of different modes of transportation, the Commission may not hold the rates of a carrier of one mode up to a particular level to protect the traffic of a carrier of another mode, if the rate proposed by the carrier is compensatory."

Finally, the bill directs the commission to "investigate and identify traffic which is moving at a rate below the variable cost of handling the traffic to which the rate applies and causes the rate promptly to be raised at least to the variable cost level." By making the foregoing changes in the substantive law of rate making, the bill also changes the "steps" through which a rate proposal must travel. Thus, it is possible that rates which might have been unlawful under the present act will be allowed to become effective. Conversely, rates which might have become effective under the present act may be found unlawful.

QUESTION: One of the Department of Transportation's arguments for reform of rate proceedings has been that the ICC takes too long to act on rate cases. What information does the department have to document such an assertion?

ANSWER: The procedures that are followed to comply with the provisions of the Interstate Commerce Act, the regulations of the ICC, and the internal practices of the commission oftentimes act to delay requested rate changes for considerable periods of time.

The commission has the authority to suspend rates either upon complaint or upon its own motion without complaint. The statute permits suspension for a period of up to seven months beyond the requested effective date of the rate change. If the rate is suspended, the case is referred for investigation that may include the presentation of both oral and written evidence and testimony. Despite the seven-month statutory limitation upon suspensions, in practice, following commission custom, the parties oftentimes voluntarily agree at ICC request not to effectuate the rate change pending disposition of the case.

Most rate suspension cases are referred directly to a review board, to Division II of the ICC, or to the full commission, thus eliminating the initial or recommended report generally used in administrative regulatory practice. Nevertheless, ICC records still indicate that cases involving suspended and investigated rail rates averaged: 9.0 months for thirty-seven cases during 1971; 7.3 months for thirty-nine cases during 1972; and 10.3 months for thirty-three cases during 1973.[2]

Specifically, reviewing the cases of recent years involving general rate increases reveals the following information:

Ex Parte 259, Increased Freight Rates, 1968. This proceeding was instituted by the railroads' petition in March 1968 for rate increases ranging from 3 percent to 10 percent, with the majority at 6 percent or less. Although the carriers were authorized increases of 3 percent pending completion of the proceeding, the ICC's final decision was not rendered until November 1968.

Ex Parte 262, Increased Freight Rates, 1969. The petitioning railroads instituted this proceeding in October 1969. Although the railroads were authorized the 6 percent requested rate increase, effective the following month and subject to refund provisions if the increase was not ultimately approved, the ICC's final decision was not served until August 6, 1970.

Ex Parte 265, Increased Freight Rates, 1970; Ex Parte 267, Increased Freight Rates, 1971. This proceeding was instituted by the railroads' petition for a 6 percent rate increase in March 1970. In June 1970, a 5 percent increase was authorized, subject to refund provisions. In September 1970, the case was consolidated with other new petitions for rate increases, ranging from 6 percent to 15 percent.

---

[2] These cases are generally concerned with many individual rates involving a substantial volume of commerce.

In November 1970, increases of 6 percent to 8 percent were authorized, subject to refund provisions. The ICC's final decision in these two merged proceedings was issued March 23, 1971.

Ex Parte 281, Increased Freight Rates and Charges, 1972. The petitioning railroads requested a 2.5 percent surcharge on bills for freight services in December 1971. In February 1972, the surcharge became effective, subject to certain conditions and a requirement that the surcharge terminate June 5, 1972. On February 28, 1972, the carriers petitioned for selective increases ranging up to 10 percent to be effective April 1, 1972. On March 6, 1972, the ICC authorized the request effective no earlier than May 1, 1972, subject to a provision for refunds. On April 24, 1972, however, after testimony in opposition was received by the ICC, the commission suspended the selective increases for the full seven-month period allowed by statute to November 30, 1972. The surcharge tariff, however, was reinstated. On October 4, 1972, the commission served its final decision.

Unit-train rates. Unit-train rates on a large scale were first applied to coal traffic in the late 1950s in response to the development of "mine-mouth" electric generation and long-distance transmission, the possibility of coal slurry pipelines, and the competition from fuel oil for electric generation at East Coast ports. In *Coal From Kentucky, Virginia and West Virginia to Virginia,*[3] the commission approved an extensive schedule of unit-train rates made to forestall the installation of long-distance transmission by the electric utilities in Virginia. The rates were filed effective August 1, 1958. At first, the rates were suspended, but later they were allowed to go into effect while still under investigation. The case was finally decided July 13, 1959. In *Coal to New York Harbor,*[4] the commission approved unit-train tariffs to forty-eight electric generating plants in the New York area after an investigation beginning on March 4, 1959. Following these decisions, the utilities and the railroads agreed on many hundreds of unit-train rates.[5]

Big John rates on grain. In 1961, the Southern Railroad published rates effective August 10, 1961, with a minimum of 450 tons shipped in 100-ton aluminum hopper ("Big John") cars. Suspension was invoked by the ICC before the rates could go into effect, and a hearing lasting two months commenced in January 1962. Upon the

---

[3] 308 I.C.C. 99 (1959).
[4] 311 I.C.C. 355 (1960).
[5] See James Sloss, "Railroad Coal Rate Policies," in *Proceedings of the Sixth Annual Meeting of the Transportation Research Forum* (December 1965); and Federal Power Commission, *National Power Survey*, part II (1964), pp. 335–45.

expiration of the seven-month period of suspension, various parties sought to enjoin the Southern Railroad from putting the rates into effect. After a series of legal maneuvers, the Supreme Court remanded the case to the commission for determination on the merits in April 1963. Meanwhile, the commission's Division II had permitted the rates to go into effect in January 1963. The full commission reversed the division in May 1963 and prescribed rates 16 percent higher, based on the ICC's cost formulas. In May 1964, a three-judge district court sitting in Cincinnati reversed the full commission and permitted the Big John rates to go into effect. In January 1965, the Supreme Court upheld the district court and remanded the case to the ICC for decision on the merits on the basis of the district court's decision. In September 1965, the commission finally approved the Big John rates as originally proposed by the Southern Railroad.

QUESTION: What specific information do you have on the number of cases (and the percentage of the total number of cases) in which the ICC has refused to allow carriers to reduce rates to a point not below the variable costs of providing the related service?

ANSWER: Some time ago we made inquiry at the ICC to see if it was possible to answer this question and several related questions. We were informed that the control over the flow of information on dockets at the ICC was not sufficiently developed to permit answers to this kind of question. Many ICC decisions are not published in the annual volumes of the ICC, and we were informed by ICC staff members that the task of determining the relative frequency of the commission's holding on a given issue is virtually impossible. Thus, for instance, we were unable to determine the percentage of the total cases in which the ICC has refused to allow carriers to reduce rates to a point not below the variable costs of providing the related service. It is simply not possible to determine the number of cases on this point nor the number of cases in which the commission has decided the issue one way or another. We did, however, undertake an analysis of this question on the basis of the annually published opinions of the commission. Table 6-3 is a partial list of cases in which the ICC has refused to allow carriers to reduce rates to a point not below the variable costs of providing the service.

QUESTION: Can you demonstrate that there would be any substantive difference in the outcome of the rate proposals if the proposed "no-suspend" zone goes into effect?

ANSWER: If the DOT proposals are adopted, traffic will bear at least the variable costs associated with the service utilized. We estimate

Table 6-3

CASES IN WHICH THE ICC HAS NOT ALLOWED A CARRIER TO REDUCE RATES TO A POINT NOT BELOW VARIABLE COSTS

1. *Freight, All Kinds, from New York to Chicago,* 308 I.C.C. 735 (1959).
2. *Tobacco from North Carolina to Central Territory,* 309 I.C.C. 347 (1960).
3. *Petroleum Oils & Greases from New Orleans,* 310 I.C.C. 703 (1960).
4. *Cigars from Jacksonville to Kansas City,* 313 I.C.C. 633 (1961).
5. *Alcoholic Liquors from New Hampshire and New York to Texas and Louisiana,* 315 I.C.C. 124 (1961).
6. *Sugar, South to Indiana,* 315 I.C.C. 521 (1962).
7. *Pig Iron from Buffalo, N.Y., to Chicago, Ill.,* 321 I.C.C. 121 (1963).
8. *Grain in Multiple-Car Shipments,* 321 I.C.C. 121 (1964).
9. *Wisconsin and Michigan Steamship Company* v. *Grand Trunk Western Railroad Co.,* 325 I.C.C. 244 (1965).
10. *Ingot Molds,* 326 I.C.C. 77 (1965); 392 U.S. 571 (1968).

an increase in rail revenues from this source at about $450 million to $500 million annually. In addition, if rates are judged on the individual carrier's cost for the proposed service, rather than on competing carriers' costs, the opportunity would present itself for the railroads to carry traffic where they have the cost advantage. If railroad management took advantage of greater rate flexibility provided by the legislation, rail revenue would increase because of rail's ability to attract and hold traffic on which rails have a competitive advantage and because of greater utilization of capacity which would result from better rate making. Shippers would have available a more efficient overall transportation system.

The Effects on Rates

QUESTION: To what extent should the following factors be considered in rate-setting procedures for rail, water, and motor carriers: (1) effective rates on movement of carriage for which rates are prescribed; (2) the need for the movement of carriage at the lowest cost consistent with furnishing service; (3) the effect of a rate for one commodity on the movement of another commodity; and (4) the effect of the rate upon the maintenance of an overall transportation system in that mode?

ANSWER: All of the factors listed have significance for rate setting. The thrust of our rate-making proposals is to place greater reliance on market forces in rate making and reduce the role of regulation. Thus, we provide rail management greater pricing flexibility in order to encourage prices to be set on the basis of costs and market conditions. We believe that more competitive pricing will lead to a more economic division of traffic and will reduce the overall freight bill, while improving the overall financial position of the transportation system. By giving management greater pricing flexibility, we would expect to see greater attention to efficient pricing. This would involve a close consideration of the effect of rates on the movement of traffic. This increased competition would encourage the movement of carriage at the lowest economic cost consistent with furnishing service. It would also encourage carriers to price more intelligently and therefore improve their overall financial health.

QUESTION: What results can be expected from a prohibition of the carriage of a commodity or a class of commodities at rates below the variable costs of providing the needed transportation?

ANSWER: The annual losses to the railroad industry from carrying commodities below variable costs are estimated to be in the $450 million to $500 million range. Increases in these rates to the level of variable costs would have two possible effects, depending upon the elasticities of demand: (1) an increase in operating revenues and a contribution to overhead burden, or (2) transfer of the traffic to other modes or reduced total movement of the commodity. In the latter case, a serious financial drain on the railroads would be removed, the net income of rails would improve, and the public would benefit from more efficient and more economical service.

QUESTION: In what instances, if any, do commodities or classes of commodities presently move at a rate or rates lower than the variable costs of providing that movement?

ANSWER: The most recent comprehensive analysis of the relationship of revenue to variable costs by commodity for railroad shipments is contained in a 1969 Department of Transportation study entitled *An Estimation of the Distribution of the Rail Revenue Contribution by Commodity Groups and Type of Rail Car*. This study contains the results of a comparison of the revenue associated with those rail movements contained in the department's 1 percent sample of rail traffic for the calendar year 1969 with the estimated variable costs which resulted from the ICC's variable costing procedure commonly known as Rail Form A. The results of this comparison indicate a substantial number of commodities which move at rates below variable costs. Table 6-4 lists the most significant deficit commodities and the relationship of their revenue to variable costs for movements within and between each of the three railroad operating territories (Official, South, and West), as defined by the ICC.

It should be noted, however, that the results of this study serve only to signal the existence of a major problem and to provide a reasonably accurate indicator of the commodities most likely involved. It is generally recognized that the costing methodology for the ICC's Form A is deficient and, in fact, the proposed bill deals with this deficiency by requiring the development of more accurate variable costing procedures and the subsequent use of these procedures by each carrier. Such a process will enable the accurate identification of those shipments in which the revenue received fails to cover at least the variable costs of the movement.

QUESTION: In cases in which a particular commodity could not move at a rate equal to or above the variable costs of providing the necessary transportation, should a carrier be permitted to move that commodity if he could subsidize that movement by charging a higher rate on another commodity? If so, when should the carrier be permitted to charge such a rate?

ANSWER: A producer of a good or service should never sell his output for less than the variable costs incurred in its production. To do so results in the uneconomic allocation of the nation's scarce resources in a process which often involves large segments of the economy.

The fact that a given commodity could not move at a rate equal to or above variable costs indicates that effective demand is inadequate to justify providing the service. This situation, in turn, is often the result of an effective competitive product or producer. To subsidize such a commodity adversely affects the market for other shippers who must bear higher rates in order to generate the funds for the subsidy.

The real burden of below-cost rates, however, is being largely borne by the carriers, as is reflected in part by low rates of return and bankruptcies. The rail carriers suffer when the shippers of the subsidizing commodities divert their traffic to other modes of transportation. As a consequence, the carrier is left with a large share of low-rated and deficit commodities and the entire transportation system suffers.

QUESTION: In the past, the Department of Transportation has criticized cross-subsidization. Is there still room for cross-subsidization

Table 6-4

LARGEST DEFICIT COMMODITIES BY TERRITORIAL MOVEMENT, 1969

Origin Territory	Destination Territory	Commodity	Ratio of Revenue to Variable Costs
Official	Official	Miscellaneous mixed shipments	0.66
		Grain mill products	0.86
		Crushed and broken stone	0.85
		Primary forest products	0.66
		Shipper associated traffic	0.81
South	South	Primary forest products	0.75
		Crushed and broken stone	0.82
		Sand	0.87
		Grain mill products	0.89
		Fertilizer	0.80
West	West	Primary forest products	0.75
		Grain mill products	0.90
		Gravel	0.73
		Crushed and broken stone	0.87
		Sand	0.79
Official	South	Crushed and broken stone	0.67
		Field crops	0.92
		Sand	0.57
		Empty trailers	0.77
South	Official	Fresh vegetables	0.78
		Fresh fruit	0.76
		Miscellaneous mixed shipments	0.86
		Field crops	0.81
		Aluminum ores	0.89
Official	West	Anthracite coal	0.88
		Meat	0.86
		Primary forest products	0.82
		Industrial sand and gravel	0.86
West	Official	Fresh vegetables	0.82
		Fresh fruit	0.76
		Field crops	0.94
		Meat	0.98
		Freight-forwarder traffic	0.91
South	West	Gravel	0.77
		Sand	0.89
		Periodicals	0.64
		Fresh vegetables	0.65
		Empty shipping containers	0.97

Source: U.S. Department of Transportation, *An Estimation of the Distribution of the Rail Revenue Contribution by Commodity Groups and Type of Rail Car,* 1969.

under the DOT proposal? For example, suppose the railroads drop their rates to variable costs to meet barge competition in the transportation of grain. Could the railroads still have higher rates to and from, say, the Granger states up to the class rate level?

ANSWER: The bill would eliminate all cross-subsidization. Properly designated as an economic concept, cross-subsidization means that some rates are below variable costs and other rates are substantially above variable costs. Since the bill requires that all rates be raised to the level of variable costs, there is a prohibition on cross-subsidization. Obviously, this does not mean that all rates on all commodities for all movements will bear the same relationship to costs. Under the bill, however, we would expect to find the relationship of rates to cost bearing a closer relationship because of the increased opportunity for the operation of market forces.

7

COST STANDARDS FOR RAIL PRICING

Stephen Sobotka and Thomas Domencich

The concept of variable-cost pricing is an important foundation block for regulatory reform in rail services. On the whole, regulated rail rates have been held above marginal or avoidable costs, and advocates of reform call for rates to be merely compensatory. Compensatory rates were defined in the Transportation Improvement Act, a bill proposed by the Department of Transportation in January 1974, as follows: "A rate is deemed to be compensatory when it equals or exceeds the variable cost of providing the specific transportation to which it applies." The bill provided further that the Interstate Commerce Commission "shall, on a continuing basis, investigate and identify traffic which is moving at a rate below the variable cost of handling the traffic to which the rate applies and cause the rate to be promptly raised at least to the variable cost level." Moreover, the bill modified existing law with respect to intermodal competition by providing that "the Commission may not hold the rate of a carrier of one mode up to a particular level to protect the carrier of another mode, if the rate proposed by the carrier is compensatory." As these quotations exemplify, variable costs is a central concept in the proposals for regulatory reform.

Variable costs represent the additional costs associated with producing additional output. Whenever rates are below variable costs, the carriers are incurring losses for performing the service. In the short run, such rates provide a partial free ride for the shipper at the

This chapter is edited from two studies prepared for the Office of the Secretary, U.S. Department of Transportation, *An Economic Analysis of Railroad Cost-Price Relationships under a Variable-Cost Regulatory Standard*, final report, April 12, 1974; and *Criteria for the Use of Short-Run Variable Cost in Railroad Pricing*, draft report, April 15, 1974. Stephen Sobotka and Thomas Domencich are economic consultants.

expense of the railroad. In the longer run, however, they destroy the railroad's ability to serve the shipper's needs by failing to provide funds with which to cover costs. As a consequence, the shipper and the railroad both suffer. A rate at or above variable costs covers the additional costs associated with producing the additional output and also makes a positive contribution to the carrier's overhead and profits.

General Principles

The variable costs incurred in providing any service may be different for different carriers depending upon a variety of circumstances. Although it is possible to discuss the basic principles which should apply in determining variable costs, the concept cannot be put into full operation without a major study that will develop the appropriate methodology to apply in determining variable costs under different circumstances. Of necessity, the present study is limited to the general principles which are applied in using the concept of variable costs. The application of the concept will be illustrated by means of three examples.

Additional Capacity Case. For some movements, there is an expanding demand for rail services. An example is the demand generated by the growing exploitation of coal reserves in the western United States. In this case, variable costs, the additional costs associated with producing the additional output, include elements not normally thought of as variable. There are requirements for new or upgraded trackage, terminals, and switching facilities; increased administrative costs; and additional cars, motive power, fuel, or labor. Only this last group of cost elements is normally thought of as variable. But, when additional expenditures for capital facilities or overhead are required in order to provide service, these expenditures are indeed variable and should be included in rate determination by carriers.

Excess Capacity Case. In some parts of the country, there now is capacity to provide more rail service than is demanded at current rates. In this case, the elements that constitute variable costs are less inclusive than when additional capacity is demanded, because only those cost elements which are dependent on the volume of service are included. The reason for this is that variable costs must include only those elements which are required to provide, on a continuing basis, the demanded services. Since the level of service demanded falls short of the available capacity, no funds are required to expand or even, in the long run, to maintain the existing facilities. Indeed, it is desirable that the capacity shrink so that the resources can be redeployed. If monies are not provided for the replacement of fixed assets, there will be a gradual shrinkage of capacity to the level demanded.

An illustration will help make this concept clearer. Suppose there is a rail facility in New England which was built primarily to serve a textile mill which has closed. There are other customers along this route, but the traffic of these other shippers and receivers is insufficient to justify any additional investment in the line. Indeed, if a decision to build this line were being made today, the line would not be built. Consequently, there is no need to provide funds for capital equipment. Nevertheless, all costs which would not be incurred (avoidable costs) if the service were not provided must be covered as long as the railroad continues to serve the customers along this route. This will happen if rates are set so that all operating costs are covered but no allocation to cover fixed charges is made. In due course, the fixed capital would have to be replaced in order to continue to provide service. It will not be replaced, however, and service will terminate because there is insufficient demand to generate funds to cover both operating costs and capital charges. In the interim, the existing capital will have been used as fully as is economical.

The adjustment process described here is the one which normally takes place in the economy. In this case, it results in shippers receiving the level of service for the time that it is economical to provide service. The railroads receive revenue sufficient to cover their avoidable costs but, because no new capital is economically justified, they receive no funds for capital or fixed charges.

In the short run, the ability of competing modes to attract traffic along this route is adversely affected by the existence of excess rail capacity. In the long run, however, as rail capacity decreases, the potential traffic that is available to other modes expands. This is as it should be; rates should be set so that optimal use is made of the nation's resources. The adjustment process is analogous to the one that takes place when a large commercial tenant moves out of the area. In the short run, all rents tend to fall, new investment in commercial property is discouraged because rents are insufficient to recover the required capital funds. The low rents attract some new tenants and some buildings that are "marginal" are torn down or converted to other uses.

Adequate Capacity Case. "Adequate" capacity requires explanation. In one sense, there typically is unused capacity in all industries—for example, airplanes fly with some empty seats, taxicabs cruise for passengers, and businesses carry inventories. Unused capacity is not necessarily excess capacity. The alternative to having some unused capacity is having people always wait for airplane seats and taxis and having businesses unable to fill orders promptly. That would result in underutilization of the resources of users or customers; this is another kind of excess capacity, as well as a cost.

In the case of rail services as in almost all businesses, some spare capacity is needed to cover random fluctuation in demand and to provide service during periods of peak demand—to assure that an economically justified level of service is provided. Because this is not excess capacity, rates have to be adequate to provide for spare capacity. The pertinent costs for rate determination then include capital or overhead charges as well as labor, fuel, and so forth. The presence of some spare rail capacity should not be reason to reduce rates below compensatory levels. For example, businessmen do not reduce prices drastically as long as inventories are in line with their expected level of sales.

There are cases of spare capacity which call for differential rates. These are commonly identified as "peak/off-peak" and "prime-haul/backhaul" rates. In these cases, it is appropriate for the peak (prime-haul) users to pay the full costs of services rendered and facilities used. The capacity provided should be that which peak (prime-haul) users are willing to pay for. This will result in more capacity being provided than is demanded by off-peak (backhaul) users. It is appropriate that the rates for the latter class of users incorporate only those costs which result from their demands. If rates to both classes of users were equalized at the average cost, less capacity would be provided than peak users are willing to pay for; hence, there would be unfulfilled demands. And, off-peak users would be discouraged from making as full use of facilities as they should.

Conclusions. Variable-cost pricing is forward-looking. Its intent is to insure that optimal use is made of existing facilities for as long as they can economically be used. Variable-cost pricing also provides proper incentives for new capital investment both in the railroad industry and in competing modes. Of course, cost determination inevitably must be influenced by experience and thus historic or accounting costs are relevant. They cannot be the sole guides, however, because the ultimate purpose of rate setting is to provide for present and future costs. Consequently, rate decisions must be forward-looking.

Variable-cost pricing is workable and, as shown by the examples, is a basic rule of pricing in industry generally. It is essential if the scarce resources used by the various transportation modes—and, indeed, also those of their customers—are to be used efficiently.

Criteria for Use

It was argued above that it is proper for railroads to set rates on the basis of short-run marginal costs (avoidable costs) when excess capacity exists in that portion of the system for which the rate applies. There is, however, concern that, in practice, such a rule may lead to a worsening of the economic position of the railroads or of the whole economy, unless limitations are set which circumscribe the use of this rule. Four areas of concern will be examined and then some limitations will be proposed. The areas of concern are as follows:

(1) The rule may lead to destructive competition.
(2) Managerial ineptitude in applying the rule may lead to a worsening of the economic position of the railroads or of their competitors.
(3) The rule may not take due account of the social costs of rail or of other modes of transportation.
(4) There may be overriding public interests for maintaining the facilities which, if the rule is used, will be phased out in the long run.

The following limitations on the use of avoidable-cost pricing are suggested:

(1) The carrier should demonstrate the existence of excess capacity. For purposes of this rule, excess capacity can be defined to exist when the traffic generated at rates based on long-run marginal costs is not sufficient to justify constructing facilities to replace existing ones as they wear out.
(2) The carrier should also provide assurance that the new rate will result in capacity being brought into line with demand in the long run.

An income criterion has also been proposed for railroad rate making—namely, that the carrier initiating the rate should demonstrate that the rate would improve its net income. We have determined, however, that this criterion could inhibit proper long-run adjustments.

Destructive Competition. It can be argued that a railroad may choose to use avoidable costs as a rate basis in order to drive another railroad or a competing mode out of business with the expectation of then raising rates sufficiently to recover the revenue losses incurred in the "price war" and also to make additional profits as a result of the demise of the old competitor. This argument has a long history, as applied to railroads as well as to many other industrial enterprises. In order for this argument to apply to railroads, the following conditions must be met:

(1) The avoidable costs of the railroad engaging in this practice have to be lower than those of any competing carrier. Otherwise, it cannot drive out the competition.

(2) The railroad has to have adequate financial resources to last out the "price war," or the competing carriers must have inadequate resources. This condition, however, is relevant only if the capital markets do not function properly.

(3) The railroad must expect to be able to charge a higher rate after the competition has been driven out than it can charge in the presence of the competing carriers.

(4) The railroad must be assured that, once the competing carriers are driven out, they will not reenter, even at the higher rates that would then prevail. Otherwise, the railroad has no incentive to try to drive out the competition in the first place.

There is no doubt that destructive competition has taken place in some instances in some industries. It is unlikely, however, that it would occur in today's transportation markets.

The primary competition to railroad service is likely to be truck service. The truck industry, however, has comparatively few fixed facilities specialized to particular routes or services. Consequently, there is little chance that reentry would be barred for economic reasons. Hence, there is little incentive for a railroad to engage in destructive competition. If, however, the railroad expected that reentry could be barred by means of protectionist legislation or regulation, such destructive rate setting would make sense.

The appearance of destructive competition will arise in two sets of circumstances that are separable but similar. They represent, not destructive competition, but the normal adjustments of the marketplace.

Before turning to these two situations, it is useful to consider briefly the kinds of market forces generated and the adjustments that normally take place in the economy where excess capacity exists. Consider a town where a bypass has just been built, thereby diverting economic activity from the central business district. As a result, all commercial rents in the central business district drop. The rents may drop so low that they do not cover the avoidable costs of some buildings, and these buildings will be boarded up. At this point it may well be that no building owner is recovering his fully allocated costs. Total rent receipts will be down, and yet nobody will be engaging in "destructive competition." This is simply the normal workings of the economy in the presence of overcapacity. In the long run, some buildings might be torn down or converted to other uses; some buildings might be expanded; and some new buildings that are more suited to new demands might be built. In a market where pricing is unconstrained, this adjustment process will take place until capacity is brought into line with demand. Any rule that limits pricing decisions would inhibit and distort this adjustment process. A rule requiring that rents must at least cover avoidable costs would be unnecessary, because it would not be in the interests of the building owners to rent buildings at less than their avoidable costs. An income test—that is, a rule requiring that rents can drop to avoidable costs only if such a drop improves the building owner's net income—would not work because total rental income drops in this situation.

Long-run adjustments may not resemble short-run adjustments. For example, one building that is boarded up in the short run might be rehabilitated and rented in the long run, whereas another building that is initially rented at reduced prices might well be abandoned and torn down in the long run. In economists' terms, the first building might have relatively high marginal costs in the short run but low marginal costs in the long run. The opposite might be true for the second building.

Returning to the railroad industry, consider first the case of two or more competing railroads which, in total, have excess capacity over the portions of the system where they compete. In this case, rates should drop to short-run marginal costs to encourage adjustment of capacity to demand and to assure that maximum economic use is made of the existing facilities. Unless substantial traffic is diverted from competing modes by the new rates, revenue for all competing railroads will drop. Hence, an income test would be inappropriate and would only impede the proper adjustments. The reduction of rates to short-run marginal costs is the result of normal competitive forces and is socially desirable. This reduction is not the result of management ineptitude, even though net income decreases, and it is not "destructive competition."

Next, consider an example of truck–rail competition. Again, the assumption is that there is more rail capacity than is demanded at rates set on the basis of the railroad's long-run marginal costs. Under the proposed marginal-cost pricing rules, we would expect the railroad to drop rates below its own long-run marginal costs to increase utilization of its capacity. The railroad may well drop rates below the competing mode's short-run marginal costs to further increase utilization of its capacity. In no case, however, would the railroad have any incentive to drop rates below its own short-run marginal costs.

In this case, it is unclear whether railroad income would increase or decrease. Hence, an income test would not be desirable because it could lead to perverse results. Whether rail income would rise or fall with rate reductions depends on the price elasticity of demand for all transportation over the route involved and the price elasticity of supply for competing modes.

Disinvestment will take place. If the railroad initially set rates below the short-run marginal costs of competing modes, then the latter will immediately disinvest on these routes. At these rates it is impractical for the railroad to invest. After some time, however, capital replenishment is required. At that point, the mode with the lower long-run marginal costs will make the investment. This may well be the truck industry rather than the railroad industry.

The above example illustrates a case in which there may be unemployment as well as idle capacity in the truck industry until trucking capacity shrinks. The duration of this adjustment depends on the ability of resources, including labor, to find other uses and on the longevity of trucks. Eventually the demand for trucking will increase as railroads disinvest. This could be a slow process, however, because railroad assets are long-lived and partial replacements might be economical. From the point of view of the economy as a whole, this is a desirable adjustment process and it is not destructive competition. But one can expect this process to be bitterly opposed by the trucking industry.

Also, there are two other problems with such an adjustment process. First, there may be a deterioration in rail safety. Second, it is reasonable to expect railroads to attempt to secure legislative or regulatory protection against reentry by the trucking industry.

Managerial Ineptitude. A possible objection to the allowance of marginal-cost pricing in the railroad industry is that managerial ineptitude in applying it may lead to an unwarranted worsening of the railroads' financial situation. This objection rests on the belief that railroad managements are worse than managements of other industries. There is no objective proof that this is so, and probably no way to prove it. Insofar as it may be true, the reason might be that the regulatory process does not allow enough managerial scope to attract highly qualified management.

Actions which may appear to be inept in that they are accompanied by a worsening of railroads' net income may simply be the outcome of the normal workings of competition in the presence of excess capacity. As was noted above, we would expect competition in the presence of excess capacity to lead to rates below the railroads' long-run marginal costs until capacity is brought into line with demand. This is socially desirable, even though railroad revenues and income drop.

It was suggested above that an excess-capacity test be applied to any railroad initiating a rate lower than long-run marginal costs. This is to insure that managements have properly considered the relevant facts in proposing such a rate decrease; it is not a measure to place limitations on the railroads' pricing flexibility. An income test was also considered, but such a test could bar desirable adjustments.

Private Costs versus Social Costs. It could conceivably be argued that not all of the social costs of providing railroad transportation are borne by the railroads; that society as a whole subsidizes railroads. It could also be argued that, relative to other modes, railroads bear a smaller share of their social costs. If the facts were to bear out either of these arguments, then pricing based on the marginal costs of railroads could result in an underpricing of rail services because the difference between social and internalized costs would not be recovered in rail rates.

There is no known evidence that there is a significant subsidy to railroad users, except in the case of Amtrak (the National Railroad Passenger Corporation). It may be that competing modes such as trucks and barges are the beneficiaries of a capital subsidy. Thus, it appears that railroad freight services are not subsidized either directly or relative to competing modes. Consequently this argument against avoidable-cost pricing is not plausible.

Overriding Public Interest in Maintaining Rail Freight Services. It can be argued that there is some form of social value in the existence of rail freight services that is not paid for by shippers. This argument goes as follows: nonshippers benefit in some unusual way from the existence of rail services. If avoidable-cost pricing leads to abandonments, then the value received by nonshippers is lost.

This argument is usually expressed in terms of the need for railroads as a matter of national defense. In this form, the argument states that rail services are unusually valuable to society as a whole and must be preserved. It is wrong, however, to apply this notion in opposition to avoidable-cost pricing. First, if rail services have an overriding social value, it is inappropriate to charge only rail users and railroad owners for the costs of providing this value. The costs should be shared by all those who benefit. Second, most economic activity confers social value and this in itself is no argument for subsidy. It has not been demonstrated that rail services are unusual in this regard.

8

RAIL-BARGE COMPETITION AND PREDATORY PRICING: AN ECONOMIC PERSPECTIVE

P. David Qualls

In 1974 the U.S. Department of Transportation proposed legislation known as the Transportation Improvement Act which would have greatly increased the railroads' pricing freedom. The water carriers then proposed two amendments to the proposed legislation. One amendment would provide for legislation of minimum rail rates on routes where railroads compete for traffic with water carriers. As stated, the amendment would provide that on such routes rail rates for given commodities should not be allowed to *fall below* a level at which the ratio of the rate to the unit cost of carrying the cargo is equal to the ratio of the commodity rate to the unit cost of carrying the cargo on rail routes not subject to water competition. A second amendment would provide for legislation of maximum rail rates on transportation routes involving a rail "leg" and a water "leg." The commodity rate on the rail leg would not be allowed to *rise above* a level at which the ratio of the rate to unit cost on the rail leg is equal to the ratio of the rate to unit costs on any "alternative" through rail transportation provided by railroads.

In other words, amendment number one provides that on any route between, say, points A and B, where there is intermodal competition between rail and water, the rail rate can be no lower relative to cost than the rail rate (relative to cost) for similar commodities between, say, points C and D, where there is no water competition. Amendment number two states that on any route between, say, points E and G, involving rail transportation from E to point F and water

This chapter is edited from a paper entitled "Economic Analysis of Legislative Amendments Proposed by Water Carriers Dealing with So-Called Discriminatory Pricing Practices of Rail Carriers," prepared for the U.S. Department of Transportation in the fall of 1974. P. David Qualls is a professor of economics at the University of Maryland.

transportation from F to G, the rail rate can be no higher relative to cost on the E to F route than on an alternative through rail route from E to G.

The arguments advanced by the water carriers in favor of these amendments are as follows: Without amendment number one, it is argued, railroads will engage in predatory price cutting on routes subject to water competition in order to injure the competitive position of the water carriers. In the long run, the competitive position of the water carriers will be destroyed and shippers, deprived of the benefits of competition, will be forced to pay monopolistic rail rates. This will happen even though the water carriers might be more "efficient," at least with respect to certain types of traffic. Without amendment number two, it is argued, railroads will establish artificially high rates on the rail "leg" of rail-water routes in order to shift the traffic over to the alternative all-rail routes where railroads will be able to make monopolistic profits.

The amendments were presented as being necessary to preserve viable intermodal competition between rail and water and to maintain the economic "efficiency" in the allocation of the nation's resources that such competition promotes. However, the supporting arguments, although superficially plausible, do not stand the test of economic analysis. It is extremely unlikely that, without the amendments, the market behavior of the railroads would be as predicted by the water carriers. It is unlikely that even a single-firm, unregulated, national railroad monopoly would behave in such fashion. It is probable that the water carriers' amendments were motivated not so much by considerations of overall efficiency in transportation as by a desire to provide a certain degree of economic protectionism—that is, insulation of the water carriers against intermodal competition from the railroads.

Amendment Number One: "Antisharpshooting"

It may well be true that the forces of market competition will lead to somewhat lower rail rates and somewhat lower railroad profits on routes that are subject to intermodal rail and water competition than will be the case on those few isolated rail routes on which one or a very few rail carriers are not faced with water competition or other forms of competition.[1] It is a major proposition of economic theory

---

[1] On the other hand, there no doubt are some water transportation routes on which water carriers are faced with little effective rail competition. With just a few water carriers operating on such routes, we would expect water rates and water carriers' profits to tend to be higher on these routes than on those where water carriers are faced with significant rail competition.

that less "competition" will tend to lead to higher average prices (relative to costs). Many, if not most, economists would lament the situation which leads to higher rates relative to costs on some routes than on others. However, it is not the fact that rates are lower (on the average) than quasi-monopolistic levels on some or most routes that is basically objectionable. It is the fact that the rates are somewhat higher (on the average) than purely competitive levels on a few routes that is socially deleterious.

The water carriers' rule would do little, if anything at all, to correct this situation. It is true that, if the rule were effectively enforced, it would tend to bring about an equality in the ratios of rates to costs on both types of rail routes (those that are subject and those that are not subject to water carrier competition). However, this equality would most likely be accomplished not by rail rates being established at *lower* levels on routes not subject to water competition, but by rates being *higher* on those routes where water and rail do compete.

Implementation and enforcement of the water carriers' amendment would have several consequences. First, such action would fail to do much, if anything, to correct or diminish the slight degree of monopolistically discretionary pricing power that railroads might have on those few isolated routes or systems not subject to intramodal or intermodal competition. Second, it would build inflexibility in rate making back into the system. Rate flexibility in the face of changing competitive conditions of demand and/or costs is eminently desirable in and of itself. Such flexibility will enable a market price system to allocate transportation resources more efficiently between both time and place points. Rules which force equality of ratios of rates to costs across different transportation markets effectively preclude rate flexibility and the social economic benefits that flexibility confers. Third, implementation and enforcement of the amendment would inhibit intermodal competition between rail and water, and would therefore lead to generally higher rates on those routes where railroads and water carriers would otherwise compete for traffic. It would make little sense to add to reform legislation an amendment that would hamper market competition, which such legislation is designed to promote.

The water carriers do not agree that the effect of this amendment would be as just indicated. Their view is that, since the amendment allows for railroads to lower rates to levels required to "meet such water competition, considering both the rate or charge and the economic utility of the rail service in comparison with the rate or charge and the economic utility of the water service," the rule does not preclude water-rail competition. Secondly, in their view the amendment is needed to prevent predatory behavior on the part of the railroads, which in the long run would destroy water competition.

Let us consider each of these in turn. A major difficulty with the first argument is that the difference in "utility" between water service and rail service is likely to be different for different types of shippers. It is administratively and conceptually impossible for the regulator to assess accurately this different utility. Even if it were possible for the regulator to make such an assessment, the rule would still be objectionable. With comparative rates for rail and water which reflected exactly the difference in utility of the different services, individual shippers would be "indifferent" about whether to ship by rail or by water. Choices of the shippers between rail and water presumably would be based on random selection which would not economically allocate resources between water and rail.

With free and open competition between rail and water, comparative rail and water rates will tend to reflect comparative rail and water costs. A shipper for whom the water rate was lower and the utility of the water service was greater would choose to ship by water. A shipper for whom the rail rate was lower and the utility of the rail service was greater would ship by rail. A shipper for whom the rail rate was higher but for whom the utility of the rail service was greater would make his decision whether to ship by rail or by water depending on whether the difference between the rail and the water utility was greater than or less than the difference between the rail and the water rates. Similarly, any shipper for whom the water rate was higher and for whom the utility of water service was greater would decide to ship by water or by rail depending on whether the difference between the utility of water service and the utility of rail service was greater than or less than the difference between water and rail rates.

It is in this fashion that free and open competition between water and rail carriers would tend to allocate water and rail transportation among shippers so as to maximize the net utility or benefit to shippers (and, ultimately, to the consuming public). Implementation of the water carriers' rule would prevent this desirable market outcome from occurring.

Another major objection is that the rule would lead to higher rates in general, for both rail and water, than would otherwise be the case. For a seller to be a viable, effective competitor who constitutes a constraining influence on his market rivals' pricing policies, he must have the potential power and ability to undercut his rivals' effective prices and to take business away from them, not just to meet their prices. The rule clearly would have the effect of inhibiting the potential power of the railroads to win "business" from the water carriers by engaging in effective price competition. It tends to place the water carriers alone in the position of determining water rates *and* rail rates on routes where water carriers and railroads would otherwise be competitors. Therefore, it would most likely lead to higher rates, for both rail and water, than would otherwise be the case on such routes.

The second argument—that "predatory" pricing by the railroads would destroy the competitive water carriers—is very unlikely. Economic theory suggests that, for this sort of activity to be practically feasible, dominating firms must have the financial means (perhaps monopoly profits from other markets) and a profit motive. The water carriers are a viable, efficient, competitive service. For the railroads to mount a predatory-pricing campaign to destroy the water carriers would be very expensive in terms of economic losses and foregone profits. It is very unlikely that the railroads have the financial capability to underwrite such a campaign of price warfare. More important than this, however, is the fact that there would be little, if anything, for the railroads to gain, even in the long run, by such activity. The usual argument is that a predatory firm, once having destroyed the competition, will be able to recoup its losses, plus something extra, by engaging in subsequent monopoly pricing. This probably would not be possibile for the railroads. They would still be faced with intermodal competition from truckers and other types of carriers. Moreover, the inland water transportation industry is not characterized by severe barriers to entry. If the railroads attempted to recoup by charging monopoly prices, the water carriers would reenter the market. Predatory pricing on the part of the railroads would involve cost outlays for little or no potential gain. Therefore, it seems unlikely that the railroads would engage in such pricing.

In addition, the water carriers have other legal and administrative recourse to protect themselves against overwhelming predation. The proposed legislation, the Transportation Improvement Act, provides that railroads shall not be allowed to price below cost. This should be all the protection that viable, efficient competitors such as the water carriers would need to protect themselves against overt predation.

There is one further unfortunate characteristic of the water carriers' first amendment. Because it would effectively limit the ability of the railroads to engage in free and open price competition with the water carriers, it would set up an incentive for the railroads to adopt covert "extramarket" competitive strategies. These could take such forms as secret rate rebating, bribing freight forwarders, and the like. Such practices are socially wasteful and might truly be labeled "predatory." It is bad public policy to establish incentives for firms to engage in such behavior.

Amendment Number Two: "The Price Squeeze"

The water carriers' second amendment would establish maximum-rate rules for railroad pricing on rail legs of combined rail-water transportation routes. The argument of the water carriers is that without this legislation of maximum rates, the railroads will price at artifically high levels designed to shift the traffic to all-rail routes where the railroads will maximize their profits.

In order to understand and analyze this argument, a basic point must be understood. Any rational, cost-conscious shipper moving his goods over a rail-water combination route from, say, point E to point G, involving rail transportation from E to F and water transportation from F to G, would be concerned solely with the total price of the total service from E to G. The shipper would not care how that sum was broken down into rail and water components. If the total price for the total service was $100, for example, the shipper would be completely unconcerned whether the rail price was $90 and the water price $10, or whether the rail price was $10 and the water price $90. The shipper would only be concerned with the fact that the total price was $100. The "demand" of the shipper is for the total transportation service from point E to point G.

Once this basic notion is understood, one gains insight into the possible motive of the water carriers in attempting to establish legally maximum rates on the rail leg. If the shipper is willing to pay $100 for the total service from E to G and the railroad charges $90 for the service from E to F, the shipper is willing to pay only $10 for the water service from F to G. If, on the other hand, the railroad charges only $10 for the service from E to F, the shipper is willing to pay $90 for the water service from F to G. If by administrative means the water carriers can minimize the rail charge, they thereby maximize the residual demand for their services on the water leg of the transportation route.

What about the water carriers' argument that the railroads will price to drive traffic off the rail-water routes? Is this likely? The water carriers claim this will happen even though the rail-water route is the more efficient route, that is, it is the route with the lower total cost. What about the effect of the water carriers' pricing rule for the railroads? Will it, as the water carriers claim, lead to a more efficient pattern and allocation of resources in transportation?

Theoretic Market Model. The received body of economic literature on market theory does not deal with this sort of market structure. Therefore, in order to analyze the operation of this sort of market structure, a theoretic model of the market was developed. The model incorporated the following assumptions:

(1) There is a rail-water route from, say, point E to point G involving rail service from E to F and water service from F to G.

(2) There is alternative all-rail service between E and G.

(3) From the point of view of the shippers concerned, these two alternatives are perfect substitutes. The individual shipper will choose between rail-water service and all-rail service solely on the basis of price. If all-rail service is cheaper, he will go that way. If rail-water service is cheaper, he will go that way.

(4) The railroad is a single-firm, unregulated monopoly. All the rail service provided is provided by the railroad at unregulated, monopolistically determined prices.

(5) The water carriers providing service on the water leg are essentially competitive. They do not individually have monopoly power to set prices above their marginal costs (in the long run, such prices would yield "competitive" rates of return on water carriers' investments).

These assumptions about the market structure seem to be more favorable to the water carriers' case than any other assumptions that could have been adopted.[2] In addition, algebraic cost functions (for the water leg, the rail leg, and the all-rail route) and a service-demand function were assumed. It was assumed that the railroad would price so as to maximize its profits.

The first question posed, using the model, was whether the railroad would price so as to move the traffic over the all-rail route or over the rail-water route. The answer was that the outcome depended on the comparative total costs of the two alternative services. If the total costs on the rail-water route (the costs of the railroad and the costs of the water carriers) were lower than the rail costs on the all-rail route, the railroad would price so that the traffic would move over the rail-water route. If the total costs of providing the all-rail service were lower than the total costs of providing rail-water service,

---

[2] When this analysis was presented to and discussed with a representative of the water carriers and their economic consultant, it was agreed that these were the most favorable possible assumptions.

the railroad would price so that the traffic would move over the all-rail route.

This represents economic efficiency in the sense that the traffic is moving over the least-cost route. A given volume of traffic is being moved at the lowest cost in terms of society's resources.

All-rail as lower cost route. What effect would the implementation of the rule have on the allocation of traffic between routes? Assume that the all-rail route is the lower total cost route. Without the rule, the railroad would price so the traffic would move by the all-rail route. Given the demand for traffic and the cost of providing service, there is some all-rail rate, R_a (and thus some ratio of rate to cost, R_a/c_a), which maximizes the railroad's profit on the all-rail route. The railroad rate on the all-rail route would be lower than the total price on the rail-water route, and shippers would not demand service on the rail-water route.

If, however, the rule were implemented and the railroad were required to provide service on the rail leg at a rate, R_L, at which the ratio of rate to cost, R_L/c_L, was equal to R_a/c_a, the total price for service on the rail-water route might be lower than the price on the all-rail route.[3] The traffic would therefore shift to the rail-water route. In one way this is good—the price is lower; in another way it is bad—the traffic is moving over the high-cost route. In this situation, the railroad would make less profit than by providing service only on either the rail leg or the all-rail route.

In this instance, the railroad would have three options whereby it might try to increase its profits. First, the railroad might cease offering service on the all-rail route. Then it could increase its rate on the rail leg. There would be no all-rail alternative ratio of rate to cost for use in regulating the rate on the rail leg. This would be unfortunate because, as it turns out, the rate on the rail leg which would maximize the profits of the railroad (assuming service is not offered or provided on the all-rail route) is higher (when added to the water rate, which is still assumed to be equal to the marginal costs of the water carriers) than the profit-maximizing rate on the all-rail route (assuming no service on the rail leg). This outcome of the implementation of the rule seems to be the worst possible. It would have the

---

[3] This might not be the case if the difference between the unit cost of providing service on the all-rail route and the rail leg is small and the unit cost of the water carrier service is large. In this event, implementation of the rule would mean that the total price—rail rate plus water rate—on the rail-water route would still be higher than the monopoly rate on the all-rail route. Since in this case no traffic would shift from all-rail service to rail-water service, implementation of the rule would have no effect.

traffic (a smaller total volume) moving over the higher cost route and paying a higher total rate.

A second strategy that the railroad might attempt would be to increase the rate on the all-rail route to a level *above* that at which it otherwise would be established in the absence of the rule enforcement. By bringing up the rate on the all-rail route, the railroad might satisfy the rule and make more profits than if the ratio of the profit-maximizing rate to cost on the all-rail route were used for rate making on the rail leg of the rail-water route. Compared with the situation if the rule were not implemented, this would be unfortunate. The traffic might move over the higher cost route and, in any event, the volume of traffic would be lower and the total rate would be higher than if the railroad were allowed to maximize its profits by providing service on the lower cost all-rail route at a profit-maximizing rate level.

A third strategy the railroad might adopt would be to establish a ratio of rate to cost on the rail leg equal to the ratio of the profit-maximizing rate (assuming that service is not offered on the rail leg) to cost on the all-rail route and then attempt to deny service on the rail leg. The water carriers' amendment states that such service must be provided; however, there may be "extramarket" means whereby the railroad might attempt to limit demand for service on the rail leg. Such tactics might take the form of bribes and rebates to freight forwarders, shipping agents, and the like, to induce them to ship over the higher priced all-rail route. If such tactics were effective, the market outcome would be similar to the situation if the rule were not enforced, except for the costs involved in the socially wasteful "extramarket" activity.

Summing up, in the event that the all-rail route is the lower cost route, implementation of the water carriers' rule can have two possible types of effects—"none" and "bad." In the absence of the rule, the monopoly railroad would price so the traffic would move over the lower cost all-rail route. Enforcement of the rule may or may not have an effect on the railroad's pricing policy. If it does, the behavioral response of the railroad is likely to be such that market performance is worse than it would be in the absence of the rule.

Rail-water as lower cost route. Assume now that the rail-water combination is the lower cost route. In this case, the railroad would maximize its profit by establishing a rate on the rail leg of the rail-water route which, when added to the competitive water rate, would be lower than the putative rate on the all-rail route. Shippers for whom the two routes were perfect substitutes would ship on the rail-water route and would not demand service on the all-rail route. The traffic would be moving over the lower cost route.

In this situation, it would appear that implementation of the water carriers' rule would have no effect; no service is being demanded by shippers on the all-rail route. However, this may not be the case. There may be some shippers for whom the alternatives of all-rail service and rail-water service are not really good substitutes. These shippers will be demanding service on the all-rail route. The rate which maximizes the railroad's profit from providing service to these shippers on the all-rail route may be lower relative to cost than the profit-maximizing rate (relative to cost) on the rail leg of the rail-water route.[4] Administrative enforcement of the water carriers' rule might attempt to force the rail rate on the rail leg of the rail-water route down to a point at which the ratio of rate to cost on the rail leg was equal to the ratio of rate to cost on the all-rail route. The railroad might react by raising the rate (relative to cost) on the all-rail route. In either event, with the ratio of rate to cost being the same on the all-rail route and the rail leg of the rail-water route, a unit of traffic volume would yield more profit to the railroad if it moved over the all-rail route than if it moved over the rail-water route. Therefore, enforcement of the rule would set up an incentive for the railroad to engage in "extramarket" tactics designed to shift traffic from the lower cost rail-water route to the higher cost all-rail route.

In the case where the rail-water route is the lower cost route, enforcement of the rule can have two possible types of effects—"none" and "bad." If enforcement has an effect, the effect will be a tendency to raise rates in general and perhaps to shift some traffic from lower cost routes to higher cost routes. Such shifts would be accomplished by socially wasteful "extramarket" activity.

Water carriers as monopolistic. Given the foregoing, one might very well ask: What is the motivation of the water carriers in seeking such an amendment and its enforcement? The answer to this question no doubt follows from a recognition that the water carriers do not really constitute a "perfectly competitive industry." The water carriers' industry can be characterized as "low-grade oligopoly"—that is, it is an industry with moderately high seller concentration and moderate barriers to entry. Economic theory suggests, and empirical evidence confirms, that firms in such industries typically charge higher

---

[4] This clearly will be the case if the price elasticity of the nonsubstitute demand for service on the all-rail route is equal to the price elasticity of demand for service for which the all-rail and rail-water routes are substitutes. The total "price" on the rail-water route would still be lower than the "price" on the all-rail route, however.

prices and make larger profits than would be the case if the industry were perfectly competitive. In the usual case, this is accomplished because the established firms avoid competitive tendencies and price at levels at which moderately disadvantaged potential entrants do not find entry into the industry to be a profitable prospect.

In the case of the water carriers outlined above, however, the pricing power of the railroad on the rail leg of the rail-water route constitutes an additional constraint on the pricing power of the water carriers on the water leg of the route. Any rule which, when enforced, leads the railroad to price at a lower level than it otherwise would at least partially relieves this constraint.

Consider the model outlined above, but with one change. Assume that the water carriers, instead of being a competitive industry, are in effect a monopoly firm. Assume also that rail-water is the lower cost route. If the water carrier monopolist priced at marginal costs (the competitive price level), monopoly pricing by the railroad would yield a lower total price on the rail-water route and the traffic would move there. The water carrier monopolist could raise price above cost up to the point at which the difference between price and cost for the water carrier was equal to the difference between total costs of service on the rail-water route and the all-rail route before railroad pricing would shift the traffic to the all-rail route. If, however, implementation of the rule proposed by the water carriers led to an increase in the ratio of rate to cost on the all-rail route (a not unlikely effect), the water carrier could raise price further above cost without shifting the traffic to the all-rail route. At the same time, with equal ratios of rate to cost on both the all-rail route and the rail leg of the rail-water route, the railroad would have an incentive to adopt "extramarket" tactics designed to shift the traffic to the all-rail route. Implementation of the rule would tend to lead to higher prices and would, perhaps, shift some of the traffic to the higher cost route.

Assume now that the all-rail route is the lower cost route. Unregulated pricing by the railroad would yield a lower total shipping rate on the all-rail route. The traffic would move on the all-rail route. If, however, the railroad were forced to provide the same service on the rail leg at the same ratio of rate to cost, it might respond by increasing the rate on the all-rail route. In any event, with equal ratios of rate to cost on both routes, the railroad would find it more profitable to move a unit of traffic volume on the all-rail route. Yet, the water carrier can price above cost to some extent and still keep the total rate on the rail-water route equal to or slightly lower than the rate on the all-rail route. In response to relative prices, the traffic might tend to shift from lower cost all-rail service to higher cost rail-water service. This would enable the water carrier to make some monopoly profit; however, the railroad would have an incentive to adopt "extramarket" tactics to try to shift traffic back to the all-rail route.

In short, implementation of the rule in this case would tend, in general, to put an upward pressure on rates, to shift traffic from low-cost to high-cost routes, and to set up incentives for the railroad to engage in "extramarket promotional" activity.

Conclusions. This is, as a general matter, the thrust of the rule. Where the railroad has some amount of discretionary monopolistic pricing power, implementation of the rule carries the danger of placing an upward pressure on rates, creating pressure for the traffic to move over higher cost routes and giving rise to incentives for predatory pricing. Where the water carriers have some potential monopolistic pricing power, implementation of the rule might tend to shift some monopoly power from the railroad to the water carriers. In and of itself, this might not be regarded as socially obnoxious—it might just depend on whether one liked railroads or water carriers better. Because of the "side effects" listed above, however, significant economic costs would be imposed on shippers, consumers, and society in general.

In short, without the rule, railroad and water carrier pricing will tend toward efficiency in the allocation of transportation resources. With the water carriers' rule, the water carriers may tend to gain vis-à-vis the railroads; however, incentives leading to higher rates and prices and to inefficiency in allocation of resources are created.

The water carriers may argue that the model is wrong when it concludes that, where rail-water routes are more efficient (low cost), the railroad will price so the traffic flows over that route. The argument may be that this does not occur now. The railroad uses every means at its disposal to move traffic over long-haul all-rail routes rather than over rail-water routes, even in cases where the rail-water route is demonstrably the lower cost route.

The answer to this, if it does occur, is that this situation is the result of the past and current system of rate regulation. With regulated rates, long hauls tend to be more profitable than short hauls. With nonregulated rates, lower cost routes—whether they are long haul or short haul—will tend to be more profitable. Implementation of the water carriers' rule would perpetuate the inefficiencies of the old system.

There is an additional difficulty with the water carriers' rule, namely, that the rule might create a disincentive to technological innovation. There may be some technological innovations which can be expected to be profitable if they are adopted on long-haul all-rail routes but unprofitable if they are installed on short-haul rail legs. If implementation of the water carriers' rule meant that service provided with the new technology on the all-rail route would also have to be provided on the rail leg of a rail-water route, the "attractiveness" of adopting the innovation (from the point of view of the railroad) would be diminished. Consequently, the innovation may not be adopted. Shippers on the all-rail route (and ultimately the consuming public) would be denied the benefit of technological change.

The water carriers may argue that their rule would not have this effect because it provides an escape clause for the railroad where "that rail service having substantially the same characteristics as the all-rail service cannot feasibly be provided on the rail portion of the rail and water service." There may, however, be a wide gulf between what is "feasible" from the point of view of the regulatory authority and what is "profitable" from the point of view of the railroad. Thus, implementation of the rule may depress the railroad's incentive toward technological innovation.

Overall, the public interest is not served by the water carriers' amendments to the legislation that has been proposed to reform regulation of the railroads.

9

RAIL-BARGE COMPETITION AND PREDATORY PRICING: A LEGAL PERSPECTIVE

Glen E. Weston

The rail reform legislation proposed by the Department of Transportation in January 1974—specifically, the bill known as the Transportation Improvement Act—contained provisions designed to permit greater flexibility in rate determination by carriers so that competitive incentives would operate more freely among transportation firms. One of the key provisions in the legislation prevented the Interstate Commerce Commission from suspending railroad rate increases or decreases of 7 percent for the first year, 12 percent for the second year, and 15 percent for the third year. This would thus be an experiment in gradual deregulation of rates, which, if successful, would be extended.

The water carriers, however, expressed concern that the greater rate flexibility would permit the railroads to engage in unfair competition. Specifically, the water carriers objected that the railroads would charge lower rates on routes competitive with water routes for the purpose of injuring or destroying competition by water carriers. Moreover, they said that railroads would charge higher rates on the rail segments of combined rail-water routes in order to exert a "price squeeze" on the water carriers that were attempting to compete with all-rail shipments to the same destination.

The Creedy Proposal

John A. Creedy, president of the Water Transport Association, proposed certain amendments to the Transportation Improvement Act

This chapter is edited from a paper entitled "Comparison of the Economics and Administration of the Unfair Competition Doctrines of the Antitrust Laws and Proposals of John Creedy to Amend the Surface Transportation Improvement

which were introduced by Congressman Bob Eckhardt (Democrat, Texas) and given active consideration by the House Committee on Interstate and Foreign Commerce. These amendments are designed to limit the flexibility of rate establishment by railroads by creating a private right of action for damages by a carrier injured by rate discrimination. The amendments read as follows:

(g) (A) The purpose of this subparagraph (g) is to assure that the provisions of paragraphs (7) (b) and (c) will not be employed to effectuate monopoly or predatory practices destroying other modes of transportation, and this subparagraph shall apply only to rates and charges effectuated in accordance with the provisions of subparagraphs (b) and (c) of this paragraph. It is recognized, however, that the protection of the vitality of intermodal competition and not the protection of individual carriers as such against such competition is the paramount purpose of paragraphs (7) (b) and (c). Without in any manner altering the application of other provisions of the Act, the immediately succeeding subparagraphs are intended to designate with greater specificity certain monopolistic or predatory practices which are prohibited and to provide remedies.

(B) No carrier shall discriminate in the rates or charges assessed on a route where intermodal competition exists versus the rates or charges which it assesses for the same or similar traffic on another route, where the purpose or effect is substantially to lessen competition between the carriers and a carrier of another mode, but the prima facie unlawfulness of such discrimination having the above effect may be rebutted by an affirmative showing that the lower rate or charge creating the discrimination is not below the point necessary in good faith to meet the rate or charge of a competitor.

(C) No carrier acting alone or in concert with another carrier shall maintain a higher rate or charge, difference in cost considered, for that segment of an actual or potential rail and water route over which it carries shipments than it maintains on the same or similar traffic over a competitive all-rail or all-water route, where the purpose is to monopolize or the effect is substantially to lessen competition between it and a connecting carrier or tend to create a monopoly of the traffic in question.

Act," prepared for the U.S. Department of Transportation, April 8, 1975. Glen E. Weston is an attorney and a professor of law at the George Washington University Law School.

(D) Any carrier which shall be injured in its business or property by reason of engagement by a carrier in any predatory or discriminatory practice or monopolizing which is forbidden by the foregoing provisions of this subparagraph (g) may sue therefor in any district court of the United States in the district in which the defendant resides or is found or has an agent and shall recover the damages by it sustained, and the cost of suit, including a reasonable attorney's fee.

(E) Before any damage action under subparagraph (D) may be filed in a Federal district court, the Commission shall determine the lawfulness of the practices or rates. The determination of the Commisison shall be conclusive, subject to judicial review, as to the issue of the lawfulness of such practices or rates in any subsequent damage suit under this subsection.

(F) All actions pursuant to subparagraph (E) above shall be commenced within 4 years from the time the cause of action accrues, and not after.[1]

Difficult questions arise concerning the necessity of the so-called Creedy Amendment, its probable effect on intermodal rate competition, its relationship to other provisions against other types of discrimination, and its compatibility with the objectives of the rail reform legislation. This paper will evaluate the amendment in the light of its relationship to economic criteria of fair competition and will compare the amendment to fair competitive standards of the Sherman, Clayton, and Robinson-Patman antitrust acts. The paper will also discuss specific problems of the language of the amendment and present an alternative draft that is designed to achieve the principal objectives of the Creedy proposal with less adverse impact upon competitive pricing flexibility under the deregulation experiment.

Price Discrimination in Economic Theory

There are significant differences of opinion among economic theorists about whether price discrimination is a serious problem requiring specific regulation to preserve competition. The long prevailing economic theory, reflected in early decisions under the Sherman Act and in the detailed prohibitions of the Robinson-Patman Amendment to the Clayton Act, regarded price discrimination as a substantial means by which business concerns with superior financial resources could elimi-

---

[1] U.S. Congress, House, Committee on Interstate and Foreign Commerce, *Report to Accompany H.R. 5385*, 93d Congress, 2d session, 1974, H. Rept. 1381.

nate their smaller competitors from the market and achieve monopoly power.[2]

In recent years, however, there has been an expanding body of economic literature (particularly by economists trained or influenced by economists at the University of Chicago) that strongly questions whether such predatory price discrimination either is theoretically likely or exists in practice to any major extent.[3] These theorists suggest that the cost of driving competitors out of business by price discrimination is so excessive that rational competitors would not be likely to attempt it. Such objectives can usually be achieved at far less cost by other means, such as merger or other accommodation. These costs could not easily be recouped where higher prices would invite new entry or would reactivate dormant capacity. Moreover, Professor John S. McGee has reviewed the record of "classic" monopolization cases, such as the 1911 *Standard Oil Company of New Jersey* v. *United States* case, where predatory price discrimination was cited as a major means used in obtaining monopoly power. Professor McGee has asserted that, in reality, predatory price discrimination was not employed by Standard Oil.[4]

The views of these "Chicago School" theorists are probably not generally accepted. Nevertheless, their critiques have contributed to an almost uniform skepticism about the earlier assumptions that predatory price cutting is a common practice and that detailed prohibitions and vigorous enforcement are needed to prevent such price discrimination. In 1968 President Lyndon B. Johnson's White House Task Force on Antitrust Policy recommended thorough revision of the Robinson-Patman Act. The task force recognized that "price discrimination has an adverse effect on competition only in exceptional cases" and that in some cases "price discrimination improves the functioning

---

[2] See Joel B. Dirlam, *Fair Competition: The Law and Economics of Antitrust Policy* (Westport, Conn.: Greenwood Press, 1954), chapters 7 and 8; W. Stevens, *Unfair Competition* (Chicago: University of Chicago Press, 1917), chapter 1; Robert C. Brooks, Jr., "Injury to Competition under the Robinson-Patman Act," *University of Pennsylvania Law Review*, vol. 109 (1961), pp. 777 ff.

[3] See, for example, John S. McGee, "Predatory Price Cutting: The Standard Oil (N.J.) Case," *Journal of Law and Economics*, vol. 1 (1958), pp. 137 ff.; McGee, "Some Economic Issues in Robinson-Patman Land," *Law and Contemporary Problems*, vol. 30 (1965), pp. 530 ff.; Ward S. Bowman, "Restraint of Trade by the Supreme Court: The Utah Pie Case," *Yale Law Journal*, vol. 77 (1967), pp. 70 ff.

[4] McGee, "Predatory Price Cutting." See also Roland H. Koller II, "The Myth of Predatory Pricing—An Empirical Study," *Antitrust Law and Economics Review*, vol. 4 (1971), pp. 105 ff.; Richard A. Posner, "Separate Statement to Report of ABA Commission to Study the FTC," 1969, p. 113, n. 40. According to Posner, "Predatory pricing is now regarded by most students of antitrust as largely a mythical beast."

of the competitive system."[5] Similarly, in 1969 President Richard M. Nixon's Task Force on Productivity and Competition recommended reform of the Robinson-Patman Act because secret price cutting in oligopolistic industries is likely to lead to general lowering of prices and to be beneficial to competition.[6]

Many enforcement officials within the Antitrust Division of the Department of Justice have long been skeptical about whether predatory pricing can adequately be controlled by the Sherman Act alone. The Antitrust Division, along with the Federal Trade Commission, has full powers to enforce the Robinson-Patman Act. The division has rarely enforced the act, however, because of doubts about the inherent consistency of the Robinson-Patman Act with the policy of the Sherman Act.[7]

Within the Federal Trade Commission itself, the prevailing economic theory concerning price discrimination has changed radically in recent years. The views of former Commissioner Philip Elman, which previously were dissenting from the majority,[8] have apparently become the current prevailing views in the FTC.[9] Official pronounce-

---

[5] White House Task Force on Antitrust Policy, *A Report to the President* (Neal Report), 1968.

[6] Task Force on Productivity and Competition, *A Report to the President* (Stigler Report), 1969. See also National Commission on Food Marketing, *A Report to the President*, 1966; this report called for a study and reappraisal of the Robinson-Patman Act in light of current economic conditions and overall antitrust policies.

[7] See Frederick M. Rowe, *Price Discrimination under the Robinson-Patman Act* (Boston: Little, Brown and Company, 1962). Rowe counted only six criminal and four civil actions by the Justice Department from 1937 to mid-1961; most of these were ultimately dismissed. Compare Edward H. Levi, "The Robinson-Patman Act—Is It in the Public Interest?" *ABA Antitrust Section*, vol. 1 (1952), pp. 60–61: "The Robinson-Patman Act tends to be a price fixing statute hiding in the clothes of anti-monopoly and pro-competition symbols. . . . The conflict between the Robinson-Patman Act and the Sherman Act is this: The Robinson-Patman Act promotes that uniformity of prices and control over prices which the Sherman Act and also the Federal Trade Commission Act deem to be illegal."

[8] Philip Elman, "The Robinson-Patman Act and Antitrust Policy: A Time for Reappraisal," *Washington University Law Review*, vol. 42 (1966), p. 1.

[9] See *Report of the ABA Commission to Study the Federal Trade Commission* (Chicago: American Bar Association, 1969), pp. 67–68 and 99–102. This was the report of a study group chaired by Miles Kirkpatrick who later became chairman of the FTC. See also Henry M. Banta, Jr., and H. Robert Field, "FTC Orders under the Price Discrimination Law: An Evaluation," *Antitrust Law and Economics Review*, vol. 3 (1970), p. 89. Banta and Field are FTC lawyers who conclude: "(1) that there is no satisfactory evidence that price discrimination is significantly related to the general phenomena of concentration in American industries; (2) that there is no persuasive evidence that the Commission's enforcement of the Robinson-Patman Price Discrimination Act has had any significant effect on either the structure, conduct, or performance of any important American industry."

ments of the FTC rarely indicate the dramatic change that has occurred in the attitude of the FTC toward the Robinson-Patman Act
because of concern about the reactions of Congress. Nevertheless, the
drastic decline in enforcement activities is ample proof of a complete
turnabout of FTC enforcement policy.[10]

A recent analysis of predatory pricing that appears to represent
the "mainstream" of current economic theory is found in an article
by Phillip E. Areeda and Donald F. Turner of Harvard Law School.[11]
Professors Areeda and Turner recognize that there is such a thing as
"predatory pricing" that may be relatively rare but that justifies antitrust remedies under section 2 of the Sherman Act. However, they
suggest that two conditions are essential for predatory pricing: (1)
the predators must have superior resources to provide greater staying
power to achieve the purpose to drive rivals out of the market, and
(2) there must be very high barriers to entry to permit recouping of
losses from predatory pricing. They assert that "extreme care must be
taken in formulating" antitrust rules against predatory pricing "lest
the threat of litigation, particularly by private parties, materially deter
legitimate, competitive pricing." After extensive analysis of alternative ways of formulating tests for predatory pricing, Professors
Areeda and Turner conclude that the most appropriate criterion for
predatory pricing that would be administratively workable because of
limitations upon data available would be that of "reasonably anticipated average variable cost." They thus propose rules that a price
below "reasonably anticipated average variable cost" should be conclusively presumed unlawful and a price above such level should be
conclusively presumed to be lawful.[12]

---

[10] Compare the views expressed in Frederic M. Scherer, *Industrial Market Structure and Economic Performance* (Chicago: Rand McNally and Co., 1970), pp.
504–05. Scherer, currently the chief economist of the FTC, said: "The Act is a
jungle but not impossible; however, a fresh legislative start may be needed to
discourage systematic predatory discrimination but permit desirable unsystematic
discrimination."

[11] Phillip E. Areeda and Donald F. Turner, "Predatory Pricing and Related
Practices under Section 2 of the Sherman Act," *Harvard Law Review*, vol. 88
(1975), p. 697.

[12] Compare Joe S. Bain, *Industrial Organization*, 2nd ed. (New York: John Wiley
and Sons, 1968), pp. 563–67. According to Bain, the adverse economic effects of
the Robinson-Patman Act appear substantially to outweigh any favorable effects.
Editor's Note: Subsequent to the preparation of this paper, the article by Professors Areeda and Turner, "Predatory Pricing and Related Practices under Section 2 of the Sherman Act," has been relied upon strongly in judicial decisions
under the Robinson-Patman Act and Sherman Act in rejecting claims of predatory pricing. See International Air Industries, Inc. v. American Excelsior Co.,
517 F.2d 714 (5th Cir. 1975), certiorari denied, 424 U.S. 943; Pacific Engineering
& Production Co. of Nevada v. Kerr-McGee Corp., 551 F.2d 790 (10th Cir. 1977),
certiorari petition pending (1977). The article has also stimulated a lively de-

Fair Competitive Pricing Standards of the
Sherman and Robinson-Patman Acts

Section 2 of the Sherman Act, which prohibits monopolizing and attempts to monopolize, has occasionally been applied to predatory pricing practices. In *Standard Oil Company of New Jersey* v. *United States*, Standard Oil was held to have monopolized through various activities, including formation of a holding company which held the stock of forty separate oil companies controlling 90 percent of the market.[13] One of the practices cited as a means used to gain monopoly power was the use of local price cutting for the purpose of suppressing competition by smaller local competitors. In the companion case of *United Sates* v. *American Tobacco Co.*, it was held that section 2 of the Sherman Act was violated by American Tobacco Company which controlled 95 percent of domestic cigarette output and large percentages of plug tobacco and other products. American Tobacco was found to have engaged in "ruinous competition" with manufacturers of plug tobacco by lowering prices "below its cost" and to have sustained severe losses, successfully forcing five large competitors to sell out to American Tobacco.[14]

In numerous other cases dealing with section 2 of the Sherman Act, price discrimination has been a part of a course of conduct found to constitute monopolization or an attempt to monopolize.[15] These cases, however, have nearly always involved practices other than predatory pricing, and the decisions do not provide clear guidelines or standards for determining when pricing is unlawful beyond the use of such terms as "predatory" or "ruinous price warfare" or "below

bate. See Frederic M. Scherer, "Predatory Pricing and the Sherman Act: A Comment," *Harvard Law Review*, vol. 89, p. 869 (1976), a reply in Areeda and Turner, "Scherer on Predatory Pricing," *Harvard Law Review*, vol. 89, p. 891 (1976), and a rejoinder in Scherer, "Some Last Words on Predatory Pricing," *Harvard Law Review*, vol. 89, p. 901 (1976).

In 1977 a Department of Justice Report on the Robinson-Patman Act (Government Printing Office) recommended repeal or drastic revision of the Act, but a *Report of the Ad Hoc Subcommittee on Antitrust, the Robinson-Patman Act, and Related Matters of the House Committee on Small Business* (1977), concluded that the act should not be "repealed nor emasculated nor weakened in any way whatsoever."

[13] Standard Oil Company of New Jersey v. United States, 221 U.S. 1, 43 (1911).
[14] United States v. American Tobacco Company, 221 U.S. 106 (1911).
[15] Story Parchment Co. v. Patterson Parchment Paper Co., 282 U.S. 555 (1931); United States v. E.I. du Pont de Nemours & Co., 188 Fed. 127, 140 (C.C.D. Del. 1911) (monopolizing of gunpowder and explosive powder in which "disastrous price warfare" against competitors was used); United States v. United Shoe Machinery Co., 110 F. Supp. 295 (D. Mass. 1953), affirmed per curiam, 347 U.S. 521 (1954) (discriminatory pricing policy on shoe machines was part of the method used to retain an 85 percent share of the market).

cost." For a practice to constitute monopolizing, the defendant must have acquired or maintained "monopoly power" (usually proved by a 75 percent or greater share of a "relevant market" by exclusionary means).

An "attempt to monopolize" under section 2 of the Sherman Act requires specific intent to gain monopoly power or to exclude competitors and anticompetitive conduct that is designed to achieve the objective, such as predatory, below-cost price cutting. The prevailing view also requires proof of a dangerous probability that monopoly power will be achieved in a "relevant market." This normally requires that the defendant have a large share of the "relevant market."[16] A minority view, however, would regard an "attempt to monopolize" as requiring only proof of conduct that is predatory or anticompetitive and that is specifically intended to eliminate competitors from a substantial segment of a market.[17] Under this minority view, predatory pricing intended to eliminate a particular significant competitor may be sufficient to violate section 2. Professors Areeda and Turner suggest that pricing below the reasonably anticipated average variable costs should be considered conclusively unlawful under section 2, but there is at present no precedent for this view.[18]

Section 2 of the Clayton Act of 1914 was enacted for the purpose of providing a specific prohibition against discriminatory pricing that may have the effect of substantially lessening competition or tending to create a monopoly. The focus of the 1914 provision was upon preventing injury to competition with the discriminating seller (first-line injury). The Robinson-Patman Amendment in 1936 added the dimension of probable injury to competition on the buyer level (second-line injury) and to customers of the buyer level (third-line injury). In this connection, the amendment added the underlined language so that the clause now reads as follows:

> [Price discrimination is unlawful] where the effect of such discrimination may be substantially to lessen competition or tend to create a monopoly in any line of commerce, *or to injure, destroy or prevent competition with any person who either grants or knowingly receives the benefit of such discrimination, or with customers of either of them.*

---

[16] Mackey v. Sears, Roebuck & Co., 237 F.2d 869 (7th Cir. 1956); United States v. Charles Pfizer & Co., 245 F. Supp. 801 (E.D. N.Y. 1965); Don T. Hibner, Jr., "Attempts to Monopolize: A Concept in Search of an Analysis," *ABA Antitrust Law Journal*, vol. 34 (1967), p. 165.

[17] Donald F. Turner, "Antitrust Policy and the Cellophane Case," *Harvard Law Review*, vol. 70 (1956), p. 281; Lessig v. Tidewater Oil Co., 327 F.2d 459 (9th Cir. 1964).

[18] Areeda and Turner, "Predatory Pricing and Related Practices."

This provision has created ambiguity that is not yet fully resolved about whether the act reaches discrimination which merely injures individual *competitors* or whether a general injury to *competition* in the market must be shown.[19] The prevailing view is that injury to *competition* is required.[20] Some decisions, however, have held that predatory pricing that is intended to injure a single firm's ability to compete will constitute a sufficient injury to competition.[21] Another court has suggested a distinction between, on the one hand, cases where competitive injury at the *seller* level (first-line injury) is claimed, in which a *general injury* to competitive conditions in the market must be shown, and, on the other hand, cases where injury at the *buyer level* (second-line injury) is alleged, in which injury to *individual competitors* is sufficient.[22]

The type of injury relevant to the proposed Creedy Amendment is seller-level (first-line) injury. The standards for determining violation of the Robinson-Patman Act in seller-level injury cases are still surprisingly unclarified. This is partly because only a small percentage of the cases brought under the Robinson-Patman Act have primarily involved seller-level injury, and partly because a continual tug-of-war has been waged between the economic objectives of the act and the social and political objectives of preserving small businesses for egalitarian purposes.

Some of the earlier decisions seem to suggest that price discrimination that may merely cause a "substantial diversion" of trade from competitors may be sufficient to constitute a violation of the act.[23] Later decisions, however, required proof of substantial market dislocation rather than merely diversion of trade.[24]

Most of the successful seller-level injury cases brought by the Federal Trade Commission or by private plaintiffs have involved find-

---

[19] See the collection of cases in S. Chesterfield Oppenheim and Glen E. Weston, eds., *The Lawyer's Robinson-Patman Act Sourcebook: Opinions of the FTC and the Courts, and Related Materials*, vol. 1 (Boston: Little, Brown and Co., 1971), pp. 369–93.

[20] Anheuser-Busch, Inc. v. Federal Trade Commission, 289 F.2d 835 (7th Cir. 1961); Atlas Building Products Co. v. Diamond Block & Gravel Co., 269 F.2d 950 certiorari denied, 360 U.S. 834 (1960).

[21] Lloyd A. Fry Roofing Co. v. Federal Trade Commission, 371 F.2d 277 (7th Cir. 1966); Dean Milk Co., CCH Trade Reg. Rep., par. 17,357 (FTC 1965).

[22] Foremost Dairies, Inc. v. Federal Trade Commission, 348 F.2d 674 (5th Cir. 1965), certiorari denied, 382 U.S. 959 (1965).

[23] Samuel H. Moss, Inc. v. Federal Trade Commission, 148 F.2d 378 (2d Cir. 1945), certiorari denied, 326 U.S. 734 (1945); Rowe, *Price Discrimination under the Robinson-Patman Act*, pp. 151–53.

[24] Minneapolis-Honeywell Regulator Co. v. Federal Trade Commission, 191 F.2d 786 (7th Cir. 1951), certiorari dismissed, 344 U.S. 206 (1952); Anheuser-Busch, Inc. v. Federal Trade Commission; Dean Milk Co., CCH Trade Reg. Rep., par. 17,357 (FTC 1965), reversed in part, 395 F.2d 696 (7th Cir. 1968).

ings of "predatory" pricing.[25] The leading analytical treatise on the act indicates, however, that pricing which is not predatory may violate the act where: (1) the discriminating seller has an overpowering position in wider markets than those in which he cuts prices; or (2) there is proof of aggressive objectives aimed at smaller rivals, or there has been deep, sustained undercutting of a rival's prices or elimination of an established price spread between a "premium" and a lesser product; or (3) there have been persistent sales below the seller's "cost"; or (4) there is actual or impending demise of the seller's sole rival in a particular market because of the price cutting.[26]

Another type of predatory pricing that has been recognized is "disciplinary" pricing, where selective price cuts by a large seller are designed to punish a smaller competitor who deviates from general industry price levels.[27]

In the most recent Supreme Court decision involving seller-level injury under the Robinson-Patman Act, the Court held that three national sellers of frozen fruit pies violated the act by "predatory" pricing of their pies at below "cost" after entering a local market that was dominated by a local bakery, which continued to have the largest market share and to make a small profit.[28] The Court did not define what it meant by "cost"—whether below variable costs, marginal costs, fully distributed costs, et cetera. Moreover, in its dicta the Court indicated that predatory or below-cost pricing is not essential to a violation of the act:

> We believe that the Act reaches price discrimination that erodes competition as much as it does price discrimination that is intended to have immediate destructive impact. In this case, the evidence shows a drastically declining price structure which the jury could rationally attribute to continued or sporadic price discrimination.[29]

There are also several court decisions which create further uncertainty about whether price discrimination that is not below cost can be held to violate the Robinson-Patman Act. These decisions turn on the issue of "causation"—that is, whether competitive injury can be considered as the "effect" of price discrimination in the absence of proof that the lower prices are being "subsidized" by higher prices in other markets or to other customers. In *Shore Gas & Oil, Inc.* v.

---

[25] See the cases collected in Oppenheim and Weston, eds., *The Lawyer's Robinson-Patman Act Sourcebook*, vol. 1, pp. 403–638.

[26] Rowe, *Price Discrimination under the Robinson-Patman Act*, pp. 161–62.

[27] Lloyd A. Fry Roofing Co. v. Federal Trade Commission, p. 285.

[28] Utah Pie Co. v. Continental Baking Co., 386 U.S. 685 (1967).

[29] Ibid.

Humble Oil & Refining Co., for example, the court held that lower prices on gasoline to a taxicab company could not "cause" competitive injury to rival sellers of gasoline because the low prices were "self-sufficient" (not below cost) and were not supported by higher prices to others.[30] On the other hand, in *Lloyd Fry Roofing Co.* v. *Federal Trade Commission*, the court rejected any requirement of proof of "subsidization" of the lower prices; the court distinguished the *Shore Gas & Oil, Inc.*, and the *Balian Ice Cream Co.* cases as being, not FTC cases, but *private suits* in which plaintiffs must prove actual damages to themselves.[31] In a later decision, however, the same circuit court criticized an FTC finding of injury to competition because the commission failed to show that higher prices in other markets "supported" the lower prices in the market where competition was claimed to be injured.[32]

Section 3 of the Robinson-Patman Act is a criminal prohibition against: (1) knowingly being a party to a discriminatory transaction, (2) geographical price discrimination for the purpose of destroying competition or eliminating a competitor, and (3) selling "at unreasonably low prices" for the purpose of destroying competition or eliminating a competitor. It has rarely been used by the Department of Justice because of doubts about whether it adds significantly to the substantive reach of the Sherman Act and also because of its substantial ambiguity as a criminal statute. In *United States* v. *National Dairy Products Corp.*, the Supreme Court held that the prohibition against selling at "unreasonably low prices" was not unconstitutionally vague as applied to an indictment alleging sales "below cost."[33] The Court did not, however, indicate what the criterion of "cost" is. Upon remand, the court of appeals held that the jury could find that sales below "fully distributed costs" are "unreasonably low," even though the defendant had not sold below "direct costs" of production.[34] A specific intent is clearly required. No private right of action for damages can be based upon section 3, and complaining parties are seldom able to persuade the Department of Justice to use it.

The above cases illustrate that the standards of the Robinson-Patman Act for determining when price discrimination is unlawful because of possible injury to competing sellers are distressingly un-

---

[30] Shore Gas & Oil, Inc. v. Humble Oil & Refining Co., 224 F. Supp. 922 (D. N.J. 1963). See also Balian Ice Cream Co. v. Arden Farms Co., 231 F.2d 356 (9th Cir. 1955), certiorari denied, 350 U.S. 991 (1955).
[31] Lloyd Fry Roofing Co. v. Federal Trade Commission.
[32] Dean Milk Co. v. Federal Trade Commission, 395 F.2d 696 (7th Cir. 1968).
[33] United States v. National Dairy Products Corp. 372 U.S. 29 (1963).
[34] National Dairy Products Corp. v. United States, 350 F.2d 321 (8th Cir. 1965), vacated on other grounds, 384 U.S. 883 (1966).

clear, despite detailed prohibitions that have been subjected to almost three decades of judicial and administrative interpretation. As the two presidential task force reports cited above indicate, there are many economists who believe that, because of this ambiguity, price competition has been discouraged rather than improved. This experience would suggest that great caution should be exercised before borrowing the language or the concepts of the Robinson-Patman Act for other legislation. Moreover, the Sherman Act decisions reaching predatory pricing do not provide clear-cut guidelines; they provide only general formulations such as "predatory pricing," "selling below cost," or "ruinous price competition." The Sherman Act does, however, provide substantial flexibility which is lacking in the Robinson-Patman Act precedent. The general prohibition of the Sherman Act permits full consideration of the particular circumstances to identify the purpose and the effect of the conduct involved.

Is There a Need for the Creedy Amendment?

The railroad and water carrier transportation interface would appear to present a borderline case as to whether there is a need for specific prohibitions against predatory pricing practices. Some of the conditions which most economists seem to regard as permitting predatory price cutting appear to be present. Railroads do, in general, have substantially greater resources and greater staying power than water carriers. Barriers to entry into the water carrier industry exist both in the form of substantial capital and equipment requirements and in the form of government certificate requirements. These barriers, however, are not clearly so great as to assure railroads that they would gain long-lasting monopoly pricing benefits from sustained predatory rate cutting on routes that are competitive with water carriers. The generally higher operating costs of railroads and the ultimate power of the Interstate Commerce Commission to stop such price cutting would seem to be substantial limitations on the ability of railroads to recoup their short-term losses from predatory pricing. Moreover, the explicit provision in section 4(2) of the Interstate Commerce Act, which prevents a railroad that has lowered rates in competing with water carriers from raising them without showing changed conditions other than elimination of water carriers, stands as a warning that recoupment of losses may be difficult.

The "price squeeze" tactic of charging higher rates on the rail segment of a combined rail-water route for the purpose of limiting competition with all-rail traffic would appear to be a practice more

likely to occur. Unlike predatory price cutting, there would sometimes be a short-term gain, instead of a loss, from an attempt to use
this device to eliminate water carrier competition. The principal deterrent would be the likelihood that the ICC would ultimately invali-
date the higher rate. However, if the rail segment is substantially
profitable in itself, or if the total volume of traffic exceeds the capacity that could be handled by the all-rail route alone, or if motor carrier competition is a feasible alternative for a significant amount of
the rail segment traffic, the incentive to use such a tactic would be
minimized or nonexistent.

Even assuming that there should be a significant ultimate need
for specific prohibitions to prevent these forms of predatory pricing
by railroads if railroad rates are eventually deregulated, there is serious
question about whether they are needed in the initial experiments at
deregulation. Since the initial experiment provides for only a 7 percent
upward or downward flexibility for the first year, there is little leeway
for serious predatory pricing. Moreover, there is a strong likelihood
that the result of the Creedy proposal in such an experimental period
would be to destroy the experiment by limiting changes to increases
and deterring decreases on any routes that are subject to significant
intermodal competition. The experience of the Robinson-Patman Act
would seem to indicate the likelihood that detailed prohibition may
inhibit price competition. Professor Corwin D. Edwards, formerly
chief economist of the FTC, has indicated that the Robinson-Patman
Act has tended to create price inflexibility because of risk of liability:

> Excessive scope in the law has tended to reduce the vigor
> of competition. Even where there is no predatory purpose
> and no problem of the large enterprise, sellers and buyers
> tend to play safe as a precautionary measure. . . . Price
> structures that have proved to be legally safe tend to be
> continued because change would involve new risk.[35]

Analysis of Problems in the Creedy Amendment

Assuming that an amendment is deemed desirable to protect water
carriers against predatory pricing by railroads, there are nevertheless
a number of ambiguities and problems in the proposed Creedy
Amendment, as introduced by Congressman Eckhardt. Some of the
more significant of these problems will be analyzed below and an
alternative version or draft will then be proposed.

---

[35] Corwin D. Edwards, *The Price Discrimination Law* (Dobbs Ferry, N.Y.:
Oceana Publications, 1959), p. 630.

Subsection (B). As quoted above, subsection (B) provides that there will be no discrimination that injures intermodal competition.

Unnecessary scope in applying to other carriers. This provision is made applicable to all carriers; it is not limited to railroads and water carriers. However, there appears to be no reason to believe that the conditions for predatory pricing exist for motor carriers or water carriers. Motor carriers and water carriers do not, in general, have such superior resources vis-à-vis other intermodal carriers as to make sustained predatory pricing likely. Also, there would appear to be little incentive for railroads or water carriers to engage in predatory pricing to drive out motor carriers, because barriers to new entry are relatively low for motor carriers and the cost advantages for motor carriers would make the costs of such predatory pricing excessive. It is therefore recommended that the scope of the proposed amendment be limited to the problem complained about—namely, the use of predatory pricing by railroads against water carriers.

The indefiniteness of comparable routes and the concept of "discrimination." Subsection (B) contains a serious ambiguity in not indicating clearly what routes may be compared. This would permit water carriers to search for the highest rate routes of a railroad for comparison rather than a truly comparable route. Similarly, there is no definition of "discrimination" and, particularly, no required relationship to costs. Thus, as in the case of the Robinson-Patman Act, the concept of "discrimination" that is used appears to be the legalistic concept of "price differences" rather than the economist's concept of "discrimination" by charging rates that are higher in relation to costs. Thus, a railroad could be found to have "discriminated" by comparing rates on routes having widely different costs. This would compel economic discrimination. Unlike the Robinson-Patman Act, this section has no provision for a carrier to defend its rates based on a justification of the costs.

It is therefore recommended that the provision be rewritten along the lines suggested by Professors Areeda and Turner as a prohibition against selling below reasonably anticipated average variable costs, rather than as a discrimination prohibition.

The "meeting competition" defense. The defense of rates based on "meeting competition" contains several ambiguities similar to some of those not yet fully resolved under the Robinson-Patman Act. It is not clear, for example, whether a carrier may exactly match the rate of a competing carrier of another mode even though there may be differences in the desirability to shippers. Or, must some type of differential be maintained to compensate for the qualitative differences in the services of the competing modes? Can a carrier cut its rate below variable costs for the purpose of meeting competition? Suppose the competitor's rate is below variable costs—would that be a "lawful" rate?

Subsection (C). As quoted above, subsection (C) provides that there will be no "price squeeze" on rail-water routes.

The "potential" rail and water route problem. The inclusion in this prohibition of the prevention of a mere "potential" rail-water route may create problems in view of the fact that a purpose to prevent such competition is not required where there is an "effect" shown. This makes it possible for damages to accrue where a "potential" rail-water route is possible, even though it may not have been actually perceived or proposed. It would seem preferable either to omit the reference to potential routes entirely or, at the least, to require the complaining carrier to seek first the establishment of the potential rail-water route through notice to the other carrier or through a petition to the Interstate Commerce Commission.

The "similar traffic" ambiguity. The reference to "the same or similar traffic" creates considerable ambiguity. Freight rates on different commodities are extremely complex and it is uncertain whether this subsection would be applicable even where a different rate is generally established for a different but "similar" commodity. Since section 2 of the Interstate Commerce Act prohibits discrimination among commodities and uses the words "a like kind of traffic," it would seem preferable to use the same language in this amendment so as to lessen the ambiguity involved in using new and undefined words. A better approach, however, would limit this subsection to a prohibition against rates that are "unreasonably high" for the purpose of destroying or preventing competition.

Inflexibility of prohibition. The prohibition of a "higher" rate is inflexible, except to the extent that it refers to differences in cost or requires showing of a competitive effect. It would be improved by adding a further note of flexibility by limiting it to charging "unreasonably high rates."

Subsection (D). Subsection (D) permits any carrier "injured in its business or property" to sue for actual damages, costs of suit, and attorney's fee. The most serious problem with this is that there is no requirement for submission of any complaint to either the offending carrier or the ICC before damages begin to accrue. Thus, a water carrier could sit back and allow damages to accrue, based merely upon "effect" rather than actual intent and based merely upon prevention of a "potential" rail-water route. The water carrier could then complain to the ICC just in time to prevent the running of the four-year statute of limitations. I would recommend an amendment requiring complaint to the ICC before damages begin to accrue.

There is no indication of how damages are to be measured. However, since there is some authority under the Robinson-Patman Act for allowing recovery of either the lost anticipated profits or the "going-concern value" of a concern driven out of business, the damages could be substantial. Therefore, the requirement of some type of warning to give the offending carrier an opportunity to correct the practice and minimize damages seems a desirable means of achieving compliance and avoiding unnecessary litigation.

The Complexity of Superimposing a New Regulation of Discrimination upon the Preexisting Disparate Prohibitions. The Interstate Commerce Act already contains several distinct provisions prohibiting four types of discrimination: (1) personal discrimination, (2) discrimination among commodities, (3) discrimination among localities, and (4) discrimination among long hauls and short hauls.[36] "Personal discrimination" refers to discrimination among shippers of like commodities between the same points. It is covered by the prohibition in section 2 of the act against "unjust discrimination" by charging "a greater or less compensation" to one shipper than to another for "a like kind of traffic." Discrimination among commodities and localities is covered by the prohibition in section 3 of the act against "any undue or unreasonable preference or advantage" to any shipper, locality, region, district, or "any particular description of traffic, in any respect whatsoever." Section 4 of the act is the so-called long-and-short haul clause which prohibits charging more for a short haul than for a long haul over the same line, or charging more for a through route than the aggregate of the intermediate rates.

The superimposing of a fifth distinct prohibition against rate discrimination on top of these already complex prohibitions would seem likely to raise possibilities of conflicts that are difficult to anticipate fully without a detailed examination of the possible conflicts by a thoroughly experienced expert in rate regulation. At a minimum,

---

[36] See Kenneth W. Dam, "The Economics and Law of Price Discrimination: Herein of Three Regulatory Schemes," *University of Chicago Law Review*, vol. 31 (1963), pp. 14–18, for discussion and comparison with the Robinson-Patman Act.

however, it would suggest caution in adopting an additional complex regulation of discrimination. The objective of an experiment in deregulation could be substantially undermined by substituting a new and uncertain form of partial regulation.

Alternative Draft of Amendment

My primary recommendation is that the initial experiment in rate deregulation be tried without risking its partial nullification by substituting the new form of rate regulation represented by the Creedy Amendment. Nevertheless, I have prepared an alternative version or draft to ameliorate some of the problems referred to above. It might provide a compromise position that would not likely result in destroying the flexibility of rate determination.

Proposed Draft. The proposed alternative draft of the amendment reads as follows:

> (B) No railroad shall maintain rates or charges which are below reasonably anticipated variable costs, as determined by the commission, for the purpose or with the effect of substantially lessening competition between the railroad and water carriers.
> (C) No railroad, acting alone or in concert with another carrier, shall maintain rates or charges that are unreasonably high, in relation to reasonably anticipated variable costs, for the rail segment of an actual or potential rail and water route over which it carries shipments, for the purpose of destroying or preventing competition with water carriers.
> (D) Any carrier which shall be injured in its business or property by reason of engagement by a carrier in any predatory practice or monopolizing which is forbidden by the foregoing provisions of this subparagraph (g) may sue therefor in any district court of the United States in the district in which the defendant resides or is found or has an agent and shall recover the damages by it sustained, and the cost of suit, including a reasonable attorney's fee.
> (E) Before any damage action under subparagraph (D) may be filed in a federal district court, the complaining carrier must first file a petition with the commission complaining about the lawfulness of the rates concerned. No damages shall begin to accrue until the filing of such a petition. The determination of the commission shall be conclusive, subject to judicial review, as to the issue of the lawfulness

of such rates in any subsequent damage suit under this subsection.

Explanation of Changes in New Draft. The following comments explain the reasons for some of the changes from the Creedy Amendment to the proposed alternative draft.

Subsection (B).

1. Change from "no carrier" to "no railroad": The purpose of this change is to limit the scope of the new type of regulation to the carriers where predatory pricing may be a realistic problem and where complaints have been made. It is based upon the principle that the least regulation necessary is the best rather than on a desire for reciprocal rights of action for the sake of symmetry.

2. Change from a "discrimination" prohibition to a "below reasonably anticipated variable costs" prohibition: The purposes of this change are to avoid problems of comparing rates on routes that are not really comparable, to avoid a legalistic "price difference" approach rather than an "economic discrimination" concept, to avoid ambiguities and litigation over whether there is "causation" without proof of "subsidization" of lower prices, and to provide greater flexibility of pricing both downward and upward than a "discrimination" concept would permit.

3. The use of "reasonably anticipated variable costs": "Variable costs" is a concept that is already used in the industry, and the data is therefore readily ascertainable. This does not constitute a flat prohibition against pricing below variable costs. The prohibition exists only where the purpose or effect is to injure competition with water carriers. It is also further qualified by the requirement in subsection (E) that damages shall not begin to accrue until a complaint is filed with the ICC.

4. Change from lessening intermodal competition generally to "between the railroad and a water carrier": Here again the purpose is to limit this new type of rate regulation to the situations of necessity where predatory pricing is likely—railroads with superior resources injuring water carriers where barriers to entry are great enough to make some incentives for predatory pricing.

Subsection (C).

1. Change from "no carrier" to "no railroad": As in subsection (B), the purpose is to limit the regulation to the area of necessity—railroads injuring water carriers.

2. Change from "maintain a higher rate" to maintain rates that are "unreasonably high in relation to reasonably anticipated variable

costs": The purpose here is to provide greater flexibility by use of the "unreasonable" standard rather than merely any "higher" rate. The "variable costs" criterion is again invoked to provide greater clarity by use of known or readily ascertainable data.

Subsection (E).

1. The requirement of complaint to the Interstate Commerce Commission: The purpose here is to provide a warning to the railroad that its rate changes may subject it to a damage claim by a water carrier, particularly for a mere "potential" combined rail-water route. This will give the railroad an opportunity to comply with the statute and avoid expensive litigation. It should effectively prevent any long-term predatory pricing by railroads without running as much risk of discouraging the short-run flexibility of competitive pricing.

Conclusion

Predatory pricing is probably not a very common practice, but it may exist where one concern has substantially greater resources than its competitors and where there are substantial barriers to entry. Sustained systematic price discrimination is the principal form of predatory pricing. On the other hand, sporadic or unsystematic price discrimination is frequently a beneficial form of price competition which exerts useful downward pressures upon price levels. In unregulated industries, section 2 of the Sherman Act provides a useful but flexible means of regulating predatory pricing by the largest firms. The Robinson-Patman Act, however, is an exceptionally detailed prohibition of price discrimination which is quite inflexible in reaching not merely predatory pricing but even those types of price discrimination which most economists consider beneficial. The purpose is not purely economic but also protectionist for small business concerns on the buyer level, sometimes at the sacrifice of price competition at the seller level.

In the regulated surface transportation industry, railroads may sometimes have the resources to engage in predatory pricing in competition with water carriers. The antitrust laws are inapplicable, but the Interstate Commerce Act regulates such practices. Water carriers are concerned, however, with the significant time lag before the ICC can act under the provisions of the proposed rail reform legislation. This legislation precludes the ICC from suspending rate increases or decreases of 7 percent for the first year, 12 percent for the second year, and 15 percent for the third year. The water carriers' proposed amendment would adopt regulation similar to the Robinson-Patman

Act, with a private right of action for damages by a carrier injured by rate discrimination. It is debatable whether such regulation is needed. For the first year or two, the amount of pricing flexibility is quite limited, and the ICC has power ultimately to regulate any predatory pricing. There are substantial arguments against inclusion of the Creedy Amendment in the experimental period. It is likely that the Creedy Amendment will discourage some rate decreases and will tend to give the deregulation experiment an inflationary bias, thereby jeopardizing its success.

The Creedy Amendment is somewhat less of a deterrent to price flexibility than the Robinson-Patman Act. This is because the amendment provides for single damages only; it is concerned solely with seller-level injury; and it requires either intent or actual effect on competition rather than merely a "reasonable possibility" of injury. However, the amendment presents some inflexibilities and uncertainties that the alternative draft endeavors to ameliorate. Although I recommend against any amendment of this nature, the alternative draft presents a compromise that should not be too detrimental to the experiment.

10

RAIL ABANDONMENTS AND THEIR IMPACTS

U.S. Department of Transportation

Extent of Uneconomic Light-Density Lines Outside the Northeast

The issue of abandonment and service termination of light-density railroad lines can be viewed from a number of perspectives. A most important perspective is one of scale; that is, how important is this matter nationally as well as from the regional and state viewpoints? This section reviews the question of the scale of abandonments of light-density lines in light of recent experience and indicates changes which are likely to result from the recent rail legislation. The most significant findings presented in this section are estimates of mileage, carloads, and tonnage of various commodities that originate and terminate on uneconomic, light-density lines outside of the northeastern region of the United States.

Recent and Pending Abandonments Nationwide. When a railroad wishes to cease providing service on a particular line, it must petition the Interstate Commerce Commission for permission to abandon that line. This must be done not only when an existing service is to be terminated, but also when the service is to be taken over by another railroad or when the service has already been suspended as a result of storm damage or because there are no longer any users on the line.

In recent years, the ICC has annually approved the abandonment of 1,000 to 2,000 railroad route miles. Table 10-1 shows the number of abandonment petitions and the corresponding route mileage annually approved for abandonment since 1970. The peak year by both

This chapter is edited from *Railroad Abandonments and Alternatives: A Report on Effects Outside the Northeastern Region*, report of the secretary of transportation to the United States Congress pursuant to section 904 of the Railroad Revitalization and Regulatory Reform Act of 1976, May 1976.

measures was 1972, with 3,279 miles approved for abandonment in 231 separate cases. The subsequent decline in approvals, to 634 miles in 1974, was caused in part by the *Harlem Valley* decision, which required at the outset of all abandonment proceedings an assessment of the impact of the abandonment on the environment,[1] and by the Regional Rail Reorganization Act of 1973 (RRR Act), which transferred jurisdiction over the seven northeastern railroads undergoing reorganization to the United States Railway Association (USRA).[2] The table also shows the Association of American Railroad's data for year-end route miles of roadway for all line-haul railroads (switching and terminal companies are excluded).

Data for abandonments approved by the ICC since 1970 are summarized by state in Table 10-2. Also shown are the number of cases currently pending and the mileage that would be affected by such abandonments (excluding potential abandonments of lines of railroads in reorganization under USRA's Final System Plan). Nationally, there are 216 such abandonment petitions totaling 6,050 route miles pending before the ICC. This is in addition to the 5,757 miles of active roadway omitted from the Final System Plan.

Experience with Light-Density Lines in the Northeast. Information developed as the result of the reorganization of bankrupt railroads in the Northeast is utilized throughout this study as a basis for the analysis of the problems related to light-density lines outside the Northeast. This section reviews key elements in the Northeast situa-

---

[1] Harlem Valley v. Stafford, 5 ERC 1503 (S.D. N.Y., July 6, 1973). This decision resulted in a delay in approving abandonment applications while the ICC developed the capability for preparing the required environmental impact statements. This U.S. district court decision was upheld by the U.S. Court of Appeals for the Second Circuit, but was subsequently modified by the U.S. Supreme Court in another case in which it was ruled that an environmental impact statement does not have to be prepared until the commission makes a recommendation or report concerning the application for abandonment. The commission's capability for preparing the required statements has now been established, but the preparation of these statements has increased the time required for processing abandonment applications. See Interstate Commerce Commission, *Annual Report*, 1974, pp. 23–24, 80–81, and 1975, pp. 17, 71–72.

[2] The Regional Rail Reorganization Act of 1973 established the USRA to carry out the special reorganization of the bankrupt railroads of the Northeast. One of the responsibilities of the USRA was to analyze the lines of the region's railroads to determine which lines were not profitable and should come under the subsidy provisions of Title IV of the act or be abandoned. The initial output of the USRA was the Preliminary System Plan which was reviewed, critiqued, and refined to produce the Final System Plan. The Final System Plan listed branch lines which were determined to be excess. Such lines could be purchased by other regional carriers; purchased by private industry to maintain railroad service; subsidized by local, state, and federal agencies to maintain service; or abandoned.

Table 10-1

ABANDONMENTS APPROVED BY THE INTERSTATE
COMMERCE COMMISSION, 1970–1976

Year	Number of Cases	Miles Granted	Mileage in Railroad System (year end)[a]
1970	113	1,718	206,265
1971	180	1,938	205,220
1972	231	3,288	203,299
1973	103	1,221	201,585
1974	51	634	200,000 (est.)
1975	73	1,668	. . .
1976 (through March 11)	10	113	. . .
Cumulative since 1970:	761	10,580	

[a] The decline in mileage reflects the lag between the date of approval and the date of abandonment. The total decline in mileage is also somewhat less than that approved for abandonment because some new lines have been built to serve recently developed industrial facilities and deposits of natural resources, and because some lines approved for abandonment have been taken over by other railroads (sometimes by a shortline railroad company which has been established for this purpose).

Sources: Data for number of cases and miles granted are from unpublished information supplied by Interstate Commerce Commission, Section of Case Control and Information. Data for mileage in railway system are from Association of American Railroads, *Yearbook of Railroad Facts* (Washington, 1975). Data are for route miles of roadway and exclude yards and sidings. Jointly used track is counted only once.

tion, that is, traffic and mileage distribution throughout the rail network and the route miles and annual carloads subject to abandonment.

Typically, major portions of traffic tend to be concentrated on relatively small segments of transportation systems. Such patterns can be found in highway and airport systems as well as railroad systems. In 1955, an historical analysis of the traffic density of the railroad system in the United States indicated that 10 percent of the mileage carried 50 percent of the traffic (measured in net ton-miles), while 30 percent of the mileage carried only 2 percent of the total net ton-miles.[3]

Analyses made during the past five years indicate that such skewed traffic distributions continue, and that they are probably even more pronounced today than they were in 1955. The following statements summarize the findings of four of those studies:

[3] John W. Barriger, *Super-Railroads for a Dynamic American Economy* (New York: Simmons-Boardman Publishing Corp., 1955), p. 7.

Table 10-2

RECENT AND PENDING ABANDONMENTS BY STATE

State	Approved by ICC since 1970[a] Cases	Miles	Currently Pending Before ICC[a] Cases	Miles	Miles in Railroad System[b]
Alabama	6	136	3	72	4,541
Alaska	0	0	0	0	538
Arizona	5	79	3	72	2,034
Arkansas	2	24	0	0	3,559
California	37	178	5	72	7,335
Colorado	9	110	4	50	3,499
Connecticut	6	39	0	0	656
Delaware	1	5	1	9	291
District of Columbia	0	0	0	0	30
Florida	11	142	3	69	4,143
Georgia	8	60	3	76	5,414
Hawaii	0	0	0	0	0
Idaho	4	82	5	59	2,659
Illinois	29	349	20	574	10,607
Indiana	27	265	2	16	6,419
Iowa	33	700	21	478	7,644
Kansas	10	254	6	158	7,621
Kentucky	7	55	2	34	3,518
Louisiana	7	133	5	103	3,752
Maine	2	24	3	40	1,667
Maryland	10	38	3	51	1,099
Massachusetts	9	42	0	0	1,405
Michigan	41	564	16	498	6,032
Minnesota	24	619	14	280	7,382
Mississippi	4	129	3	223	3,645
Missouri	16	470	6	96	6,082
Montana	6	142	2	69	4,900
Nebraska	10	337	7	306	5,334
Nevada	1	61	0	0	1,573
New Hampshire	6	94	3	140	751
New Jersey	25	212	0	0	1,708
New Mexico	3	58	1	14	2,087
New York	36	537	2	75	5,325
North Carolina	6	212	2	33	4,115
North Dakota	4	145	3	28	5,079
Ohio	36	385	5	184	7,746
Oklahoma	11	521	4	217	4,946
Oregon	7	71	2	22	3,041

Table 10-2 (Continued)

RECENT AND PENDING ABANDONMENTS BY STATE

State	Approved by ICC since 1970[a]		Currently Pending Before ICC[a]		Miles in Railroad System[b]
	Cases	Miles	Cases	Miles	
Pennsylvania	164	858	9	245	8,064
Rhode Island	2	51	0	0	139
South Carolina	9	165	3	57	3,016
South Dakota	13	461	5	322	3,363
Tennessee	7	121	6	131	3,207
Texas	19	530	12	558	13,320
Utah	7	44	1	4	1,734
Vermont	9	109	2	77	765
Virginia	2	109	1	9	3,873
Washington	20	269	5	47	4,807
West Virginia	24	109	7	130	3,508
Wisconsin	21	319	6	350	5,832
Wyoming	5	86	0	0	1,780
Totals	761	10,497	216	6,050	201,585

[a] As of March 11, 1976; excludes potential abandonments resulting from USRA's Final System Plan.

[b] As of December 31, 1973.

Source: See Table 10-1.

- The Federal Railroad Administration estimated in 1971 that approximately $57 million could be saved by terminating service on 21,000 miles of light-density lines. This mileage, approximately 10 percent of the national network, generated only one-half of one percent of all carloads moved by rail.[4]
- The trustees of the Penn Central asserted in February 1972 that about 80 percent of the Penn Central's freight revenues were attributable to approximately 11,000 miles of its 20,000-mile network.[5]
- The report of the secretary of transportation entitled *Rail Service in the Midwest and Northeast Region* in February 1974 found

---

[4] Task Force on Railroad Productivity, *Improving Railroad Productivity*, report to the National Commission on Productivity and the Council of Economic Advisers, November 1973, pp. 160–61.

[5] Report of the Penn Central Trustees on Reorganization Planning, February 15, 1972. As cited in U.S. Congress, Senate, Committee on Commerce, *The Penn Central and Other Railroads*, 92d Congress, 2d session, December 1972, pp. 78–80 and Appendix D, Exhibit 54, p. 623.

that 15,757 of the total 61,184 miles of railroad line in the region's railroad network accounted for only 4 percent of the total traffic originated and terminated in the region during 1972.[6]
- The USRA analyzed approximately 25,000 miles of railroad line operated by the railroads under reorganization in the Northeast. Of this total, 5,757 miles of active roadway (23 percent) were recommended for abandonment or subsidy. These lines generated only 2.2 percent of the traffic originated or terminated in the region in 1973.[7]

Although the uneven distribution of traffic on the nation's railroads no doubt accounts for many of the problems associated with light-density rail lines, many other factors have also contributed to the poor financial health of the railroad industry and bankruptcy of certain carriers. Among the factors most often cited by various authors are:[8]

- labor productivity losses because of inefficient work rules;
- noncompensatory rates;
- regulated rates and restricted price flexibility;
- unprofitable passenger operations;
- redundant and inefficient main-line and terminal rail operations;
- noncompensatory rate divisions;
- discriminatory state taxation; and
- public subsidy of competing modes.

Certain of these problem areas have been addressed by recent rail legislation. AMTRAK (the National Railroad Passenger Corporation) has taken over intercity railroad passenger service. The Railroad Revitalization and Regulatory Reform Act of 1976 (4R Act) provides for greater rate flexibility, increased consolidation efforts to eliminate redundant facilities, and the gradual elimination of discriminatory state taxation of railroad property. Both the RRR Act and the 4R Act provide for the public subsidization or abandonment of unprofitable

[6] Secretary of Transportation, *Rail Service in the Midwest and Northeast Region*, U.S. Department of Transportation, February 1, 1974, pp. 2 and 69–74.
[7] United States Railway Association, *Final System Plan for Restructuring Railroads in the Northeast and Midwest Region Pursuant to the Regional Rail Reorganization Act of 1973*, July 26, 1975, vol. 2, pp. 2–3.
[8] See Thomas G. Moore, *Freight Transportation Regulation* (Washington, D.C.: American Enterprise Institute, 1972); U.S. Congress, Senate Committee on Commerce, *The Penn Central and Other Railroads*; Task Force on Railroad Productivity, *Improving Railroad Productivity*; Secretary of Transportation, *Rail Service in the Midwest and Northeast Region*; USRA, *Preliminary System Plan for Restructuring Railroads in the Northeast and Midwest Region Pursuant to the Regional Rail Reorganization Act of 1973*, February 26, 1975; and USRA, *Final System Plan*.

light-density lines, thus freeing the private carriers from the financial burden of cross-subsidization.

In addition to the operating deficit incurred by and attributable to the unprofitable light-density lines, it should also be remembered that there is substantial capital invested in these lines which is not available for reinvestment on profitable segments of the system. The capital requirement for the main-line system and the profitable branch lines has been recognized by the Congress in Title V of the 4R Act. The immense capital investment required to rehabilitate many unprofitable light-density lines to minimum safety standards may not be financially justifiable.

Potentially Uneconomic Light-Density Lines outside the Northeast. The data presented earlier showed that there are 216 petitions now before the ICC involving requests to abandon 6,050 miles of railroad line, approximately 70 percent of which is outside of the Northeast. Those figures do not, however, provide a complete picture of the potentially uneconomic light-density lines outside of the Northeast.

Railroad companies have generally filed abandonment petitions only when they felt that there was a good chance of receiving approval for abandonment by the ICC. This has usually been when the railroad expected that the ICC would find that the financial benefits of abandonment to the railroad outweighed the costs to the public and the rail users. Thus, abandonment has usually been sought only for the most unprofitable of lines.

In planning for the Consolidated Rail Corporation (ConRail), USRA rejected the concept of cross-subsidization of uneconomic light-density lines by profitable traffic, and consequently omitted from the Final System Plan those lines which did not meet certain criteria of economic viability. Continued operation of these lines will depend upon federal and state subsidies as provided for in the RRR Act and the 4R Act or upon the implementation of some alternatives for the existing rail freight service.

In order to gain a preliminary understanding of the implications of light-density lines outside the Northeast, estimates of the number of miles of unprofitable rail lines are needed. Furthermore, estimates of the volume of freight, by region and commodity, moving over those lines are also needed. To develop such preliminary estimates within the short time allowed for this report, it was necessary to employ readily available data. It was not possible to undertake a detailed individual analysis of the economic viability of each railroad line in the country as had been performed by USRA on the several hundred lines in the Northeast. Therefore, special situations, such

155

as those related to the military and "high and wide" shipments, could not be addressed. In addition, it was not possible to wait until the railroads publicly identified all lines which are "potentially subject to abandonment," as they are required to do under section 802 of the 4R Act. Instead, a computerized analysis was conducted using data from the Federal Railroad Administration (FRA) describing the nation's railroad system and the freight shipments which it handles, together with selected information about the viability of light-density lines obtained from USRA's more detailed study of the Northeast.

This analysis has produced preliminary estimates of the total railroad mileage outside the Northeast that could be considered uneconomic if categorized by the criteria used by USRA in developing its Final System Plan. Estimates were also made of the carloads and tonnage of shipments which would be affected if service were discontinued on this mileage.

Analytical procedure. The computerized analysis was performed in two steps. First, the FRA preliminary network data base of the nation's railroad system was used to select a set of light-density line segments and to obtain the length of each segment.[9] The network data represent the complete national railroad system except for some simplifications involving complex urban-area network configurations.

The segments selected for analysis are those directly represented in the network data model, served by a single carrier, and identified as carrying 1 million gross tons or less per year.[10] Because of the unavailability of data on terminating traffic for railroads with average annual operating revenues of less than $3 million,[11] lines operated by such railroads were excluded from the analysis.

The second step of the procedure involved a test on the selected segments to determine their economic viability based on the volume of traffic originated and terminated on each segment and the impor-

---

[9] See *Federal Railroad Administration Network Model: General Information* (Gaithersburg, Md.: International Business Machines Corp., Federal Systems Division, November 1975); and W. W. Cantey and T. T. Bouve, "The Use of Analytical Models and Related Data in the State Rail Planning Process" (paper presented at the National Rail Planning Conference, U.S. Department of Transportation, Federal Railroad Administration, New Orleans, May 19–22, 1975).
[10] The year for which this density data was compiled by FRA varies from railroad to railroad.
[11] Prior to 1965 the ICC defined Class I railroads as those railroads with average annual operating revenues of $3 million or more. This revenue figure has since been raised to $5 million and effective in 1976 to $10 million. Waybill data, however, are collected from all railroads generating revenues of $3 million or more. Seventy-seven railroads were included in the analysis. The waybills from which the sample was drawn accounted for approximately 85 percent of all carloads shipped during 1972–1974.

tance of the segment to the connectivity of the main line. Traffic data were obtained from the 1972, the 1973, and the 1974 "carload waybill statistics." These data represent a systematic sample of audited revenue waybills for all domestic shipments terminated by railroads with annual operating revenues of $3 million or more. A three-year period was used to increase the size of the sample and thereby increase the statistical reliability of the viability test. The enlarged data base also serves to reduce the effect of the business cycle, the weather, and other temporary influences on traffic volume.

The economic viability criterion used was based upon prior work by USRA and modified for this effort. The criterion requires that each segment originate and/or terminate an average of seventy carloads per mile per year. This criterion was used to test individual line segments and, where appropriate, sets of contiguous segments. Data limitations, however, made it impractical to test portions of a segment. Thus, the procedure was limited to designating an entire segment as viable or nonviable even when its primary traffic generator was the middle of the segment and a more detailed study might have resulted in designating as nonviable only that part of the segment lying beyond such a midpoint traffic generator.

Results of the analysis. Carloads and miles of light-density lines which may be uneconomic have been tabulated for six regions outside the northeastern United States.[12] These six regions are shown in Figure 10-1.[13]

Table 10-3 shows the estimated miles of potentially uneconomic light-density railroad lines (PULD lines) by region. Table 10-4 depicts estimates of the carloads which are originated or terminated annually on those lines. As indicated, the West North Central Region has the greatest number of potentially uneconomic light-density lines, 28.4 percent of the region's total mileage, as well as the most carloads

---

[12] These are estimates of the potential inability of the light-density lines in their present configuration to be profitable. No recommendations are being made here to abandon any particular mileage. Each line must, of course, be understood within its own financial and operational context. Nevertheless, these estimates do provide overall statistical indications of the possible impacts of the light-density lines not meeting the traffic criteria used in this study.

Because all traffic estimates are derived from small-sample data, there is some imprecision in the estimates. All data for potentially uneconomic light-density lines have been aggregated into relatively broad groupings (regions instead of states) in order to avoid the use of estimates which go beyond this level of precision.

[13] These regions are basically Bureau of the Census regions which are used for, among other things, the Commodity Transportation Survey of the Census of Transportation. The West North Central Region and the South Atlantic Region have been slightly redefined for this report so as to encompass only those states outside the Northeast Region as it was defined in section 102 of the RRR Act.

Figure 10-1

REGIONS AND STATES INCLUDED IN THE ANALYSIS
OF LIGHT-DENSITY LINES

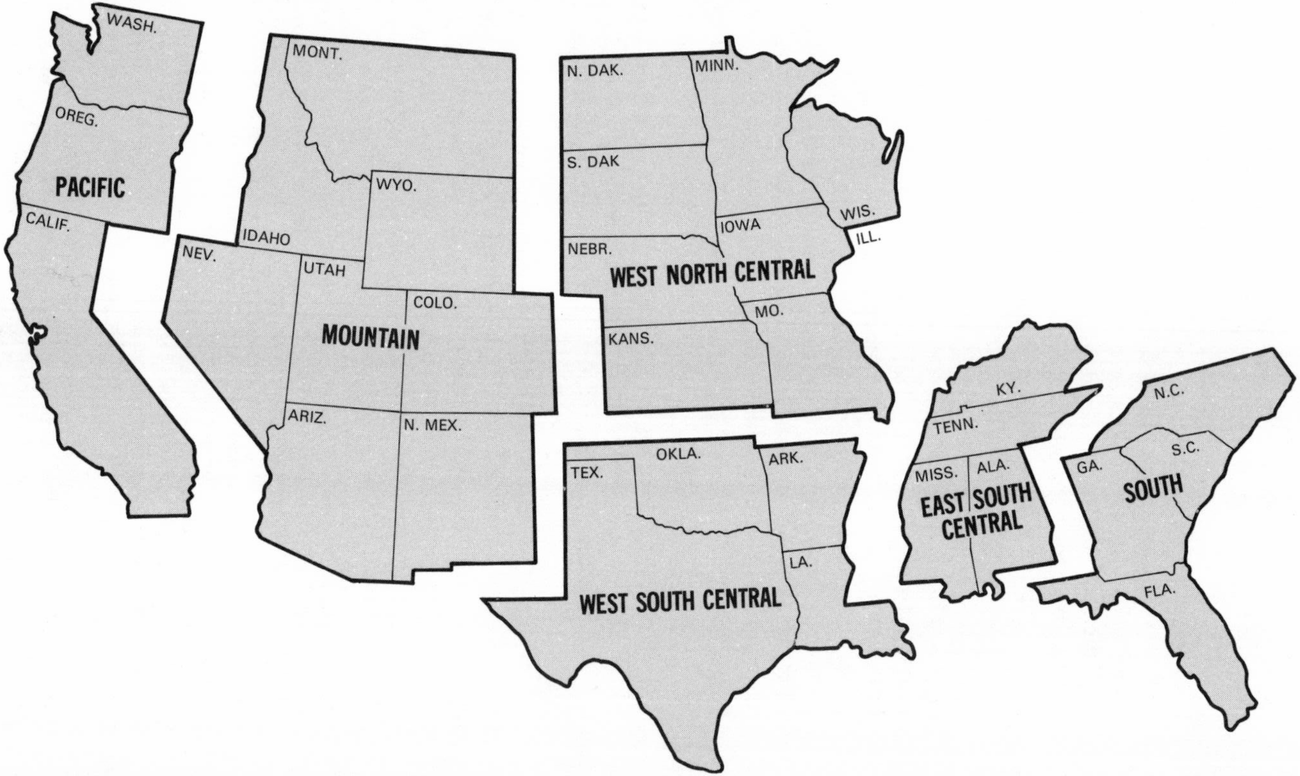

Table 10-3

MILES OF POTENTIALLY UNECONOMIC LIGHT-DENSITY LINES OUTSIDE THE NORTHEAST, 1974

Region	Existing Miles (1974)[a]	Potentially Uneconomic Light-Density Lines	
		Miles[b]	Percentage of existing miles
South Atlantic	16,688	1,100	6.6
East South Central	14,911	900	6.0
West South Central	25,577	3,600	14.1
West North Central	48,337	13,700	28.4
Mountain	20,266	3,600	17.8
Pacific	15,183	2,600	17.1
Total[c]	140,962	25,500	18.1

[a] Association for American Railroads, *Yearbook of Railroad Facts* (Washington, 1975).

[b] From computer analysis.

[c] Totals are for thirty-one states outside of the Northeast.

originating and terminating on these lines, 5.3 percent of all carloads in the region. The Mountain, Pacific, and West South Central regions show 17.8, 17.1, and 14.1 percent of their mileage designated as potentially uneconomic, with 3.1, 2.1, and 1.9 percent of their total carloads being affected. The South Atlantic and East South Central regions have relatively low levels of potentially uneconomic light-density lines, as only 6.6 and 6.0 percent of the line miles and 0.6 percent of the carloads in each region have been identified as such. In total, although 18.1 percent of the railroad mileage outside the Northeast is identified as potentially uneconomic, only 2.4 percent of all the originating and terminating carloads in the thirty-one states require the use of these particular lines. These percentage estimates are comparable to those in the northeastern region, where 23 percent of the bankrupt mileage generated 2.2 percent of the carloads and has been categorized as available for subsidy by USRA.

Because of the limitations of the computerized network analysis, the mileage and carloads identified as potentially uneconomic are somewhat overestimated. This overestimation occurs because the procedure used in the analysis was capable neither of considering the distance between lines nor of determining how close nearby lines were to their economic break-even point. Where such nearby lines are marginally unprofitable, the abandonment of one might result in

Table 10-4

SHIPMENTS ORIGINATING OR TERMINATING ON POTENTIALLY UNECONOMIC LIGHT-DENSITY LINES OUTSIDE THE NORTHEAST BY REGION

(thousands of carloads)

Region	Originating Carloads			Terminating Carloads			Overall Percent of Carloads Affected[c]
	Total[a]	On PULD lines[b]	Percent on PULD lines	Total[a]	On PULD lines[b]	Percent on PULD lines	
South Atlantic	2,188	21	1.0	2,724	10	0.4	0.6
East South Central	2,490	15	0.6	1,810	10	0.6	0.6
West South Central	2,045	49	2.4	2,344	35	1.5	1.9
West North Central	3,427	260	7.6	3,184	90	2.8	5.3
Mountain	1,296	55	4.2	1,045	17	1.6	3.1
Pacific	1,651	53	3.2	1,665	18	1.1	2.1
Total[d]	13,097	452	3.5	12,772	179	1.4	2.4

a Derived from Federal Railroad Administration carload waybill data for 1972–1974.

b Derived from computer analysis of PULD lines outside of Northeast.

c Carloads originating or terminating on PULD lines as a percentage of all originations and terminations in the thirty-one states.

d Totals are for thirty-one states outside of the Northeast. Detail may not add up to totals because of rounding.

the other's becoming profitable through shifts in traffic. The computerized analysis does not recognize this situation, however, and designates both lines as unprofitable. This situation exists for many lines in the Plains states and contributes significantly to the relatively large mileage and carloads designated as potentially uneconomic in the West North Central Region.

Table 10-5 shows the total carloads originated and terminated on potentially uneconomic light-density lines by commodity for the thirty-one states. The sector that would be most affected if service on light-density lines were discontinued is agriculture. Traffic in lumber and wood products would be moderately affected. Commodity groups which could be affected to lesser degrees are food and kindred products, chemicals and allied products, and petroleum and petrochemical products.

Primary Economic Effects

In the previous section, estimates were made of the potentially uneconomic light-density railroad mileage outside the Northeast and of the freight traffic that would be affected if service were discontinued on all such lines. In this section, estimates related to the effects on various segments of the economy are presented and discussed. These estimates are presented as indications of the nature and scale of the likely effects if no alternative actions are taken to maintain partial service on light-density lines or to provide alternative transportation service.

The Railroad Industry. If the railroad industry were relieved of the responsibility for operating approximately 25,500 miles of light-density lines outside the Northeast Region, or of the deficits resulting from such operation, the operating deficits for the industry would be reduced by approximately $150 million annually. This estimate is based on the assumption that the average deficit outside of the Northeast Region would be $240 per carload, the figure that was determined by the USRA for the bankrupt railroads of the region.[14] This deficit estimate is, of course, preliminary and subject to refinement as more information is developed on light-density lines outside the Northeast.

---

[14] An estimated 620,000 carloads of freight originate and/or terminate on these lines annually (including 11,000 carloads that both originate and terminate on these lines). Multiplying by $240 per carload yields an estimate of $148.8 million.

Table 10-5

SHIPMENTS ORIGINATING AND TERMINATING ON POTENTIALLY UNECONOMIC LIGHT-DENSITY LINES OUTSIDE THE NORTHEAST BY COMMODITY
(thousands of carloads)

STCC	Product Description	Originating Carloads			Terminating Carloads			Overall Percentage of Carloads Affected[c]
		31-state total[a]	On PULD lines[b]	Percentage on PULD lines	31-state total[a]	On PULD lines[b]	Percentage on PULD lines	
01	Farm products	1,389	249	17.9	1,278	17	1.3	10.0
11	Coal	752	6	0.8	560	6	1.1	0.9
14	Nonmetallic minerals	808	18	2.2	773	16	2.1	2.2
20	Food products	1,390	43	3.1	1,200	26	2.2	2.7
24–25	Lumber and wood products	1,691	78	4.6	1,491	18	1.2	3.0
26	Pulp and paper products	765	4	0.5	582	9	1.6	1.0
28	Chemicals	900	8	0.9	806	33	4.1	2.4
29–30	Petroleum and related products	550	7	1.3	527	12	2.3	1.8
32	Clay and concrete products	642	16	2.5	635	13	2.0	2.3
33–34	Metal products	364	4	1.1	541	12	2.2	1.8
35–37	Machinery and equipment	424	7	1.6	854	9	1.1	1.3
40	Waste and scrap	308	6	1.9	269	2	0.7	1.4
	All others	588	6	1.0	757	6	0.8	0.9
	Totals	10,571	452	4.3	10,273	179	1.7	3.0

a Derived from Federal Railroad Administration carload waybill data for 1972–1974.

b From computer analysis.

c Carloads originating or terminating on potentially uneconomic light-density lines as a percentage of all originations and terminations in the thirty-one states.

The significance of the $150 million of reduced deficit can be shown by a comparison of this figure to the average annual net income of Class I railroads for the southern and western ICC districts for a comparable period (1972–1974), which totaled approximately $820 million.[15] The annual saving resulting from termination of service on this mileage is equivalent to 18 percent of the net income for the railroads in these districts.

One of the chief problems faced by the railroad industry today is capital formation. Railroads are a capital-intensive form of transportation and have large amounts of capital committed to light-density operations which might be more effectively utilized in the profitable parts of the railroad system.

A conservative estimate of the value of the track facilities associated with light-density lines outside of the Northeast is $640 million. This is based on an average scrap value of $25,000 per mile for reusable rail and other track materials, less the cost of dismantling and removal.[16] This estimate does not include the value of grading, tunnels, or bridges, because they are not capital items that can be reinvested in other parts of the railroad system. It also does not include the resale value of abandoned rail rights-of-way, a value that is highly variable from one area to another.

The operation of unprofitable light-density lines also requires locomotive power and equipment resources which could better be utilized elsewhere on the railroad system. The 25,500 miles of light-density lines consist of approximately 1,000 line segments (average length of about 25 miles). Assuming service on two days a week requiring a full eight-hour day for each trip, approximately 832,000 annual train-hours are spent in servicing these lines. This requires the commitment of at least ninety-five locomotive units and caboose units to service these lines. Although there are several thousand freight cars utilized in serving the traffic originating and terminating on the light-density lines, only a relatively small number of freight cars will be freed for utilization on other parts of the railroad system, as much of the traffic will continue to move by rail.

The reduction in the rail network by 25,500 miles of light-density lines in the thirty-one states would have, in all likelihood, little effect on railroad employment, even though employment committed to the light-density lines is estimated at about 1,700 jobs with an

---

[15] Association of American Railroads, *Yearbook of Railroad Facts* (Washington, D.C., 1975).
[16] CONSAD Research Corporation, *Criteria for Line Retention*, report to the United States Railway Association, February 1975.

estimated annual payroll of $32 million. Because of the provisions protecting labor in most rail labor contracts, it is expected that most of these jobs would be reassigned to service on other parts of the rail system.

Agriculture. One of the more significant impacts related to any line abandonments involves the agricultural sector. Most light-density lines are located in rural areas, and agricultural products account for a major share of the traffic originating and terminating on uneconomic light-density lines outside of the Northeast. Although a large amount of agricultural supplies and products are moved by truck, certain products—particularly grain, fertilizer, and feed—are commonly transported by railroad. At issue is whether the cessation of service on some railroad lines in agricultural areas will force farmers, suppliers, and marketing cooperatives that are rail users to shift to alternative, perhaps higher cost, transport modes.

The agricultural traffic moving over uneconomic light-density lines has been analyzed in some detail and is shown in Table 10-6. All production and consumption figures are national estimates, while figures given for rail shipments and receipts on potentially uneconomic light-density lines are restricted to lines in the thirty-one southern and western states under consideration.

When the traffic moving over uneconomic light-density lines is compared to the total national production, only two cases, wheat and barley, show substantial amounts of production affected. However, even though 17 percent and 12 percent of wheat and barley, respectively, move over these lines, the abandonment of selected light-density lines could be carried out with little adverse effect on grain shipments since (1) much of the traffic goes through states with very dense rail networks and (2) grain shipments initially involve truck movements from the farm to the elevator and thus there is some flexibility as to which elevator might be used.

On a regional basis, the data show that shipments over the light-density lines form a higher percentage of regional rail shipments. Here again, the actual impact of a reduced number of light-density lines will be less severe. Another component of agricultural railroad traffic is the inbound shipment of agricultural supplies. Table 10-7 shows that, if unprofitable light-density lines were abandoned, it would have only a minor effect on receipts of fertilizer, feed, and farm machinery and equipment.

From a local viewpoint, where the effects of reduced service are most acute, the problem can best be approached by separately assessing the impacts of abandonment on several distinct types of agricul-

Table 10-6

ESTIMATED USE OF POTENTIALLY UNECONOMIC LIGHT-DENSITY LINES FOR SHIPPING AGRICULTURAL PRODUCTS
(millions of tons)

Commodity	National Production[a]	Rail Shipments[b]				Percent of National Production Shipped on PULD Lines
		National total[c]	31-state total[d]	On PULD lines[e]	Percent of 31-state total on PULD lines	
Wheat	50.5	44.5	40.9	8.8	21.5	17
Corn	148.2	31.6	18.0	3.0	16.7	2
Barley	9.2	4.9	4.9	1.1	22.4	12
Sorghum grains	22.1	6.8	6.4	0.9	14.1	4
Oats, rye, and other grains	20.9	3.8	3.3	0.7	21.2	3
Soybeans	40.5	9.4	6.4	1.0	15.6	2
Other field crops	...	16.9	5.3	0.6	11.3	...
Other farm products	...	4.8	4.4	0.3	6.8	...

Note: All production figures are national estimates, while figures given for rail shipments on PULD lines are restricted to lines in the thirty-one southern and western states under consideration.

[a] U.S. Department of Agriculture, Agricultural Statistics, 1975, tables 9, 16, 23, 38, 44, 55, 62, and 174. Figures shown are 1972–1974 averages.

[b] Total shipments may exceed total production because of reshipment.

[c] Derived from U.S. Department of Transportation, Federal Railroad Administration, Carload Waybill Statistics, 1972, 1973, and 1974.

[d] Derived from Federal Railroad Administration carload waybill data for 1972–1974.

[e] From computer analysis of PULD lines outside the Northeast.

tural users, that is, grain elevator operators, feed and fertilizer producers and distributors, and the farmer.

Grain elevators. Numerous country elevators that serve as collection, storage, and shipping facilities for local farmers are situated on light-density rail lines. Complicating the matter further is the fact that these elevators are frequently unable, because of poor track conditions, to use modern 100-ton covered hopper cars. Many of them still ship in quantities of one to three boxcars. Larger subterminal elevators—those which receive most or all of their grain from country elevators—typically receive and ship grain in sufficient volume to raise the rail line on which they are located out of the "light-density" category.

The most generally applicable alternative which would avoid the problems associated with the collection of grain from dispersed country elevators involves the construction of larger grain subterminals on nearby high-density rail lines capable of handling 100-ton covered hopper cars in unit-train service. Under this method, grain would be trucked from the country elevators to the subterminals and shipped in unit trains of fifty or more cars at a time. Studies have indicated that the saving in rail freight charges that would result could more than pay for the construction costs of the new facility as well as the additional handling and trucking costs.[17]

Other transport alternatives available to country elevators include truck/rail (without the use of subterminals), truck/barge,[18] and

---

[17] C. P. Baumel, John J. Miller, and Thomas P. Drinka, *An Economic Analysis of Upgrading Branch Rail Lines: A Study of 71 Lines in Iowa* (Ames, Iowa: Iowa State University, February 1976); C. P. Baumel et al., *Economic Analysis of Alternative Grain Transportation Systems, A Case Study* (Ames Iowa: Iowa State University, November 1973); and Floyd D. Gaibler, "Economic Impact of Abandonment on Country Grain Elevators in South-Central Nebaska" (M.S. thesis, University of Nebraska, 1974). Baumel and his colleagues estimated in their 1976 study that construction of such subterminal elevators would increase net revenue to grain producers and shippers in Iowa by $14 million to $24 million annually.

[18] A. R. Bunker and L. D. Hill have found that Iowa grain elevators with direct rail service but located within ninety miles of the Mississippi River found it more profitable to transport grain by truck to subterminals located on the river for transshipment by barge than to ship by rail directly to more distant destinations. Even for those that are somewhat farther from such a waterway, shipment by truck and barge, combined with additional subterminal facilities, may present an acceptable alternative at no more than a small increase in costs. A. R. Bunker and L. D. Hill, "Impact of Rail Abandonment on Agricultural Production and Associated Grain Marketing and Fertilizer Supply Firms," *Illinois Agricultural Economics*, vol. 15 (January 1975), pp. 12–20.

Table 10-7

ESTIMATED USE OF POTENTIALLY UNECONOMIC LIGHT-DENSITY LINES FOR RECEIVING AGRICULTURAL SUPPLIES
(millions of tons)

Commodity	National Consumption[a]	Rail Receipts				Percent of National Consumption Received on PULD Lines
		National total[b]	31-state total[c]	On PULD lines[d]	Percent of 31-state total on PULD lines	
Fertilizers	45					
Phosphates	...	10.6	6.7	0.8	11.9	1.8
All others	...	6.7	5.1	0.4	7.7	0.9
Feed	28	11.2	7.1	0.2	2.8	0.7
Grain	...	91.6	75.7	0.8e	1.1	...
Oil kernels, nuts, and seeds	...	10.2	7.3	0.1e	1.4	...
Farm machinery and equipment	...	0.9	0.7	0.1	14.0	...

Note: All consumption figures are national estimates, while figures given for rail receipts on PULD lines are restricted to lines in the thirty-one southern and western states under consideration.

a U.S. Department of Agriculture, Agricultural Statistics, 1975, tables 70 and 648. Figures shown are 1972–1973 averages.

b Derived from U.S. Department of Transportation, Federal Railroad Administration, Carload Waybill Statistics, 1972, 1973, and 1974.

c Derived from Federal Railroad Administration carload waybill data for 1972–1974.

d From computer analysis of PULD lines outside the Northeast.

e A significant portion of shipments of these commodities terminating on PULD lines are to be made into feed for local agricultural use.

truck.[19] Previous abandonments have not prevented the continued expansion of affected country elevators.[20]

Feed producers and distributors. Feed producers and distributors in "grain-surplus" areas (where more grain is grown than is used locally) also frequently use grain elevators.[21] Since feed sold in these areas is grown, ground, and mixed locally, and is rarely shipped by rail, feed operations in these areas should not be adversely affected by abandonment. Feed producers and distributors in "grain-deficit" areas, on the other hand, could be adversely affected. The most likely transportation alternative for receiving feed and feed grains in grain-deficit areas would involve the combination of rail and truck.[22]

Increased costs in these areas will, for the most part, be passed on to the firms' customers. In areas where competitors are unaffected by the loss of rail service and the increased cost of trucking cannot be passed along, the affected firms may be forced to close or terminate their feed operations. One study disclosed that, of ten feed distributors which lost direct rail service, four closed and a fifth reported a substantial decline in feed sales.[23]

Fertilizer distributors. Loss of rail service is likely to result in rail/truck transshipment of virtually all potash and most phosphate fertilizer destined for stations on the line. In the case of nitrogen fertilizers, a producer may be sufficiently close so that direct shipment by truck is feasible.

[19] Shipments to terminals or subterminals no more than 200 to 400 miles away may be transported completely by truck. See Baumel et al., *Economic Analysis of Alternative Grain Transportation Systems;* and U.S. Department of Agriculture, Economic Research Service, and Oklahoma State University, *Analysis of the Effects of Cost-of-Service Transportation Rates on the U.S. Grain Marketing System,* Technical Bulletin 1484, October 1973. Data from these studies indicate the use of 800-bushel tractor-trailers for this purpose would increase the costs about 0.015–0.035 cents per bushel (or 3–7 cents per bushel for a 200-mile shipment).

[20] Baumel et al., *An Economic Analysis of Upgrading Branch Rail Lines,* pp. 138–44. This study found that three of four elevators surveyed had increased their capacity since abandonment (from a combined total of 320,000 bushels to 2,462,000 bushels), and that all four had increased employment.

[21] See Bunker and Hill, "Impact of Rail Abandonment on Agricultural Production"; they observed that about half the feed distributors in two areas of Iowa surveyed used grain elevators.

[22] Simat, Helliesen and Eichner found that the resulting increase in costs reported by three firms which lost service as a result of previous abandonments was between $0.75 and $3 per ton. Some retailers may be close enough to a wholesaler for direct truck shipment, although even a firm only twenty-six miles away from a feed mill reported an overall cost increase of $1 per ton. See Simat, Helliesen and Eichner, *Retrospective Rail Line Abandonment Study,* rev. ed., report submitted to U.S. Department of Transportation, Office of the Secretary, 1973.

[23] Ibid.

Estimates obtained by A. R. Bunker and L. D. Hill of increased costs resulting from transshipment by rail and truck were approximately $1.50 per ton for transloading and 4 cents to 8 cents per ton-mile for trucking.[24] The resulting increase in costs may be compared to retail prices of $100 to $200 per ton for common forms of concentrated fertilizers and $8 per ton for agricultural limestone.[25] This price increase will, in all likelihood, make retailing of agricultural limestone impractical and may result in the loss of sales of other types of fertilizers to nearby distributors who do not lose rail service.[26]

Farmers. For most crops, only a relatively small number of farmers will encounter major increases in production and marketing costs if local, direct rail service is lost. In the case of feed and fertilizer, data presented previously indicate that the cost increase for these two commodities would generally be less than 2 percent, though it would be somewhat more for the lower priced fertilizers. Since fertilizers constitute only a small portion of the costs of growing agricultural crops, the overall effect on crop-production costs should be quite small. The effect of increased feed costs on livestock-production costs would be relatively larger, but would still generally be no greater than 0.5 percent of total costs.

The effect on farm incomes of increased costs for shipping grain from country elevators could be more significant. As discussed previously, a system of grain subterminals may allow the abandonment of many light-density lines without any effect on shipping costs, and perhaps even some reduction in costs. If this is not the case, however, increased shipping costs of 5 cents to 10 cents per bushel might result. Such increased costs would be primarily absorbed by farmers in the form of a lower net on grain sales, although in some cases a portion of these costs may be passed on to the consumer. Subter-

[24] Bunker and Hill, "Impact of Rail Abandonment on Agricultural Production," p. 20. The abandonments occurred in 1969 and 1971, and all data were collected by personal interview in 1974. Individual distributors interviewed by Bunker and Hill reported cost increases ranging from zero to $6 per ton; those interviewed by Simat, Helliesen and Eichner, *Retrospective Rail Line Abandonment Study,* reported increases of $1.50 to $5 per ton.
[25] U.S. Department of Agriculture, *Agricultural Statistics,* 1975. Prices are for 1974.
[26] Bunker and Hill, "Impact of Rail Abandonment on Agricultural Production," found that fertilizer dealers who lost rail service expanded both capacity and sales at a slower rate than did nearby dealers who retained their service. Of three fertilizer dealers which had closed in the two areas studied, only one had lost rail service. Simat, Helliesen and Eichner, *Retrospective Rail Line Abandonment Study,* found two distributors of nitrogen fertilizer that had closed after losing rail service and one fertilizer retailer that had discontinued sales of agricultural lime; another seven firms that sold fertilizer did not report any impact on sales volume.

minals, therefore, may play an important role in minimizing or avoiding the adverse effects that the loss of rail service may have on the farmers served by light-density lines.

Retailing and Wholesaling. In isolated areas, loss of rail service will generally have little effect on retailing operations (except for coal); in more populated areas, however, sales may be lost to competing businesses on surviving rail lines and a few firms may be forced to close. Thus, on an area-wide basis, little or no loss of jobs will result from the loss of rail service to retailers. Furthermore, since only a few commodities are still shipped by rail to retailers, increased costs for these items will not result in a perceptible increase in the cost-of-living in affected communities.

Affected wholesalers, on the other hand, may find that passing along increased costs to their customers will result in at least some loss of business, particularly on the periphery of their market area. Where sources of supply are relatively close and/or products are of at least moderate value, switching to direct shipment by truck may

Table 10-8
RAIL SHIPMENT DATA PERTAINING TO EFFECTS ON NONAGRICULTURAL RETAILERS AND WHOLESALERS
(rail receipts in millions of tons)

Commodity	National Total[a]	31-State Total[b]	Receipts on PULD Lines[c]	Percent of 31-State Total on PULD Lines	Percent of National Total on PULD Lines
Lumber	24.5	16.7	0.4	2.4	1.6
Coal	288.0	42.8	0.4	0.9	0.1
Grocery products	82.4	48.8	0.9	1.8	1.1
Motor vehicles and parts	24.7	14.0	0.1	0.7	0.4
Other consumer durables (primarily household appliances)	4.9	2.6	0.02	0.8	0.4

[a] Derived from U.S. Department of Transportation, Federal Railroad Administration, *Carload Waybill Statistics*, 1972, 1973, and 1974.
[b] Derived from Federal Railroad Administration carload waybill data for 1972–1974.
[c] Estimated from computer analysis.

170

produce reduced inventory costs that approximate the increase in transportation costs. Where sources of supply are more distant, however, loss of rail service may result in a somewhat greater increase in costs. Since wholesale operations are generally not capital intensive, relocation of operations to a site served by a surviving rail line may be a practical alternative. The data portrayed in Table 10-8 show the extent to which the nonagricultural retailers and wholesalers located on potentially uneconomic light-density lines use rail service. Only in the cases of lumber and grocery products is more than 1 percent of receipts in the thirty-one states transported over such lines (and in those cases only 2.4 percent and 1.8 percent, respectively).

Manufacturing. For certain kinds of manufacturing firms, the effects of the termination of service on light-density lines could be substantial. Firms producing a relatively low-value product, one which is processed from a rather ubiquitous raw material and is typically moved in bulk (usually by rail), may well experience a marked increase in production costs subsequent to the cessation of rail service. Grain, lumber, and paper mills typify this kind of production process. Table 10-9 presents selected production and transport data for these types of mills.

In the case of grain-mill products other than animal feed, nearly one-third of total national production is shipped by rail, yet only 0.3 percent of this production originates on uneconomic light-density lines in the thirty-one states under study (that is, 200,000 tons of a total of 53 million tons). On a regional basis, 1.5 percent of rail shipments made in the thirty-one states originate on these lines. Potential abandonments could have a greater impact on feed mills than on grain mills; perhaps 5 percent of the nation's production could be affected (as much as 800,000 tons out of 17.4 million tons of grain to be milled,[27] as well as 200,000 tons out of 11.2 million tons of feed shipped by rail).

Paper mills are dependent on the railroads for the movement of more than two-thirds of their production, but only 0.2 percent of these shipments originate on uneconomic light-density lines in the thirty-one states, and potentially affected shipments represent only 0.4 percent of all rail shipments made in this region. In the case of lumber mills, 5.1 percent of the nation's rail shipments and 4.9 per-

---

[27] In the case of feed mills, rail is more important as a means of transporting grain *to* the mills (particularly in grain-deficit areas) than as a means of transporting the feed *from* the mills. The estimated 800,000 tons of grain which could be affected includes grain received by all grain mills, though it is likely that the bulk of this is received by feed mills.

Table 10-9

RAIL SHIPMENT DATA PERTAINING TO EFFECTS ON GRAIN, LUMBER, AND PAPER MILLS

(millions of tons)

Commodity	National Production[a]	National Rail Shipments[b]	31-State Rail Shipments[c]	Plants on PULD Lines			
				Total rail shipments[d]	Percent of 31-state rail shipments	Percent of national production	Rail receipts of primary inputs[d]
Feed mills	53	11.2	7.2	0.2	2.8	0.4	...
Other grain mills	63	20.1	13.0	0.2	1.5	0.3	0.8[e]
Lumber mills	...[f]	24.5	23.6	1.2	5.1	...[g]	0.1[h]
Paper mills	53	35.7	26.8	0.1	0.4	0.3	0.1[i]

Note: All production figures are national estimates, while figures given for rail shipments and receipts on PULD lines are restricted to lines in the thirty-one southern and western states under consideration.

a U.S. Bureau of the Census, *Census of Manufactures, 1972: Industry Series.*

b Derived from U.S. Department of Transportation, Federal Railroad Administration, *Carload Waybill Statistics,* 1972, 1973, and 1974.

c Derived from Federal Railroad Administration carload waybill data for 1972–1974.

d Estimated from computer analysis of PULD lines outside the Northeast.

e Grain, assumed to be received primarily by feed mills.

f Production data in census generally not specified in units of weight.

g Not estimated.

h Sawlogs.

i Pulpwood logs and wood chips.

cent of those in the thirty-one states originate on potentially uneconomic light-density lines.

In each of these instances the percentage of production that might be affected is somewhat overestimated since some of the output could be transported via other modes or might originate from a relocated mill. For example, in at least one case, the abandonment of a line serving an area with the potential for profitable logging did not prevent the subsequent development of both logging operations and lumber mills in the area despite the absence of rail service.[28]

Other types of manufacturing firms generally will be less affected by a loss of rail service than the mill-type operations discussed above. Table 10-10 presents data summarizing the extent to which firms in various industries ship over uneconomic light-density lines, while Table 10-11 discloses similar data summarizing the extent to which various industrial inputs are received on these lines.

From the data presented in Table 10-10, it might be presumed that the food processing industry would be most noticeably affected by a cessation of rail service. However, three retrospective abandonment studies found that, of the thirteen food processors surveyed, none had closed or reduced employment after the abandonment of its line, although two firms did transfer some or all of their operations to other locations in the area.[29]

Overall, significant effects on manufacturers should be generally limited to relatively small plants in a few industries which are heavily dependent on rail service to provide lower cost transport of relatively low-valued commodities.

Mining. Data summarizing the movements of products of the mineral industries on uneconomic light-density lines in the thirty-one states are shown in Table 10-12. As can be seen, only about 0.2 percent of the nation's bituminous coal production moving by rail is shipped over potentially uneconomic light-density lines in these states (that is, 500,000 tons out of 288 million tons). In turn, less than 1 percent of output in the thirty-one states is affected. In addition, after interviewing the operators of five coal mines which had lost rail service

[28] John F. Due, "Long Term Impact of Abandonment of Railway Lines," Transportation Research Paper 7, University of Illinois at Urbana-Champaign, College of Commerce and Business Administration, June 6, 1975.

[29] See Simat, Helliesen and Eichner, *Retrospective Rail Line Abandonment Study;* Boston University Bureau of Business, "The Economic Impact of the Discontinuance of the Rutland Railway," in *Studies on the Economic Impact of Railway Abandonment and Service Discontinuance*, U.S. Department of Commerce, Transportation Research, June 1965; and Benjamin J. Allen, "Economic Effects of Rail Abandonments on Communities: A Case Study" (Ph.D. diss., University of Illinois at Urbana-Champaign, 1974).

Table 10-10

ESTIMATED USE OF POTENTIALLY UNECONOMIC LIGHT-DENSITY LINES FOR SHIPMENT FROM MANUFACTURING PLANTS

(millions of tons)

Commodity	National Production[a]	Rail Shipments				Percent of National Production Shipped on PULD Lines
		National total[b]	31-state total[c]	On PULD lines[d]	Percent of 31-state total on PULD lines	
Food processors						
Meat	57	4.6	3.9	0.2	5.1	0.4
Canned and preserved foods	..[e]	8.6	7.1	0.4	5.6	...
Others[f]	..[e]	43.2	30.8	0.7	2.3	...
Chemicals	140	83.0	61.0	0.5	0.8	0.4
Petroleum products	..[e]	43.4	24.8	0.3	1.2	...
Hydraulic cement	80	19.6	11.4	0.4	3.5	0.5
Concrete, gypsum, and plaster	..[e]	9.0	5.0	0.2	4.0	...
Processed nonmetallic earths and minerals	30	27.0	16.5	0.4	2.4	1.3
Primary metal products	478	60.0	15.3	0.2	1.3	0.04
Fabricated metal products, machinery, and equipment	...	41.5	11.7	0.1	0.9	...
All other manufacturing products	...	30.4	19.9	0.3	1.5	...

Note: All production figures are national estimates, while figures given for rail shipments on PULD lines are restricted to lines in the thirty-one southern and western states under consideration.

[a] Estimated from U.S. Bureau of the Census, *Census of Manufactures, 1972: Industry Series.*

[b] Derived from U.S. Department of Transportation, Federal Railroad Administration, *Carload Waybill Statistics,* 1972, 1973, and 1974.

[c] Derived from Federal Railroad Administration carload waybill data for 1972–1974.

[d] Estimated from computer analysis of PULD lines outside the Northeast.

[e] Production data in census generally not specified in units of weight.

[f] Excluding grain, lumber, and paper mill products (all covered in Table 10-9), and bakery products.

Table 10-11
ESTIMATED USE OF POTENTIALLY UNECONOMIC LIGHT-DENSITY LINES FOR RECEIVING MATERIALS USED BY MANUFACTURING PLANTS
(millions of tons)

Commodity	National Production[a]	Rail Receipts				Percent of National Production Received on PULD Lines
		National total[b]	31-state total[c]	On PULD lines[d]	Percent of 31-state total on PULD lines	
Agricultural products (except grain, oil kernels, nuts, and seeds)[e]	...	17.1	5.6	0.2	3.6	...
Coal	569	288.0	42.8	0.4	0.9	0.07
Other minerals	1,100	185.2	20.2	0.3	1.5	0.03
Chemicals	100	50.0	40.3	1.0	2.5	1.0
Petroleum products	...[f]	43.4	23.3	0.5	2.2	...
Processed nonmetallic earths and minerals	30	27.0	13.8	0.3	2.2	1.0
Primary metal products (primarily iron and steel)	478	60.0	27.0	0.4	1.5	0.08
Fabricated metal products, machinery, and equipment	...	15.3	8.4	0.2	2.4	...
Other industrial materials	...	45.6	18.0	0.2	1.1	...

Note: All production figures are national estimates, while figures given for rail receipts on PULD lines are restricted to lines in the thirty-one southern and western states under consideration.

a Estimated from U.S. Bureau of the Census, *Census of Manufactures, 1972: Industry Series.*

b Derived from U.S. Department of Transportation, Federal Railroad Administration, *Carload Waybill Statistics,* 1972, 1973, and 1974.

c Derived from Federal Railroad Administration carload waybill data for 1972–1974.

d Estimated from computer analysis of PULD lines outside the Northeast.

e See Table 10-7 for receipts of grain, oil kernels, nuts, and seeds.

f Production data in census generally not specified in units of weight.

Table 10-12

RAIL SHIPMENT DATA PERTAINING TO EFFECTS ON MINING

(millions of tons)

Commodity	National Production[a]	Rail Shipments				Percent of National Production on PULD Lines
		National total[b]	31-state total[c]	On PULD lines[d]	Percent of 31-state total on PULD lines	
Metallic ores	600	135.0	10.0	0.1	1.0	0.02
Coal[e]	569	288.0	56.1	0.5	0.9	0.09
Crushed and broken stone	623	52.9	22.2	0.7	3.2	0.11
Sand and gravel	943	43.4	26.3	0.4	1.5	0.04
Other nonmetallic minerals	700	50.5	12.8	0.3	2.3	0.04

Note: All production figures are national estimates, while figures given for rail shipments on PULD lines are restricted to lines in the thirty-one southern and western states under consideration.

[a] Estimated from U.S. Bureau of the Census, *Census of Mineral Industries, 1972: Industry Series.*

[b] Derived from U.S. Department of Transportation, Federal Railroad Administration, *Carload Waybill Statistics,* 1972, 1973, and 1974.

[c] Derived from Federal Railroad Administration carload waybill data for 1972–1974.

[d] Estimated from computer analysis of PULD lines outside the Northeast.

[e] Excluding anthracite.

in 1969, Simat, Helliesen and Eichner concluded that lack of service "did not seriously injure" any of the firms.[30]

For other mining activity, the situation is similar. The only instance in which more than 1 percent of the present rail shipments in the thirty-one state region is affected involves the movement of crushed and broken stone (see Table 10-12). Even in that case, however, only 0.1 percent of the nation's output would be affected. It is clear that most mining locations generate sufficient rail traffic to preclude the lines serving them from being classified as light-density.

Logging. Logging companies rely upon railroads to transport logs and wood chips to saw and paper mills to a greater extent than firms in the mining sector. As the figures in Table 10-13 indicate, between 3.8 percent and 5.4 percent of the nation's rail shipments of logging products could be affected by cessation of service. The loss of rail service would result in increased transportation costs to the logging company. The retrospective studies indicate, however, that the larger and more profitable logging companies will generally be capable of

---

Table 10-13

ESTIMATED USE OF POTENTIALLY UNECONOMIC LIGHT-DENSITY LINES BY LOGGING COMPANIES
(rail shipments in millions of tons)

Commodity	National Total[a]	31-State Total[b]	Shipments on PULD Lines[c]	Percent of 31-State Total on PULD Lines	Percent of National Total on PULD Lines
Sawlogs	4.3	1.6	0.2	12.5	4.6
Pulpwood logs	34.3	30.1	1.3	4.3	3.8
Wood chips	22.2	20.8	1.2	5.8	5.4
Other primary forest products	2.2	1.5	0.1	6.7	4.5

[a] Derived from U.S. Department of Transportation, Federal Railroad Administration, *Carload Waybill Statistics,* 1972, 1973, and 1974.
[b] Derived from Federal Railroad Administration carload waybill data for 1972–1974.
[c] Estimated from computer analysis of PULD lines outside the Northeast.

---

[30] Simat, Helliesen and Eichner, *Additional Retrospective Rail Line Abandonment Studies,* report submitted to U.S. Department of Transportation, Federal Railroad Administration, and Office of the Secretary, March 1975.

Table 10-14

ESTIMATED USE OF POTENTIALLY UNECONOMIC LIGHT-DENSITY LINES FOR RECEIVING CONSTRUCTION MATERIALS

(millions of tons)

Commodity	National Production[a]	Rail Shipments			Percent of 31-state total on PULD lines	Percent of National Production Received on PULD Lines
		National total[b]	31-state total[c]	On PULD lines[d]		
Lumber	...[e]	24.5	16.7	0.4	2.4	...
Crushed stone	623	52.9	22.2	0.5	2.2	0.08
Sand and gravel	943	43.4	25.5	0.3	1.2	0.03
Hydraulic cement	81[f]	19.6	12.5	0.3	2.4	0.4
Other construction materials	...[e]	22.1	12.7	0.2	1.6	...

Note: All production figures are national estimates, while figures given for all receipts on PULD lines are restricted to lines in the thirty-one southern and western states under consideration.

[a] U.S. Bureau of the Census, *Census of Manufactures, 1972: Industry Series.*

[b] Derived from U.S. Department of Transportation, Federal Railroad Administration, *Carload Waybill Statistics,* 1972, 1973, and 1974.

[c] Derived from Federal Railroad Administration carload waybill data for 1972–1974.

[d] Estimated from computer analysis of PULD lines outside the Northeast.

[e] Production data in census generally not specified in units of weight.

[f] Estimated from census data.

Table 10-15

ESTIMATED USE OF POTENTIALLY UNECONOMIC
LIGHT-DENSITY LINES BY SCRAP DEALERS
(rail shipments in millions of tons)

Commodity	National Total[a]	31-State Total[b]	Shipments on PULD Lines[c]	Percent of 31-State Total on PULD Lines	Percent of National Total on PULD Lines
Scrap metal	31.4	10.2	0.2	2.0	0.6
Other scrap	7.1	4.2	0.1	2.4	1.4

[a] Derived from U.S. Department of Transportation, Federal Railroad Administration, *Carload Waybill Statistics*, 1972, 1973, and 1974.
[b] Derived from Federal Railroad Administration carload waybill data for 1972–1974.
[c] Estimated from computer analysis of PULD lines outside the Northeast.

absorbing these costs.[31] In one case, logging operations were not begun until after the rail line serving the location had been abandoned.[32]

Other Industries. Two other types of "processing" firms are also identifiable as possibly being affected by the potential abandonment of light-density rail lines outside the Northeast. These are construction companies and scrap dealers.

Table 10-14 presents data on the use of potentially uneconomic light-density lines for receipt of building materials. These materials are received by construction companies as well as by retailers, wholesalers, and industrial firms. Only in the cases of lumber, hydraulic cement, and crushed stone are more than 2 percent of the region's inbound shipments transported over these lines. To the extent that receipt of materials by construction companies may occur at the construction site, to which the materials must already be transshipped by truck, construction firms will encounter smaller cost increases than firms which receive all shipments at a private siding. Furthermore, since the construction industry is labor intensive, the increase in transport costs resulting from any loss of service will be relatively small in relation to total costs. Affected firms would be able to pass along these cost increases with little negative effect on their operations.

Large-volume scrap dealers also use the railroads to transport scrap to their industrial customers. Data on the amount of scrap

---

[31] Ibid.; Simat, Helliesen and Eichner, *Retrospective Rail Line Abandonment Study;* Due, "Long Term Impact of Abandonment."
[32] Due, "Long Term Impact of Abandonment," pp. 38–39.

transported over potentially uneconomic light-density lines outside the Northeast are presented in Table 10-15. The data indicate that only about 2 percent of present rail shipments of scrap—whether scrap metal or other scrap—outside the Northeast is shipped via these lines. Interviews with two scrap iron and steel dealers who had lost direct rail service through abandonments determined that in each case they encountered increased shipping costs but had maintained a steady volume of shipments and continued to operate profitably.[33]

[33] Simat, Helliesen and Eichner, *Retrospective Rail Line Abandonment Study;* and Simat, Helliesen and Eichner, *Additional Retrospective Rail Line Abandonment Studies.*

PART THREE

IMPLEMENTATION OF REFORMS

On February 6, 1976, President Ford signed into law the Railroad Revitalization and Regulatory Reform Act of 1976. The 4R Act is landmark rail legislation dealing with a wide variety of rail issues: financial assistance, restructuring of the rail system in the Northeast, mergers, abandonments, ICC procedures, and railroad pricing.

Although not all of the Ford administration's reform provisions were adopted, many of the basic reform ideas suggested by the Railroad Revitalization Act are reflected in the bill which the President signed. Under the 4R Act, however, implementation of the reform is left to the Interstate Commerce Commission. The eventual outcome of the reform provisions thus depends to a great degree on the way the ICC administers them.

In this part we present papers dealing with the implementation of the reform provisions. The first essay by John W. Snow and Mark Aron is based upon a memorandum prepared for Secretary of Transportation William T. Coleman, Jr., assessing the reform provisions of the 4R Act in December 1975—that is, after the bill had been passed by both houses of Congress but before it went to conference. The second essay is an analysis prepared by the Department of Transportation staff of the implementation tasks required by the 4R Act. Many of the reform provisions were not self-implementing but required administration by the ICC.

The final two papers deal with implementation of the most significant pricing provision in the act—the so-called market dominance provision. Under this provision—section 202(b) of the act—railroads were given broad pricing freedom, except where the ICC found that railroads had market dominance. The ICC docketed a proceeding (Ex Parte No. 320) to issue its regulations for administering the market dominance provision. The essay by Norman Jones, Jr., an economic consultant, is an analysis of market dominance and competition in the rail industry prepared for the Department of Transportation in connection with this proceeding. On March 10, 1976, the ICC issued its final rules on market dominance. There was considerable sentiment in the rail industry and in the administration that the ICC had misapplied the market dominance concept, taking too narrow a view of competition. The Department of Justice filed an appeal of the ICC's action in the U.S. Court of Appeals for the District of Columbia Circuit. The final essay is drawn from the brief which the DOJ filed in the circuit court, arguing for a modification of the ICC's action.

11

ASSESSMENT OF THE REGULATORY REFORM SECTIONS OF THE RAILROAD REVITALIZATION AND REGULATORY REFORM ACT

John W. Snow and Mark Aron

Overview

Overall the regulatory reform sections of the Railroad Revitalization and Regulatory Reform Act are good. The changes are all positive, and some are quite substantive and far-reaching. Although the bill does not provide for all of the regulatory reform which the Ford administration sought, it does represent a significant break with the past regulatory policy of the Interstate Commerce Commission. The substance of most of the reforms we sought is contained in the bill, although often in a somewhat modified form and in the case of rate bureaus in a weakened form.

The cornerstone of the administration's regulatory reform proposal was pricing flexibility, and we can be pleased by the fact that the bill provides for a substantial amount of pricing flexibility by the railroads. The bill adopts the substance of the administration's proposal on a number of pricing-flexibility issues:

(1) Railroads can freely raise rates which are below cost up to variable costs ("going-concern value").

(2) Railroads can reduce rates down to variable costs ("going-concern value").

(3) The ICC may not engage in "umbrella" rate making.

This chapter is edited from two documents prepared within the U.S. Department of Transportation: an analysis of the Railroad Revitalization and Regulatory Reform Act prepared by the DOT staff in December 1975, and a "covering memorandum" concerning the analysis from the deputy under secretary (John W. Snow) to the secretary of transportation (William T. Coleman, Jr.), dated December 23, 1975. The principal author of the staff analysis is Mark Aron, an attorney in the Office of the General Counsel, U.S. Department of Transportation.

(4) The 7 percent "no-suspend zone" was adopted in a some-what modified form on a two-year experimental basis.

(5) Further restrictions on the power of the ICC to suspend rate changes were adopted along the lines we proposed.

(6) Our proposed time limits for action by the ICC on rate cases were adopted.

(7) The "Big John" provision was adopted.

(8) The intrastate rate-making provision was adopted.

The bill also provides that the ICC loses jurisdiction over rates where railroads do not have market dominance. This provision is of tremendous potential significance; it reflected the Senate's compromise with us on the issue of up-side rate flexibility. Moreover, the bill provides significant reforms with respect to rate bureaus. Although the reforms fall short of what we sought, they certainly represent significant changes in the rate bureau powers—changes which promise much more attention to the pricing of individual commodities than has been the case in the railroad industry.

The bill provides a number of other desirable reforms, which are found in the sections on divisions, exemptions, cost accounting, unit trains, mergers, and discriminatory state taxation. We estimate that the intrastate rate-making provision and the discriminatory taxation provision will save the industry approximately $100 million annually, while the ability to raise rates up to variable costs is worth between $50 million and $250 million annually to the industry. Of course, the biggest gain will come from the increased ability of management to test their markets, experiment with new services, adjust prices quickly in response to cost changes and so forth.

The principal problem with the bill lies in the fact that certain concepts in the bill, such as variable costs and market dominance, are ambiguous. Consequently, the commission is left with a large amount of discretion which could be used to frustrate the overall objective of the legislation. However, the policy declaration, which precedes the regulatory reform part of the bill, is strong and provides the kind of policy direction which we desire. There is really no way to eliminate agency discretion except by eliminating the regulatory agency. This is an inherent problem with the regulatory process.

In sum, we have had reasonable success in our effort to reform regulation. We must, however, await the ICC's action in implementing the various reform provisions before declaring a victory. In large part, we got the substance of our regulatory reform provisions, and we certainly obtained more regulatory reform than was considered possible. We have probably obtained the maximum regulatory reform we could reasonably expect to achieve from this Congress. If regulatory issues are opened up in subsequent consideration of the bill, we will lose ground. The rate bureaus are unhappy with the section on rate bureaus. Many shippers are unhappy with the concepts of up-side flexibility and market dominance. The water carriers are extremely unhappy with the down-side flexibility, as are the truckers. In addition, the truckers are unhappy about the reforms of the rate bureaus. The truckers view the reforms of the rate bureaus and the pricing flexibility as a prelude to similar reform of motor carrier regulation. The ICC is unhappy with the whole thrust of the legislation and would be most pleased to see it undone. Thus, if the regulatory issues are reopened, there will be strong efforts made to weaken the bill, and we stand to lose a substantial amount of ground, while the prospects for gain are slight at best. Therefore, it is strongly recommended that we seal the regulatory part of the bill.

Every administration since that of John Kennedy has called for substantial regulatory reform in the rail industry and until now nothing had been achieved. This is the first success any administration has had on the issue. It is a real success (even though short of our goal) and represents all that we could reasonably have expected to achieve and more than our critics thought we would achieve. Beyond its significance for the railroad industry, the regulatory reform sections of the bill provide the basis for extending these reforms to the motor carrier and aviation industries.

Analysis

The regulatory reforms of the Railroad Revitalization and Regulatory Reform Act (4R Act) are significant but not as extensive as those recommended by the administration. The two principal problems of the act are, first, the vagueness of the language which might lead to very costly litigation and, second, the failure of the act to go as far as we recommended. It should be recognized, however, that the 4R Act does provide significant regulatory reform, more than anyone thought we could achieve. The reforms in the bill represent a definite break with the past and provide a good deal of pricing flexibility and reform of the archaic ICC procedures.

In evaluating the regulatory reform of the 4R Act, three additional points should be considered. First, all of the regulatory changes are positive in nature. At one point the House bill would have confused the abandonment section of the Interstate Commerce Act. The House provision, however, was dropped. Second, there are numerous "minor provisions" in the regulatory section of the 4R Act. The significance of each of these individual provisions is not great, but when added together their adoption should have a substantial beneficial impact. Finally, the provisions in the 4R Act form a good precedent for future changes in the motor and air carrier regulatory programs. The rail provisions were weakened because both the House and the Senate inserted certain "exceptions," especially in the area of rate bureaus. These exceptions, however, are not particularly important in the motor carrier industry, and we would have a very strong provision on motor carrier rate bureaus if we could enact the 4R Act's provisions for rate bureaus in the Motor Carrier Reform Act. We will now discuss the individual regulatory provisions of the 4R Act.

Policy declaration. The final bill adopted much of the strong policy language of the administration's proposal. Some of the bill's vagueness is overcome by the policy declaration.

Divisions. The final bill adopts a provision placing a time limit on divisions cases and making a few other procedural changes. This is a beneficial provision. It was not in our proposal, but we did support reform of the procedure for divisions cases in our testimony.

Minimum rates. The administration proposed that railroad carriers could lower their rates to variable costs without ICC interference. The 4R Act does not adopt the precise language of the administration's proposal, but it is very close. The act provides that a carrier may reduce its rates free of ICC interference except where doing so would reduce the "going-concern value." This "going-concern value" standard is a more ambiguous test than the administration's proposal, but the 4R Act adds a strong presumption tying "going-concern value" to variable costs. Section 202 of the act provides that a rate which equals or exceeds variable costs shall be presumed to contribute to the "going-concern value" unless such presumption is rebutted by "clear and convincing evidence" to the contrary.

Umbrella rate making. The administration proposed to amend section 15(a)(3) of the Interstate Commerce Act to delete the reference in the last sentence to the national transportation policy (NTP) which has formed the basis for the commission's umbrella rate-making policy. The 4R Act accomplishes this reform, although the language is somewhat different from the administration's proposal. The act adds section 202(f), which provides that nothing in the 4R Act modifies the application of sections 2, 3, or 4 of the Interstate

Commerce Act or makes lawful any competitive practice "which is unfair, destructive, predatory, or otherwise undermines competition which is necessary in the public interest." The Senate bill contained the above language, but also provided that nothing in the act was meant to nullify the application of the NTP to any provision of the Interstate Commerce Act. Section 202(f) is a vague provision that some might use to argue that the commission still has the authority to engage in umbrella rate making. Both the Senate and the House reports, however, are quite specific in limiting the vague reference to "predatory" practices to rates below variable costs. In addition, the failure of the conference report to adopt the reference to the NTP and the strong language of the policy declaration also argues that the Congress intended to enact meaningful reform of section 15(a)(3).

Maximum rates. The administration proposed only modest changes with respect to the commission's authority over maximum rates. We proposed that carriers could increase below-cost rates to a level equal to cost without commission interference. The 4R Act adopts this proposal, although it again uses the indirect reference to "going-concern value," which is then related to variable costs, rather than the direct variable costs approach.

The 4R Act goes beyond the administration with respect to maximum rates. It provides that the commission has no authority with respect to maximum rates unless a carrier has "market dominance." Market dominance is defined as the lack of effective competition. The Senate staff adopted the market dominance approach as an alternative to the increase part of our "no-suspend zone." Both the House and Senate had certain presumptions of market dominance to help clarify the definition. The House presumptions were quite confusing, but the Senate presumption was helpful. Unfortunately, the Senate presumption is not in the 4R Act.

No-suspend zone. The administration proposed a gradually increasing, permanent "no-suspend zone." In addition, the administration proposal would have imposed a seven-month time limit for rate-making cases and would have made all suspensions, even those outside the zone, more difficult to obtain.

The 4R Act adopted a two-year no-suspend provision, with a 7 percent zone for each of the two years. A two-year no-suspend zone is a valuable mechanism for rate flexibility in the transitional period before the commission and the courts adequately define "going-concern value" and "market dominance." The value of the two-year zone is considerably diminished, however, because the zone does not apply where there is market dominance or to a rate decrease which is "unfair, destructive, or predatory." Given the limited time for decision in suspension cases, the no-suspend provision, to be effective, should have read in terms of specific and uncontestable numbers, rather than vague statutory standards.

The 4R Act did pick up our provision limiting rate-making cases to seven months and imposing certain new conditions on all suspension cases.

Recyclables. The administration did not have a section dealing with recyclables. The 4R Act does have a section dealing with discrimination against recyclables. The language appears to be innocuous, but there is some feeling that this language would impose new regulatory requirements. The railroads have indicated that they will have no problems with this section.

Big John. The administration proposed a new expedited procedure for rates involving capital investments of $1 million or more. In addition, these new rates, once approved, cannot be found unlawful for a period of five years. The 4R Act adopted the administration's proposal.

Exemptions. The 4R Act provides that the commission can exempt certain goods or carriers from the requirements of the Interstate Commerce Act if it determines that such an exemption is in the public interest and is consistent with the NTP. The administration did not propose such a section, although we testified in favor of it and we informally submitted a provision to exempt grain and flour from the regulations. Although the effect of this provision is uncertain, it might be valuable if there were a change in attitude at the commission.

Rate bureaus. The administration proposed substantial changes with respect to rate bureaus. Our bill would have limited discussion, agreement, and voting to only those participating in a particular movement. Our proposal would also have applied to general rate increases, except for those related solely to increases in fuel and labor costs.

The 4R Act adopts the form of our proposal (although it does not apply to discussions) but then provides a significant exemption for all general rate increases and for all so-called broad tariff changes. This latter category would include so-called group rates, which constitute a large part of all rates. Nevertheless, there is some reform in the 4R Act's provision dealing with rate bureaus in the area of individual single-line and joint-line rates. It should be emphasized that the act, through the no-suspend and Big John provisions, dramatically increases and in some ways forces increased reliance on individual rate changes—the very area where the act's provision for rate bureaus is more effective. Also, the bill limits the ability of the bureaus to protest independent action. The 4R Act carefully took the best of the House and Senate bills to maximize the potential for reform.

Intrastate rate making. The administration proposed an amendment to clarify the relationship between state regulatory agencies and the Interstate Commerce Commission. This amendment was intended to expedite the consideration of intrastate rail rates. The 4R Act adopted this reform.

Discriminatory state taxation. The administration proposed outlawing discriminatory state taxation of rail carriers and other carriers. This provision was adopted without the language in the Senate bill which would have "grandfathered" Tennessee.

Uniform cost accounting. The substance of the administration's proposal for uniform cost accounting was adopted in the 4R Act, although the function was given to the Interstate Commerce Commission rather than to the Department of Transportation.

Unit train. The 4R Act adopted a provision which will greatly increase the availability of unit trains in the coal industry. We did not propose such a change in our legislation, but we petitioned the ICC in a regulatory proceeding to make such a change.

Mergers. The administration proposed changing the substantive standard for mergers and proposed expediting the procedure. The 4R Act adopted a time limit for mergers but made no substantive changes with respect to the standard for mergers. The act does, however, provide a significant planning role for the secretary.

Abandonments. The administration proposed no changes in the substantive standard for abandonment, but did propose certain procedural changes designed to liberalize abandonments. The bill passed by the House would have made a detrimental change of the abandonment standard. The House language was not adopted, and the 4R Act in its final form would adopt some of the procedural changes proposed by the administration.

12

IMPLEMENTATION OF THE RAIL ACT

U.S. Department of Transportation Staff

ICC Plans for Implementation

On February 12, 1976, the Interstate Commerce Commission announced plans for implementing the Railroad Revitalization and Regulatory Reform Act of 1976 (4R Act). The plans included the following schedule of proceedings and studies:

> A list of the planned proceedings in which public participation will be requested is attached. The dates for the institution of these proceedings and for the period during which public comment will be received are tentative, *but in no event will the final date for receiving public comment be earlier than that indicated.*
>
> Public announcement will be made prior to the initiation of each proceeding. Each such announcement will identify and categorize the areas to which comment should be directed. This should simplify the process for the public, allowing those interested to zero in on areas of particular interest and further early decisions in each area.

Rates and Related Matters

- Establish standards and procedures for determining whether a railroad has "market dominance" over a particular service.

This chapter is edited from two documents: a news release of the Interstate Commerce Commission on February 12, 1976, entitled "Commission Announces Plans for Implementing New Railroad Legislation"; and a U.S. Department of Transportation staff memorandum on "Implementation of the RRRR Act at the ICC," March 2, 1976.

To be instituted: about March 3, 1976
Public comments due: about April 22, 1976
Statutory deadline for decision: October 4, 1976

- Establish standards and procedures for the conduct of proceedings for the adjustment of divisions of joint rail rates and fares.
    To be instituted: about March 17, 1976
    Public comments due: about May 6, 1976
    Statutory deadline for decision: August 3, 1976

- Establish standards and expeditious procedures for establishing rail rates based on seasonal, peak, or regional demand.
    To be instituted: about April 15, 1976
    Public comments due: about May 27, 1976
    Statutory deadline for decision: February 5, 1977

- Establish expeditious procedures for the publication of rates for distinct rail services.
    To be instituted: about April 6, 1976
    Public comments due: about June 7, 1976
    Statutory deadline for decision: February 5, 1977

- Prescribe formulas for determining rates which equal or exceed variable costs and rates which do not exceed incremental costs.
    Time schedule for this proceeding to be announced

- Establish standards and procedures for determining adequate railroad revenue levels.
    Time schedule for this proceeding to be announced
    Statutory deadline for decision: February 5, 1978

Rail Abandonment Proceedings

- Determine what is a shipper who has made significant use of a rail line proposed for abandonment.
    To be instituted: about April 2, 1976
    Public comments due: about May 3, 1976

- Issue regulations governing the filing and updating by each railroad of a description of its system identifying lines which are "potentially subject to abandonment." (This matter may be handled jointly with immediately preceding item.)
    To be instituted: about April 2, 1976
    Public comments due: about May 3, 1976

192

- The Commission's Rail Services Planning Office (RSPO) must publish standards for determining the "avoidable cost of providing rail service" over a line to be abandoned.
    > To be instituted: about April 15, 1976
    > Public comments due: about June 15, 1976
    > Statutory deadline for decision: November 1, 1976

- RSPO must establish standards for computing commuter rail service subsidy payments and for computing emergency commuter rail assistance available to states in the Northeast and Midwest region.
    > To be instituted: about April 30, 1976
    > Public comments due: about June 15, 1976
    > Statutory deadline for decision: August 3, 1976

- RSPO must develop an accounting system for determining rail branch-line costs and revenues.
    > To be instituted: about June 30, 1976
    > Public comments due: about August 16, 1976
    > Statutory deadline for decision: November 1, 1976

Railroad Merger Proceedings

- Develop new procedures and application form for rail merger proceedings.
    > To be instituted: about April 2, 1976
    > Public comments due: about May 17, 1976

Car Service Regulations

- Revise present regulations, if necessary, to conform to new standards for the valuation of freight cars.
    > To be instituted: about July 13, 1976
    > Public comments due: about September 14, 1976
    > Statutory deadline for decision: August 3, 1977

Tariff Rules Revision

- Revise tariff filing rules to require that all railroad rates be incorporated into individual-carrier or rate-bureau tariffs within two years of their initial publication.
    > To be instituted: about June 30, 1976
    > Public comments due: about August 31, 1976
    > Statutory deadline for decision: February 5, 1978

Uniform System of Accounts

- Issue regulations and procedures prescribing a uniform system of cost and revenue accounting and a reporting system for all railroads.
  To be instituted: about June 30, 1976
  Public comments due: about September 30, 1976
  Statutory deadline for decision: June 30, 1977

Other Areas of Commission Responsibility upon Which Public Comment May Be Sought

- Procedures for dealing with railroad rates which are shown to be contingent upon the expenditure of $1 million in capital improvements.

- Adoption of car-service rules implementing statutory provision allowing railroads to assign cars to unit coal train service.

- Conduct investigation of the rail rate structures for the transportation of recyclable commodities.

- Conduct study of conglomerates and other corporate structures in the rail industry and determine their effects upon transportation services.

- Revise the General Rules of Practice as they relate to rail proceedings.

- Prepare and submit to Congress a proposed recodification of the Interstate Commerce Act and related statutes.

Response to the ICC Plans

At a meeting on February 23, 1976, members of the Department of Transportation staff discussed the series of proceedings that were scheduled by the ICC and made plans for preparing the DOT submissions to these proceedings. What follows is a brief description of the work to be done by the department—including the Office of Policy (TPI), the Office of General Counsel (TGC), and the Federal Railroad Administration (FRA)—with respect to the specific ICC proceedings.

194

Review of Rate Bureau Agreements. (No due date has been set for comments.) Pursuant to new section 5(b) of the Interstate Commerce Act, the ICC issued an order on February 17, 1976, requiring new agreements to be filed for approval within 100 days of its order, which will be April 27, 1976. No provision was made for interested parties to comment on such submissions. If necessary, the department will petition the ICC either to accept DOT comments or to ask all interested parties to comment.

Three rate bureau issues should be explored by DOT, perhaps in conjunction with the Antitrust Division of the Department of Justice and the Federal Trade Commission:

(1) The meaning of "any particular interline movement, unless such carrier can practically participate in such movement." The issue here is whether each new agreement should indicate how the determination will be made that a carrier can practically participate in an interline movement. Guidelines or standards could be set forth in each agreement or could be established by ICC rule.

(2) The ICC retains authority to approve agreements which allow, among other things, for joint consideration of "broad tariff changes if such changes are of general application or substantially general application throughout a territory or territories within which such changes are to be applicable." This provision presumably covers proposals to restructure rates, proposals to regroup points or rates, and similar actions. It is necessary, therefore, that the intent of the statutory language be explicitly covered in ICC rules or in the commission's approval of the new agreements.

(3) Section 5(b) provides that in any proceeding in which it is alleged that a carrier voted or agreed upon a rate in violation of the provisions of section 5(b), the burden of proof is on the party alleging such violation. At issue here is what procedures, reports, or other information should be available to the public to provide the evidence necessary for the ICC or any interested party to determine whether a violation has occurred.

The 4R Act is silent on the voting requirements and procedures used by rate bureaus in making decisions on general rate increases and similar matters. DOT could suggest additional guidelines on desirable quorums and voting and record-keeping requirements.

We believe this issue is of major significance. We anticipate that the analysis of the issues outlined above could be handled by TPI and

TGC with some discussions with shippers, the railroad industry, the Antitrust Division, and the FTC.

Analysis of Market Dominance. (Comments are due by April 22.) The following steps are required:

(1) Develop an economic analysis of monopoly, oligopoly, monopolistic competition, and perfect competition.

(2) Develop a legal analysis of market dominance which would include references to the concepts that are found in the law, especially regarding its relation to the concepts of monopolizing and monopoly.

(3) Develop a definition of market dominance in terms of the economic and legal analyses.

(4) Propose a set of criteria for determining when market dominance, as defined in (3) above, exists. In this connection:

• Secure evidence from rate cases and motor carrier entry cases and prepare an analysis in support of the definition and criteria derived.

• Collect tariff data on competitive motor rates.

The greatest requirement is in the area of data collection and analysis. Work is needed to: (1) collect published truckload rates for regulated motor carriers which are competitive with carload rates for railroads on the same commodity; (2) collect unregulated barge and truck rates that fluctuate around the corresponding rail rate in relevant markets; (3) secure evidence on the use of private trucking as an alternative to rail service; (4) secure data on operating and other costs of motor carriers in order to determine the potential cost of developing new private carrier service. We also require an economist to prepare a complete history of the concepts of monopolizing, market dominance, elasticity of substitution, cross-elasticity of demand, monopoly, oligopoly, monopolistic competition, and perfect competition.

Establishing Peak, Seasonal, and Regional Demand Rates. (Comments are due by May 27.) The purpose of this provision is to improve car utilization by providing incentives to shippers to reduce peak-period shipments, to increase off-peak demand, and to permit railroads to compete more effectively with unregulated carriers. DOT should, at the least, prepare a theoretical analysis which gives consideration to seasonal availability (supply) and seasonal demand for specific types of cars, by region and by commodity. A paper of this type can be prepared only by someone knowledgeable in the specialized areas of car supply, cost and utilization, regional demand characteristics, and the seasonal nature of commodity movements. If a substantial affirmative case is to be prepared by DOT in this proceeding, a consultant must be used to prepare the basic document. The Association of American Railroads (AAR) may be able to provide help with the statistical analysis.

Distinct Service Pricing Procedures. (Comments are due by June 7.) Two major issues under this heading are: (1) What particular features of a service classify it as separate or distinct? (2) What "special" services should be identified as such?

Unit-train service should not fall into this category. There are, however, a number of services performed by railroads that are not strictly transportation, and some of these services are included in rates for transporting the goods (for example, transit privileges for drying or storing grain or fabricating iron and steel articles). The new statutory language is designed to permit carriers to identify the cost of these special services and establish specific charges to cover them, thus aiding a shipper in determining the mode of transportation which best meets his needs.

Major DOT participation in this proceeding would require a review of all the services, other than carriage, performed by the railroads. This requires a highly specialized knowledge of railroad operations and would require extensive help from an outside consultant. Without such help, DOT can submit only a brief, theoretical paper and offer its views on proposals submitted by the ICC or the industry.

Revision of Per Diem Rules and Car Service Regulations. (No due date for comments has been announced.) Recognized issues regarding car management which can be considered in connection with this proceeding are:

- utilization and allocation of cars by the railroads;

- compensation for cars by the railroads, including incentive compensation;

- compensation by railroads to owners of private cars;

- adequacy of freight car ownership by railroads;

- tax and other financial aspects of railroad versus private ownership of freight cars;

- car service orders affecting immediate eligibility of ownership and use of freight cars.

Neither TPI nor FRA has the resources even to approach a major study of these issues in connection with this proceeding. FRA has, however, been participating in a Freight Car Utilization Research Demonstration Program with representatives of the railroads, industry suppliers, and labor.[1] One of the principal areas being studied is the impact of AAR and ICC rules, directives, and orders on car utilization. This study is several years from completion, but in this area, more even than in the other areas, concurrence of all these groups is necessary to develop workable rules.

In light of this, DOT is likely to play a minor role in this proceeding at this point. We would, however, point out to the ICC the relationship between freight car costs, individual company car ownership, and compensation to individual companies for off-line car use.

Definition of Significant Shipper Use. (Comments are due by May 3.) In this proceeding we are more likely to make responsive comments than to initiate a major statistical presentation. We would, for example, urge that the definition deal with the problems of potential use and the need for a floating or variable standard depending on the commodity (for example, "significant use" would have a different meaning for transportation of coal than for transportation of manufactured goods). We would not attempt a large-scale market or commodity analysis.

Next month, however, FRA will receive from its consultants a substantial study of seventy-one marginal branch lines in Iowa. This study will apparently address the question of use of those lines and apply a cost-benefit analysis to their abandonment. Depending on the quality of the study, we might want to ask that it be expanded in certain areas. If so, we can talk with the preparers of the study about its adaptability to this proceeding.

Establishing Standards for Determining Avoidable Costs of Providing Rail Services. (Comments are due by June 15.)[2] The DOT response to this proceeding should include the following efforts:

---

[1] The Federal Railroad Administration has invested more than $5 million of its research funds in this effort.
[2] The proposed ICC schedule has a conflict of dates regarding this proceeding or issue and the two following issues:

(1) The term *avoidable costs* should be defined, based on the concept of direct costs incurred for a specific line and not incurred if the line were not operated.

(2) An accounting system, which does not duplicate the regular accounting system of the firm, should be developed to indicate the costs of a particular line. Unless this is done, two or more accounting systems must be prescribed.

(3) The avoidable costs for a specific line will come from the subaccounts, including: wages of crew; maintenance of way, including rehabilitation thereof; maintenance of equipment which is dedicated or used on the line; taxes; and any other expense which would not be incurred if the line were not operated.

(4) Revenues attributed to the line should include local revenues collected in separate subaccounts *and* a proration of freight revenues allocated to the line on a miles-traveled-on-the-branch basis. For an abandonment, the revenues lost must be considered.

(5) Some comment should be made on off-branch costs, suggesting the use of the operating ratio and percent variable of the firm.

This submission can be assembled without outside help. We hope to establish a series of meetings with accounting firms and accountants at several major railroads in an effort to enlist their support at the commission.

Developing an Accounting System for Rail Branch Lines. (Comments are due by August 16.) DOT comments should deal with the following:

Item	Announcement Date	Response Date	Statutory Date
Avoidable costs	April 15, 1976	June 15, 1976	November 11, 1976
Branch-line accounts	June 3, 1976	August 16, 1976	November 1, 1976
Revised uniform system of accounts	June 30, 1976	September 30, 1976	June 30, 1977

Inasmuch as the first two items relate to and use the accounts of the uniform system, the order of the proceedings (and the statutory dates) appears to be in reverse order. If the dates are strictly adhered to because of the statutory deadlines, we may expect interim standards for avoidable costs and an interim accounting system for branch lines, unless the railroads are to be burdened with two accounting systems after the revision of the uniform system is implemented.

(1) The branch accounting system should be subaccounts of the uniform system, by line, showing the direct (nonallocated) expenses of operating the specific line.

(2) Does the proposed system incorporate the new revised accounts? If not, is the system an interim one until the revised system is operative?

(3) If allocations other than revenues are made to the branch, what basis is used and what is its validity?

This item can be completed without outside help.

Revised Uniform System of Accounts for Railroads. (Comments are due by September 30.) In September 1975, the ICC requested comments on a proposed revision of the chart of accounts which included: (1) natural expense accounts in a functional matrix; (2) elimination of mixed accounts; (3) a full-cost concept instead of emphasis on variable costs; (4) no branch-line or specific-line accounts; and (5) a financial orientation instead of a cost orientation. On June 30 we expect a complete chart of accounts with explanations, statements, and operating statistics. It is questionable whether any provision will be made for inflation accounting, change in right-of-way accounting (from betterment to depreciation), the introduction of standards costs, and a revision of the Annual Report Form R-1.

The 4R Act in section 307(b) is quite specific that the new accounting system identify direct and indirect cost accounts (for determining fixed-cost and variable-cost components) and costs and revenues of light-density lines as well as main lines. Thus, the DOT response to the commission should include the following considerations:

(1) Does the proposed system conform with section 307(b)?

(2) Will the system mesh with the existing responsibility accounting system?

(3) Does the proposal provide for adequate, but not excessive, disclosure of financial data? Disclosure of data by lines should *not* be routinely published.

(4) Is provision made for subaccounts, at least in the accounts identified as direct costs?

(5) Is the system proposed compatible with the branch-line accounting system proposed on June 3 by the Rail Services Planning Office of the ICC?

(6) Does the proposal provide for fixed and variable components for materials, labor, and overhead items of operating

expenses? If allocations are made, on what basis are they made?

We do not propose to include comments on betterment accounting versus depreciation accounting, nor upon inflation accounting at this time.

Preparation of this submission will not require outside help.

Establishment of Formulas for Determining Variable Costs. (No procedural dates for this proceeding have been announced.) A detailed analysis of the suggested DOT position in this proceeding is impossible to formulate at this time because of the alternative courses of action which are open to the ICC in this matter and the length of time some of the alternatives would require. Courses of action which the commission might take are:

(1) use of current Rail Form A;[3]
(2) revise Rail Form A, incorporating data from the revised uniform system of accounts; or
(3) categorize either existing or revised accounts into variable costs, fixed costs, and other (the "other" group of costs would be allocated to fixed and variable costs on a basis to be suggested).

Our best estimate is that the commission will pursue some variation of the third alternative. Under this alternative, a DOT response should consider the following items:

(1) Is the new revised accounting system used?
(2) What bases are used to categorize the accounts? (Direct expenses should be the only obvious variable expenses.)
(3) What statistical validation is used to support the categorization and the allocation bases?
(4) Where categorization appears incorrect, questions should be raised.

This submission can be prepared without the help of consultants.

Need for Consultants

A clear need exists for outside economic research on the issues of market dominance, distinct service pricing, and seasonal, regional,

---

[3] Rail Form A is the ICC form used to allocate the several rail expense accounts into fixed and variable costs.

and peak demand rates. Not coincidentally, these subjects are among our highest priority concerns. Further, the quality of FRA's forthcoming study of rail abandonments in Iowa will dictate whether we adapt it, with the aid of those preparing it, into a substantial filing on the project of significant shipper use.

Further suggestions on approaches to be taken in each of the ICC proceedings and decisions on the selection of consultants ought to be made promptly.

13

THE MEANING OF MARKET DOMINANCE

Norman H. Jones, Jr.

The Legislation and Its Intent

The Railroad Revitalization and Regulatory Reform Act of 1976 (4R Act) introduces new dimensions into transportation regulation. A basic goal of the legislation is to "foster competition among all carriers by railroad and other modes of transportation"[1] by providing new rate flexibility to the railroads. To this end, the legislation provides for the revision of the procedures and powers whereby the Interstate Commerce Commission reviews rates. The act provides a zone of rate freedom for a period of two years. According to this provision, the ICC is prevented from suspending rate increases or decreases of 7 percent a year. The act also limits the ICC's powers to find any proposed rate change too high or too low whether or not it is considered under the 7 percent rule. The railroads' new upward rate flexibility is to be restrained only where railroad behavior threatens "unfair," "destructive," or "predatory" conduct,[2] or where the proponent railroad has "market dominance," which is described only as the "absence of effective competition from other carriers or modes of transportation, for the traffic or movement to which the rate

This chapter is edited from a verified statement before the Interstate Commerce Commission by Norman H. Jones, Jr., an economic consultant, prepared on behalf of the U.S. Department of Transportation in connection with Interstate Commerce Commission, Ex Parte No. 320, *Special Procedures for Making Findings of Market Dominance as Required by the Railroad Revitalization and Regulatory Reform Act of 1976*, April 15, 1976.

[1] U.S. Congress, *Railroad Revitalization and Regulatory Reform Act of 1976: Report of the Committee of Conference on S. 2718*, H. Rept. 781, 94th Congress, 2d session, 1976, p. 4.

[2] Railroad Revitalization and Regulatory Reform Act of 1976, P.L. 94-210, 90 Stat. 31 (February 5, 1976), section 202(f); hereafter referred to as 4R Act.

applies."[3] Additionally, it was not the purpose of the legislation to modify sections 2, 3, or 4 of the Interstate Commerce Act which prohibit unfair or discriminatory rates.[4]

In the context of the 7 percent rule, carriers are accorded freedom to raise or lower rates within 7 percent of their levels on January 1 in 1976 and 1977 without fear of ICC suspension. Their freedom to set rates remains restricted, however, if the railroad proposing to change a rate has market dominance with respect to the traffic or movement covered by that rate.

After the expiration of the 7 percent rule, the concept of market dominance continues to play an important role in railroad rate making. Section 202(b) of the act, which has no expiration date, states:

> Notwithstanding any other provision of this part, no rate shall be found to be unjust or unreasonable, or not shown to be just and reasonable, on the ground that such rate exceeds a just or reasonable maximum for the service rendered or to be rendered, unless the Commission has first found that the proponent carrier has market dominance over such service.

To implement the provisions of the act dealing with market dominance, the Congress directed the ICC to "establish, by rule, standards and procedures for determining . . . whether and when a carrier possesses market dominance over a service."[5]

Market Dominance

The intent of the following discussion is to show that the railroad's erstwhile dominant position in most transportation markets has been severely eroded. There is virtually no remaining market in which a railroad does not now face intermodal competition or in which such competition would not be promptly forthcoming in response to a railroad rate increase. Some of this competition comes from wholly unregulated carriers able to enter and leave markets at will and able to raise and lower prices in a matter of minutes in response to a competitor's action. The data also show that a wide range of options are open to shippers and consignees faced with railroad rate increases and that these options (seeking new markets or plant locations, changing inventory practices, and so forth) have been taken in the past in response to railroad rate increases.

---

[3] Ibid., section 202(b).
[4] Ibid., section 202(f).
[5] Ibid., section 202(b).

This and other data draw one inescapably to the conclusion that, even when a railroad does have dominance in a given market, that dominance may be elusive. The transportation world is dynamic—dominance today does not imply dominance tomorrow. The data which support these assertions also support the contention that effective competition, not market dominance, is present in virtually every transportation market.

The Legislative Statement. As noted above, the act states that " 'market dominance' refers to the absence of effective competition from other carriers or modes of transportation, for the traffic or movement to which a rate applies."[6] The Congress was concerned that, in the absence of the discipline of effective competition, the rail carrier could charge rates that were unjust or unreasonable. The Congress felt that in such instances of market dominance it was necessary to preserve the commission's power to restrain the pricing behavior of the rail carrier. A finding of "market dominance," however, is not to "create a presumption that the [proposed] rate . . . exceed[s] a just and reasonable maximum."[7]

The concept of market dominance is developed only slightly in the House and Senate committee reports and in the report of the Committee of Conference. Although the conference committee initially considered the possibility of divorcing the concept of market dominance from the antitrust concept of "monopoly power," the committee eventually recognized the impracticality of this approach. The committee concluded that the definition of market dominance is to take into consideration the precedents of the antitrust laws but not be bound thereby.

A Description of Bargaining Position. Market dominance is essentially a description of the relative bargaining positions of parties to a (rate) negotiation. Market dominance may be cast in many terms and may encompass service as well as price. The assessment of bargaining position is conventionally expressed in terms of a firm's ability to influence price. A firm with no bargaining power is unable to affect the price through any real or threatened actions. This form of competition (that is, the "perfect competition" of economists) is seldom met in the real world. Firms are seldom completely devoid of bargaining power.

Clearly, market dominance applies alike to buyers and to sellers in a market. The buyers', as well as the sellers', bargaining position

---

[6] Ibid.
[7] Ibid.

in most negotiations will be shaped by the presence of alternative (substitute) opportunities. The range of alternatives facing buyers and sellers in a given market negotiation may be quite wide and will be determined in each instance by the time perspective of the firm and the relative costs (in the form of income foregone or expenses incurred) of adopting a given alternative. For a rail carrier, the alternative opportunities may be described as the cost of providing service and the impact on the carrier's income stemming from the responses of shippers to the carrier's pricing decisions. For the shipper/consignee, the range of choice can encompass:

(1) service from alternative rail carriers;
(2) service from common or contract carriers in other modes;
(3) service by unregulated carriage;
(4) changes in the firm's and in its customers' policies of inventory and shipment size;
(5) changes in the firm's markets;
(6) changes in the firm's products;
(7) changes in the firm's production location and production procedures.

The first three of these alternatives are popularly associated with the extent of competition in a transportation market. In the jargon of economists, these three alternatives shape the elasticity of demand for rail transportation. Presumably, they are the issues about which Congress was particularly concerned when it said that market dominance refers to an absence of effective competition.

The four remaining alternatives represent factors the firm can be expected to consider in response to price and service changes by the supplier (in this case, a railroad). These factors reflect what a firm might be willing to do in the face of greater or lesser changes in offerings of price or service by the railroad. Thus, they form a key subset of factors that determine the state of market competition as the Congress apparently envisioned it. Obviously, the richer the shipper's choices from this spectrum (that is, the lower the cost associated with each alternative), the stronger his bargaining position vis-à-vis the rail carrier.[8]

The situation which Congress sought to guard against is one in which the rail carrier enjoys a great discrepancy in its favor in its bargaining with shippers. Put very simply, this situation occurs when the shipper's (threatened) action cannot be implemented because of

---

[8] See, for example, the verified statement of R. S. Hamilton, Southern Railway Commission, in Interstate Commerce Commission, Ex Parte No. 267, *Increased Freight Rates*, 1971, pp. 2–3, 8.

the absence of "effective competition" to the rail carrier's service or because of the cost to the shipper of each of his possible alternatives.

The effect of existing or potential competition—from other rail carriers, from common and contract carriers in other modes, or from unregulated carriage—in limiting the rate freedom of a given rail carrier is well known and need not be belabored here. The effect of the other alternatives open to the shipper—changes in inventory/shipment policies, in markets served, in products offered, in production location and production procedures—and the effect of competition in the product market in limiting the rate freedom of a rail carrier, even one which enjoys an absence of carrier competition, is frequently less considered and less well understood. These considerations are central, however, to the way one defines the terms *market* and *traffic*. For that reason, the way these alternatives limit rail rate freedom needs to be explored more fully.

Nature and consequences of these alternatives. These interdependent choices of the carrier and the shipper/consignee are different from choices related purely to direct carrier competition. First, the decision of a shipper/consignee to adopt one of these alternatives is generally longer run in nature. That is, these alternatives take time to implement and they are generally very costly. It should be recognized, however, that such decisions are continually brought to the firm not just as a product of rate negotiations, but also as a result of changes in labor costs, taxes, and other input costs. Thus, the firm is continually reviewing its decisions about production location, product mix, production procedures, market, inventory, and shipment size. The impact of changes of this kind on rail traffic is rather more permanent than the impact of simply shifting traffic to another rail carrier or another mode since they lead to shifts in the demand for rail service in general.

Second, the importance of these alternatives in shaping the individual shipper's bargaining position vis-à-vis the rail carrier in any given negotiation will be a function of the shipper's (actual or potential) traffic importance to the rail carrier. This, of course, may not be (and frequently is not) reflected in the movement in question. Thus, in any given situation, large, multiplant firms will enjoy a rate bargaining position considerably stronger than small, single-plant firms. Indeed, rail carriers will argue that in many instances large, multiplant firms dominate rail rate bargaining, even though the rail carrier faces little or no direct competition for the specific movement in question.

Changes in inventory and/or shipment policies. The total-cost concept of business logistics has grown rapidly in recent years as inventory and other distribution costs have mounted. Even so, many firms still allocate traffic among transportation modes with incomplete logistical analysis, using last year's formula for this year's decisions. The basic repetitiveness of these allocative decisions is well documented by a study of the decision process of several large Pittsburgh firms.[9] As the cost-squeeze and the educational process continue, however, more comprehensive logistics planning will undoubtedly occur. Although the redesign of a firm's distribution system will probably not be all in one direction, shippers and consignees should be able to match their particular needs (for example, inventory and seasonal demand) with varying types of service priced according to the costs of each. However this redesign comes out, the need for redesign is surely accelerated by increases in rail rates, even for firms that formerly thought of themselves as "rail-bound."

Evidence of such shifts or diversions from rail carriage appears in testimony submitted to the ICC in connection with Ex Parte No. 313, *Increased Freight Rates and Charges—Labor Costs—1975*. One shipper, for example, stated:

> This trend [that is, decline in the rail traffic of a firm] is responsive to a basic change in the distribution system and to introduction of multi-product lines at its (the firm's) various plants, which, in turn was partially caused by the level of rail rates, the quality of rail service, and occasional rail equipment problems. In the final analysis, it has removed from the railroads long-haul, canned goods traffic by localizing production and distribution.[10]

Changes in markets served. Changes in freight rates affect the ability of a firm to compete in various markets. This may be illustrated in the following simple example: if the costs of production are the same for all producers competing in a market, the producer with the lowest transportation costs limits the price the other competitors can pay for transportation and still remain competitive in the product market. The lowest transportation costs are usually, but not always, paid by the shippers closest to the product market. If this is assumed to be the case, the price that can be charged for transportation from more distant sources of production will be limited by the ability of the distant producers to pay transportation costs and still compete in

---

[9] Merril J. Roberts et al., *Intermodal Freight Transportation Coordination: Problems and Potential*, prepared for the Office of the Undersecretary of Commerce for Transportation, 1966, Appendix 3-A.
[10] Verified Statement of James Hickcox, Canned Goods Shippers' Conference, Inc., in Interstate Commerce Commission, Ex Parte No. 313, *Increased Freight Rates and Charges—Labor Costs—1975*, p. 4.

the market. The more homogeneous the products competing in the market, and the more competitive the market for that product, the more effective this form of indirect competition is as a regulator of freight rates.

For example, a produce grower looking for a means of moving his product from Fresno, California, to Chicago, Illinois, can take advantage of the direct competition between two railroads and between hundreds of unregulated agricultural haulers by motor carriage to carry his produce. An astute producer is also aware of the competition *he* faces from produce growers in other parts of the country who also sell in the Chicago market. For instance, the lower the rate from other growing areas to Chicago, the lower the rate from Fresno to Chicago must be in order for the Fresno growers to be competitive enough to enter the Chicago market.

This "indirect competition" facing the rail carrier must be judged by the degree of competition for the product at its point of destination, and by the importance of transportation cost as a proportion of the total cost of selling the product in that market. The more effective the product competition in the Chicago produce market, for example, and the greater the proportion of the total cost accounted for by transportation, the more effective this indirect competitive force will be in holding down produce transportation rates to the Chicago market.

The issue is not just of academic importance. Rail carriers *are* concerned whether a rate increase will cause substitution of one commodity for another or a restriction in the extent to which a commodity can compete geographically. In this way the concept of geographical competition is central to the definition of market and, therefore, to the definition of market dominance. In statements to the commission, shippers have frequently noted the impact of rates on their ability to serve markets, on their consequent need for rail transportation, and, by implication, on the rate freedom of the rail carriers.[11]

Changes in production location and production procedures. In any firm, decisions about what products to produce, how to produce,

---

[11] See, for example, verified statements in Ex Parte No. 313 from National Industrial Sand Association, p. 2; the Southwestern Paper Traffic Conference, pp. 7–8; Radcliff Materials, Inc. & Oyster Shell Products, p. 9. See also verified statements in Interstate Commerce Commission, Ex Parte No. 314, Special Procedures for General Freight Rate Increases Based on Revenue Need, from the Pacific Northwest Grain and Grain Products Association, p. 3; Daniels Archer, Midland Co., pp. 3–4; National Industrial Sand Association, p. 4; Western Wood Products Association, p. 4; Southern Furniture Manufacturers Association, p. 4.

how much to produce, where to produce, and where to market are all closely related. In the economists' jargon these decisions are "highly interdependent." Making one of these decisions limits the choices on all the other decisions. Changing one such decision opens new alternatives for the other decisions. As was noted above, rates will affect the shippers' inventory policy and market choices. In similar fashion, rates will directly and indirectly have an impact on the decisions concerning the location of production facilities and the form of production.

Again, the issue is not just of academic importance. Rail carriers are keenly aware of the ways a shipper's decisions about location and production may limit a rail carrier's pricing freedom. The issue was well expressed by R. S. Hamilton of the Southern Railway System: "Will an increase affect plant locations, the location of warehouses, and other relevant production and distribution decisions? These are judgments which must be made in determining our pricing tactics in an attempt to control the total effect upon our revenues and traffic."[12]

Competition

Few markets in the U.S. economy fit the textbook ideal of a competitive market. Similarly, few markets in the U.S. economy conform to the textbook description of monopoly. Rather, most markets fall between these two poles on a continuum of markets; that is, they exhibit a greater or a lesser preponderance of the characteristics associated with a competitive market. The important distinction is between those markets where there is sufficient competition to rely on market forces to control and limit the behavior of an individual firm and those markets where there is not. Put another way, if a firm raises the price of the product or service it provides above a competitive level, how long will it take competitors to provide alternatives and how long will it take buyers to shift to those alternatives? In a market where there is "effective competition," the response of competitors and buyers will be prompt. In a market in which the firm has "market dominance," the response of competitors and buyers will be slow, if it occurs at all.

For market forces to control effectively the behavior of a firm, two things must occur. First, there must be alternative sources of the same product or service, or of products or services which are recognized as being close substitutes. Second, the buyers must be aware of the available alternatives and must have access to them. Under

---

[12] Filing of the Southern Railway System in Ex Parte No. 313, p. 8.

such circumstances, competition will restrain prices to a level that reflects the cost of efficient production plus a fair return on entrepreneurial activity and innovation, and that insures the continuation of adequate service.

The competition a rail carrier faces in a given market is not the product of the unfettered forces of the market. The certification process of the ICC limits entry of common and contract carriers into any given market no matter how attractive movements in that market may appear to firms outside it. Thus, a key test of market dominance is not whether competition presently exists in a given market, but whether, given freedom of entry, competition would enter the market and thus serve to limit the bargaining strength of an otherwise dominant rail carrier. If this "potential competition" is found to exist, then the ICC's most effective role would be to certificate competing carriers rather than to regulate the rate behavior of the dominant rail carrier.

The competition confronting railroads is not, however, limited to common or contract carriage. The importance of exempt carriage in selected markets is well known to the ICC. In similar fashion, private carriage has become an increasingly formidable competitor to rail in many markets. Evaluation of the extent of competition facing rail carriers and the effectiveness of that competition in controlling rail pricing behavior must take these sources of competition and their potential entry into account.

Competition in Rail Markets. Rail carriers no longer hold the dominant role they once enjoyed in the national transportation system. The extent of intermodal competition that produced this result is discussed below. Further, even in those instances where railroads currently enjoy a predominant or major share of a transportation market, this position is threatened. Common carriers in other modes and exempt and private carriage provide significant potential competition that shippers will turn to when such action is beneficial. Thus, rail market dominance cannot be considered the general rule in virtually any market.

The measure of competition. One commonly used measure of the extent of competition in a market is the extent to which individual suppliers of a commodity or a service are able to participate in the market. This participation is frequently cast in terms of the "market share" of one or more of those suppliers. The ICC has frequently used "share of traffic" as an indicator of the extent of competition in a market.[13]

---

[13] The ICC relied, in part, on such information in two relatively recent merger cases: Seaboard Air Line R.R. Co.—merger—Atlantic Coast Line, 320 I.C.C.

"Share of traffic" is, however, only a partial measure of the nature of competition in a market. It reflects, at best, the way that competition affected shippers' decisions in the past. It provides only limited information regarding the future. A reasonable presumption is that, where other carriers or modes have competed effectively enough to obtain a significant share of the traffic in a market in the past, other things being equal, they will be able to compete at least as effectively in the future. Similarly, a reasonable presumption is that, where other carriers or modes have been able to compete effectively enough to gain a significant share of the traffic of a commodity in one market, other things being equal, they will be able to compete effectively for the traffic of that commodity in other similar markets.

Almost as important as market share as evidence of the effectiveness of competition is the change in market share over time. This change provides some evidence of the dynamics of competition in the market.

Market shares in any regulated industry are not, of course, the product of the free working of the market. As already noted, the ICC's certification process limits the freedom of market entry of common and contract carriers. Thus, to some extent, market shares reflect past certification decisions and not the current, competitive realities of the market. Most especially, market shares may fail to reveal the extent of the *potential* competition that underlies a given market circumstance.[14] As suggested above, the fact that other modes have been able to gain a significant share of the traffic of a commodity in the market is prima facie evidence of the potential that had always existed for those modes to compete effectively, given freedom of entry. Obviously, where the costs of other modes are comparable to those of the carrier(s) already in the market, and where their participation in other traffic indicates a willingness to compete, it is reasonable to presume, in the absence of restraints on entry, that potential competition to the rail carrier is available. Presumably decisions of the ICC regarding entry are now and will continue to be based on determinations of the ICC about whether market dominance exists in the market to which entry is sought. Wherever the ICC determines that market dominance exists, it is incumbent upon the commission to certificate, even to encourage, new entry.

---

122 (1963), pp. 151–52; and Pennsylvania R.R. Co.—merger—New York Central R.R. Co., 327 I.C.C. 475 (1966), pp. 515–17.

[14] The importance to the rail carrier of potential competition is great. "Our field sales force strongly recommended against further increases, with reports of potential losses to trucks reaching as high as 50 percent of specific movement[s] in the shorter hauls." Filing of the Southern Railway System in Ex Parte No. 313, p. 14.

The extent of competition. In the late 19th century, railroads moved about 70 percent of the country's freight traffic.[15] Scarcely thirty years ago, railroads handled two-thirds of the nation's total traffic and received almost 70 percent of the intercity freight revenue of regulated freight carriers.[16] Today, the rail share of all intercity freight tonnage has declined to 30 percent, the rail share of all intercity ton-miles has fallen to 35 percent, and rails account for only 37 percent of the revenue of regulated freight carriers.[17] These facts, well known to the ICC, underscore the changed demand for transportation brought on by economic growth and technological development, and the changed competitive environment the rails face today.[18]

The ICC is also familiar with the nature of the intermodal competition the rails face for traffic of "exempt commodities." Thus, with respect to grain the commission stated:

> Such product appears to be particularly susceptible of diversion from the railroads because their transportation by motor carriers or when transported in bulk by water carriers is exempt from economic regulation by this Commission. Aided by technological advances in the vehicles and vessels they utilize and continuing improvements of the highways and waterways upon which they operate, the exempt truckers and barge lines have proved themselves to be forceful and *effective competitors* to the railroads in the transportation of grain and other agricultural commodities. (Emphasis added.)[19]

The ICC then went on to show that traffic from every significant grain-producing area of the country had been diverted from rail to other modes.[20]

The case of grain is not unique among the exempt commodities. Thus, in 1974 in the Chicago market, 40 percent of the broccoli unloaded arrived by motor carrier; 32 percent of the romaine lettuce unloaded arrived by motor carrier; and more than 40 percent of the potatoes arrived by motor carrier (see Table 13-1).

---

[15] Harold Barger, *The Transportation Industries, 1889–1946: A Study of Output, Employment and Production* (New York: National Bureau of Economic Research, 1951), Table B-1.
[16] Transportation Association of America, *Facts and Trends*, 9th ed. (Washington, D.C.), pp. 6, 9.
[17] Ibid., 11th ed., pp. 6, 8.
[18] Task Force on Railroad Productivity, *Improving Railroad Productivity*, final report to the National Commission on Productivity and the Council of Economic Advisers, November 1973, pp. 1–2.
[19] Interstate Commerce Commission, Ex Parte No. 270 (Sub-No. 9), Investigation of Railroad Freight Rate Structure—Grain.
[20] Ibid.

Table 13-1

PROPORTION OF SELECTED FRUIT AND VEGETABLE
UNLOADINGS CARRIED BY RAIL IN FIVE CITIES, 1974

(percent)

Commodity	Atlanta	Chicago	Cleveland	Dallas	St. Louis
Apples	10.6	14.5	19.3	1.8	10.5
Broccoli	0	60.0	61.8	0	3.4
Lettuce-romaine	9.5	68.7	42.9	0.9	55.2
Oranges	0.3	56.1	30.7	0.3	17.3
Potatoes	19.1	59.9	33.3	18.2	64.2

Source: U.S. Department of Agriculture, Agricultural Marketing Service, *Fresh Fruit and Vegetable Unloads*, 1975.

Among four eastern cities, the rail share of fruit and vegetable unloadings ranged from a high of 63 percent at New York to 30 percent at Baltimore in 1974. An examination of Table 13-2 shows that only in the case of lemons did the rails attain a market share of 70 percent or more in all four cities. In general, the material in Table 13-2 would indicate substantial intermodal competition for the transportation of fruits and vegetables to these destinations.

The evidence is equally striking in the case of manufactured goods. The original version of this paper includes exhibits which document the assertion that rail carriers face widespread intermodal competition.

Even though the dominant role of rail carriage in the nation's transportation system has eroded, there remains a general belief that railroads still dominate the longer haul, larger shipment market. There are many longer haul, larger shipment markets in which railroads have retained a significant portion of the traffic. Table 13-3 identifies those manufactured goods for which rail retains a 70 percent or greater share of the traffic moving in excess of 1,500 miles and weighing more than 90,000 pounds. In specific markets, however, rail carriers do face important competition from water carriers.

The competitive environment that rail carriers face is dynamic and changing. The importance of this is twofold. First, it means that, to be effective, rail pricing must be flexible so as to respond to competitive circumstances. Second, it means that rail carrier "market dominance" will frequently be a transitory thing.

An example of such transitory dominance is the rail share of the market in the transportation of aluminum foil. In 1971 rail carriers obtained 100 percent of the aluminum foil traffic of the Reynolds

Table 13-2

PROPORTION OF FRUIT AND VEGETABLE UNLOADINGS CARRIED BY RAIL IN FOUR EASTERN CITIES, 1974
(percent)

Commodity	Boston	New York	Philadelphia	Baltimore
Apples	21.4	34.1	32.8	24.0
Apricots	0	35.9	16.7	0
Asparagus	18.9	19.7	21.9	5.0
Beans	0.3	2.3	0.3	0
Blueberries	0	0	0	0
Broccoli	1.8	93.3	83.7	57.0
Cabbage	12.6	12.4	5.6	2.0
Cantaloupe	74.7	71.9	33.1	56.0
Carrots	77.9	84.9	73.9	62.0
Cauliflower	50.4	45.2	48.6	26.0
Celery	75.0	68.2	71.9	52.0
Cherries	52.5	57.8	37.7	39.0
Eggplant	3.0	97.0	5.9	0
Grapefruit	23.9	35.0	24.5	9.0
Grapes, table	63.8	83.0	57.3	58.0
Lemons	89.7	97.9	86.1	75.5
Lettuce and romaine	75.6	67.8	66.8	75.6
Onions, green	25.4	44.3	52.3	43.0
Oranges	75.5	64.2	52.3	29.3
Peaches	1.1	1.8	0.9	0
Pears	83.6	7.5	77.1	63.0
Peas, green	53.7	64.1	57.8	80.0
Plums and fresh prunes	78.4	86.0	65.9	51.6
Potatoes	34.2	49.1	24.7	24.5
Squash (all types)	1.7	0.3	0	0
Strawberries	45.7	51.0	27.0	24.5
Sweet potatoes	0	0.3	0	0
Tomatoes	22.3	33.7	12.4	9.4
Watermelons	8.1	47.5	18.0	1.4
Total	43.9	62.9	37.5	29.8

Source: U.S. Department of Agriculture, Agricultural Marketing Service, *Fresh Fruit and Vegetable Unloads*, 1975.

Metal Company from Louisville, Kentucky, to San Francisco, and 98 percent of the company's aluminum foil traffic from Louisville to Torrance, California. In 1974 the respective shares were 53 percent

Table 13-3

MANUFACTURED GOODS MOVING MORE THAN 1,500 MILES
AND IN SHIPMENT SIZES EXCEEDING 90,000 POUNDS
WHERE THE RAIL SHARE OF TRAFFIC EQUALS OR
EXCEEDS 70 PERCENT

(percent)

STCCª	Commodity Type	Rail Share
201	Meat: fresh, chilled, frozen	100.0
202	Dairy products	100.0
203	Canned and preserved fruits, vegetables, and seafood	98.0
204	Grain-mill products	100.0
206	Sugar beets and sugar cane	94.2
208	Beverages and flavoring extracts	94.5
209	Miscellaneous food preparations	96.2
222	Man-made fibers and silk broadwoven fabrics	100.0
243	Millwork, plywood, and prefabricated wood products	99.6
249	Miscellaneous wood products	95.1
254	Partitions, shelving, lockers, office and store fixtures	100.0
261	Pulp and pulp-mill products	99.0
262	Paper, except building paper	98.5
263	Paperboard, clipboard, and fiberboard	98.9
264	Converted paper and paperboard products	100.0
265	Containers and boxes, paperboard	100.0
281	Industrial inorganic and organic chemicals	94.6
282	Plastics materials	91.5
283	Drugs (biological and botanical products)	100.0
284	Soap and other detergents	100.0
287	Agricultural chemicals	98.5
289	Miscellaneous chemical products	100.0
299	Miscellaneous petroleum and coal products	90.2
307	Miscellaneous plastic products	100.0
322	Glass and glassware, pressed and blown	100.0
324	Hydraulic cement	100.0
325	Structural clay products	96.7
327	Concrete, gypsum, and plastic products	100.0
329	Abrasives and asbestos products	91.4
331	Steel works and rolling-mill products	94.2
332	Iron and steel castings	100.0
333	Nonferrous metal primary smelter products	99.3
335	Nonferrous metal basic shapes	96.5
336	Nonferrous metal castings	100.0

Table 13-3 (Continued)

STCC[a]	Commodity Type	Rail Share
341	Metal cans	93.5
343	Plumbing fixtures and heating apparatus	100.0
344	Fabricated structural metal products	97.6
346	Metal stampings	98.7
349	Miscellaneous fabricated metal products	100.0
351	Engines and turbines	100.0
352	Farm machinery and equipment	100.0
353	Construction and mining: materials handling machinery and equipment	99.1
359	Miscellaneous machinery and equipment	100.0
362	Electrical industrial apparatus	100.0
371	Motor vehicles and equipment	99.5
374	Railroad equipment	100.0
379	Miscellaneous transportation equipment	100.0
384	Surgical, medical, dental instruments and supplies	100.0
399	Miscellaneous manufactured products	100.0

[a] Standard Transportation Commodity Code.

Source: Appendix F of the original paper.

and 41 percent.[21] In the case of shipments of edible nuts, the rail share of traffic declined from 100 percent prior to 1967 to 95 percent in 1967, to 56 percent in 1974, and may be even lower today.[22] In 1971 Mattel, Inc., moved 85 percent of its traffic by rail and trailer-on-flatcar (TOFC). By 1974 the rail and TOFC share was down to 55 percent and was projected by Mattel to fall to 16 percent in 1975.[23] The Southwestern Paper Traffic Conference has estimated "that the railroad's share of total southwestern newsprint declined from 81 percent in 1965 to less than 52 percent in 1973."[24]

The Southern Hardwood Traffic Association showed that many member firms that had shipped a large part of their traffic by rail in 1974 had reduced that rail share markedly in 1975 in response to railroad price increases. For example, for a firm in Louisville, Kentucky, the rail share declined from 100 percent in 1974 to 26 percent in 1975; for a firm in Center, Texas, the rail share declined from 81 percent to 35 percent; for a firm in Greensboro, North Carolina,

[21] Filing of the Reynolds Metal Co. in Ex Parte No. 313, p. 12.
[22] Filing of Diamond Walnut Growers, Inc., in Ex Parte No. 313, p. 3.
[23] Filing of Mattel, Inc., in Ex Parte No. 313, p. 3.
[24] Filing of the Southwestern Paper Traffic Conference in Ex Parte No. 313, p. 2.

the rail share fell from 74 percent to 19 percent.[25] One point that is of special interest in these instances is that the largest part of the decline in the rail share was captured by private trucking.

The dynamic character of the competition facing rail carriers is shown in a more general fashion in Table 13-4, which shows the changes in the rail share of the transportation of manufactured goods from 1967 to 1972 by commodity type.

Potential Competition. With few exceptions, the preceding discussion has not distinguished between competition "in place" and "potential competition." In the case of potential competition, a rail carrier's pricing and service behavior is restrained, not by the direct threat of an existing competitor, but by the indirect threat that, should the rail carrier raise its rates, other carriers will find the traffic much more attractive than it had been and will compete for it, or that shippers will be dissatisfied with a rate increase and will make use of an alternative carrier or mode which had not seemed as attractive to them before.

The dynamic character of transportation competition is seen in the filings submitted in connection with Ex Parte No. 313 and Ex Parte No. 314, and in the general traffic statistics cited above. These filings and statistics show numerous instances where potential competition became a reality in response to rail rate action. Moreover, data about motor carrier rates and costs suggest that substantial competition would face most rail carriers should they raise their rates "too high." For example, in Table 13-5 rail rates are compared with estimates of truck costs for four commodities. This table shows that, if truck operators are able to minimize the empty backhaul, trucks will be competitive with rail carriers over a wide range of distances in these four commodities. Numerous examples of potential (and actual) motor carrier competition were cited by shippers in Ex Parte No. 313. Especially noteworthy was the large number of statements submitted in Ex Parte No. 313 by shippers which included comparative rate data. This data showed motor carriers were competitive over a wide range of commodity classes and movement characteristics.

Firms can also be expected to turn to private carriage in response to increases in rail rates, when that move is attractive. For example, the Aluminum Company of America (Alcoa) now maintains a private truck fleet at its Riverdale, Iowa, plant and has indicated that further increases in rail rates would lead to the expansion of that fleet.[26]

---

[25] Filing of the Southern Hardwood Traffic Association in Ex Parte No. 313, Exhibit A.

[26] Filing of the Aluminum Company of America in Ex Parte No. 313, p. 3.

Table 13-4

RAIL SHARE OF TRAFFIC OF MANUFACTURED GOODS BY COMMODITY, BY TONS, 1967 AND 1972

(percentage of total traffic)

STCC[a]	Commodity Type	1972	1967
201	Meat: fresh, chilled, frozen	18.7	27.4
202	Dairy products	19.4	30.1
203	Canned and preserved fruits, vegetables, and seafood	35.2	46.8
204	Grain-mill products	61.9	56.4
205	Bakery products	13.6	
206	Sugar beets and sugar cane	44.4	62.9
207	Confectionery and related products	13.0	25.4
208	Beverages and flavoring extracts	15.3	30.2
209	Miscellaneous food preparations	46.9	59.4
211	Cigarettes	51.3	53.0
212	Cigars	14.4	3.5
222	Man-made fibers and silk broadwoven fabrics	5.0	2.6
225	Knit fabrics	0.7	
227	Floor coverings	18.7	15.5
228	Thread and yarn	3.9	3.1
231	Men's, youths', and boys' clothing	2.7	3.0
233	Womens', children's, and infants' clothing	1.5	5.6
239	Miscellaneous fabricated textile products	27.2	16.2
242	Sawmill and planing-mill products	45.4	48.9
243	Millwork, plywood, and prefabricated wood products	50.2	71.6
249	Miscellaneous wood products	38.4	45.5
251	Household and office furniture	26.9	26.0
253	Public building and related furniture	38.7	40.2
254	Partitions, shelving, lockers, office and store fixtures	8.7	10.2
261	Pulp and pulp-mill products	78.0	88.1
262	Paper, except building paper	58.7	62.8
263	Paperboard, chipboard, and fiberboard	71.9	71.3
264	Converted paper and paperboard products, except containers	51.3	49.9
265	Containers and boxes, paperboard	7.2	16.0
281	Industrial inorganic and organic chemicals	45.3	54.3
282	Plastics materials	44.5	38.0
283	Drugs (biological and botanical products)	25.1	28.0
284	Soap and other detergents	21.1	24.0
285	Paints, enamels, lacquers, shellacs, and allied products	8.9	11.0
287	Agricultural chemicals	56.0	47.3

Table 13-4 (Continued)

STCC[a]	Commodity Type	1972	1967
289	Miscellaneous chemical products	30.1	33.7
291	Products of petroleum refining	8.3	4.2
295	Asphalt paving and roofing materials	20.8	23.5
299	Miscellaneous petroleum and coal products	70.1	58.2
301	Tires and inner tubes	40.9	45.0
306	Miscellaneous fabricated rubber products	11.9	10.0
307	Miscellaneous plastic products	16.8	11.9
311	Leather	4.6	2.5
314	Footwear, leather, and similar materials	1.4	5.1
316	Luggage, handbags, and other personal leather goods	2.4	9.5
321	Flat glass	26.5	46.8
322	Glass and glassware, pressed and blown	10.8	15.1
324	Hydraulic cement	15.1	32.4
325	Structural clay products	24.0	33.6
326	Pottery and related products	14.2	17.1
327	Concrete, gypsum, and plaster products	16.8	38.7
329	Abrasives and asbestos products	53.9	50.3
331	Steel works and rolling-mill products	43.7	52.1
332	Iron and steel castings	20.2	28.3
333	Nonferrous metal primary smelter products	67.2	71.5
335	Nonferrous metal basic shapes	35.4	30.8
336	Nonferrous metal castings	26.4	10.7
339	Miscellaneous primary metal products	35.8	33.7
341	Metal cans	18.9	20.9
342	Cutlery, hand tools, and general hardware	9.1	10.4
343	Plumbing fixtures and heating apparatus	16.8	19.4
344	Fabricated structural metal products	20.3	28.1
345	Bolts, nuts, screws, rivets, and washers	2.0	13.6
346	Metal stampings	53.4	31.7
348	Miscellaneous fabricated wire products	18.3	29.9
349	Miscellaneous fabricated metal products	18.2	26.9
351	Engines and turbines	21.5	22.4
352	Farm machinery and equipment	24.8	31.5
353	Construction and mining; materials handling machinery and equipment	34.3	43.5
354	Metalworking machinery and equipment	8.5	15.7
355	Special industry machinery	8.1	13.9
356	General industrial machinery and equipment	6.5	21.6
357	Office, computing and accounting machines	2.5	3.9
358	Refrigeration and service-industry machines	22.4	24.9
359	Miscellaneous machinery and parts	8.6	4.9
361	Electrical transmission equipment	15.3	22.8

Table 13-4 (Continued)

STCC[a]	Commodity Type	1972	1967
362	Electrical industrial apparatus	21.6	13.1
363	Household appliances	58.3	64.9
364	Electric lighting and wiring equipment	18.7	21.4
365	Radio and television receiving sets	18.7	21.4
366	Communication equipment	10.1	34.5
367	Electrical components and accessories	8.3	16.6
369	Miscellaneous electrical machinery, equipment, and supplies	9.3	6.7
371	Motor vehicles and equipment	57.3	55.3
374	Railroad equipment	79.9	83.9
379	Miscellaneous transportation equipment	5.5	5.6
381	Engineering, scientific, and laboratory instruments	1.1	14.6
382	Measuring and controlling instruments	7.4	4.2
384	Surgical, medical, dental instruments and supplies	17.3	10.8
387	Watches, clocks, clockwork-operated devices and parts	9.8	4.1
394	Toys, amusements, sporting and athletic goods	24.6	34.6
399	Miscellaneous manufactured products	24.9	9.9

[a] Standard Transportation Commodity Code.

Airco, Inc., is another firm that turned to private motor carriage in response to increased rail rates.[27] As has already been noted, many members of the Southern Hardwood Traffic Association turned to or expanded their use of private motor carriage between 1974 and 1975 in response to increases in rail rates.[28]

The possibility of competition from water carriers is also important to consider in this context. The potential of water carriers to compete for traffic subjected to increases in rail rates is vividly illustrated by the growth of waterway traffic in paper products. Tonnage of paper products in the Mississippi River System has expanded from 119,000 tons in 1960 to more than 750,000 tons in 1974.[29] A portion of this growth is explained by growth in the production of paper

---

[27] Filing of Airco, Inc., in Ex Parte No. 313.

[28] Filing of the Southern Hardwood Traffic Association in Ex Parte No. 313, Exhibit A.

[29] U.S. Department of the Army, Corps of Engineers, *Waterborne Commerce of the United States*, 1960 and 1974 editions, part 2.

Table 13-5

COMPARISON OF RAIL RATES WITH TRUCK COSTS FOR FOUR COMMODITIES
(cents per ton-mile)

Grain

Distance (miles)	Rail Rates	Truck Costs with Empty Backhaul:	
		25 percent	75 percent
200–400	3.2–3.5	2.4	3.4
400–1,200	2.5–2.7		

Coal

Distance (miles)	Rail Rates	Truck Costs with Empty Backhaul: 100 percent
200–300	2.2–2.9	4.0
500–600	1.6–1.8	

Canned Goods

Distance (miles)	Rail Rates	Truck Costs with Empty Backhaul:	
		0 percent	50 percent
200–300	4.0–4.4	2.2	3.3
500–700	3.2–3.5		
1,100–1,500	2.6–2.7		

Steel

Distance (miles)	Rail Rates	Truck Costs with Empty Backhaul:	
		25 percent	75 percent
175–225	4.4–5.5	2.9	4.1
400–550	2.9–4.9		
900–1,050	2.8–3.1		

Source: Association of American Railroads, Staff Studies Group, "Truck-Rail Competition and the Effect of Increased Truck Weights," Staff Memorandum 74-9, June 21, 1974.

products, but an important part is explained by the response of shippers to increased rail rates.

The effectiveness of potential competition, other than private carriage, depends on two factors: first, the ability of firms to enter markets to compete; second, the awareness of shippers of the alternatives that may (can) come into the market. At present, the barriers to market entry are sufficiently high and sufficiently time-consuming and costly that potential competing carriers cannot move freely to markets that may otherwise appear very attractive. The penalty of this barrier to entry does not fall on the large firm, since a large firm can make effective use of private carriage and since its traffic is sufficiently rewarding to warrant competing carriers incurring the costs of entry. Rather, the penalty falls on the small firm, since a small firm cannot make efficient use of private carriage because of the occasional nature of its shipments and since its traffic is not sufficiently attractive that carriers would bear the cost of entry to capture it. It is the responsibility of the ICC to assure that such uneven burdens are not borne by small shippers. Where the ICC determines that rail rates are going up over a period of years in markets where there are many small shippers, and few if any of those shippers find other means of transporting their goods, it is a fair presumption that freer entry of motor carriers should be allowed. The ICC has received, in Ex Parte No. 313 and Ex Parte No. 314, ample evidence that shippers do shift their traffic when alternatives are available.

Conclusions

The facts cited above demonstrate clearly that rail carriers no longer enjoy the dominant role they once played in the national transportation system, and that intermodal competition pervades the transportation markets in which railroads participate. It is clear that exceptions to the competitive norm are less a consequence of technological or cost considerations than they are the result of past regulatory decisions by the ICC regarding the entry of new firms into transportation markets.

The facts cited above also demonstrate that, even in those instances where railroads enjoy a large share of a transportation market, they can no longer be complacent in the assurance that competition will not appear and erode their position. Potential competition from common carriers in other modes and from unregulated carriage faces the railroads in all markets. The facts cited above show clearly that shippers and consignees will turn to these alternatives when it is in their interests. As a consequence, rail market dominance can be considered the exception rather than the rule in virtually every market.

14

ANALYSIS OF THE ICC'S FINDINGS ON MARKET DOMINANCE

U.S. Department of Justice

In 1976 Congress enacted legislation which provided that a railroad's rates may not be set aside as unreasonably high unless the railroad exercises "market dominance." Congress directed the Interstate Commerce Commission to adopt standards and procedures for determining whether and when market dominance exists. The commission adopted regulations regarding market dominance and some of these regulations have been called into question.

The Statutory Scheme

The Railroad Revitalization and Regulatory Reform Act of 1976 (4R Act) declares it to be the policy of Congress to "foster competition among all carriers by railroad and other modes of transportation" and to "permit railroads greater freedom to raise or lower rates for rail services in competitive markets."[1] To implement that policy, Congress amended the Interstate Commerce Act so as to limit substantially the authority of the ICC to find that rail rates are "unjust and unreasonable."[2] Section 202 of the 4R Act provides that the ICC may not declare a rail rate to be unreasonably low if the rate contributes to the "going-concern value" of the carrier. And, as per-

---

This chapter is edited from a brief presented by the U.S. Department of Justice in the U.S. Court of Appeals for the District of Columbia Circuit, in Atchison, Topeka & Santa Fe Railway Co. v. Interstate Commerce Commission and Commonwealth Edison Co. v. Interstate Commerce Commission, "On Petitions for Review of Orders of the Interstate Commerce Commission," Nos. 76-2048 and 76-2070, April 4, 1977.

[1] Railroad Revitalization and Regulatory Reform Act of 1976, P.L. 94-210, 90 Stat. 31 (February 5, 1976), section 101(b) (2)–(3); hereafter cited as 4R Act.
[2] Interstate Commerce Act, 49 U.S.C., section 1 and following.

225

tinent here, section 202 provides that the commission may find that a rail rate "exceeds a just or reasonable maximum" only if the commission first finds that the railroad exercises "market dominance" over the service to which the rate applies. Market dominance is defined as "an absence of effective competition from other carriers or modes of transportation, for the traffic or movement to which a rate applies."[3] If the commission finds that a railroad has market dominance in a particular case, the agency has authority to determine whether the rate that is involved is unreasonably high. In all other cases, the railroads are free to set nondiscriminatory rates at whatever levels are dictated by sound management and the forces of competition. This fundamental change in the law was "intended to inaugurate a new era of competitive pricing" in the field of transportation.[4]

The rationale of Congress in permitting greater rate flexibility for railroads is clear from the legislative history of the 4R Act. First, Congress recognized that the structure of the transportation industry in the United States had changed dramatically since passage of the Interstate Commerce Act in 1887, and that many railroads now face vigorous competition either from other railroads or from other modes of transportation:

> Railroads were the first large business to be regulated by the Federal Government. The regulation was called for by the industry's dominance of the market and its ability to price some services monopolistically while engaging in predatory competitive practices in other markets. These problems exist today but in a very different transportation environment. . . .
>
> In 1887, a single railroad often provided the only transportation available to shippers. Growth of other modes in the past century has raised [the] question whether protection against rail monopoly is any longer necessary in many markets.[5]

Second, Congress recognized that the rate rigidity imposed on the railroads in the past by the Interstate Commerce Act had undermined the financial viability of the railroads by preventing them from

---

[3] 4R Act, section 202(b).
[4] U.S. Congress, *Railroad Revitalization and Regulatory Reform Act of 1976: Report of the Committee of Conference on S. 2718*, H. Rept. 781, 94th Congress, 2d session, 1976, p. 148.
[5] U.S. Congress, Senate, S. Rept. 499, 94th Congress, 1st session, 1975, pp. 10–11: "In [1947] the railroads carried nearly two-thirds of the intercity freight; by 1973 that share had dropped to 39%. During the same period, when the gross national product grew approximately 179% . . . and while industrial production grew 219%, total U.S. rail revenue ton-miles grew only 30%, while ton-miles carried in the eastern district actually declined 17%."

successfully competing with other modes which are subject to significantly less regulation.[6] Thus, Congress determined that,

> if railroads are to increase their revenues and attract the resources necessary to revitalize the industry, they must be able to raise their rates in a timely fashion free from regulation in markets sufficiently competitive to prevent abuses of monopoly power.[7]

In short, the new market dominance provision is based on Congress' judgment that railroads today generally face substantial competition and that maximum rate regulation is no longer either necessary or desirable where effective competition exists.

To implement the market dominance provision, the ICC was directed to establish rules "designed to provide for a practical determination without administrative delay" and to "solicit and consider the recommendations of the Attorney General and of the Federal Trade Commission in the course of establishing such rules."[8] In entrusting the ICC with responsibility for formulating rules about market dominance, Congress expressly cautioned the agency against frustrating the underlying purpose of the market dominance provision by adopting "a too narrow or protectionist attitude or by [a] desire to retain jurisdiction over competitive markets."[9]

Proceedings before the Commission

On March 10, 1976, the ICC issued a notice setting forth proposed market dominance rules which reflected the very "narrow [and] protectionist attitude" that Congress had warned against. The ICC's proposed rules provided that a presumption of market dominance would arise in the following seven situations, or fact patterns:

(1) Where the rate in issue has been discussed or considered in proceedings before a rail carrier rate bureau acting under an agreement filed and approved by the commission pursuant to section 5(b), or the former section 5(a), of the Interstate Commerce Act;

---

[6] See ibid., p. 11: "More than half of all truck shipments are by unregulated carriers. Water carriers are for the most part unregulated. Pipeline regulation has been minimal."

[7] Ibid.

[8] 4R Act, section 202(b).

[9] U.S. Congress, House, Committee on Interstate and Foreign Commerce, H. Rept. 725, 94th Congress, 1st session, 1975, p. 70.

(2) Where no other carrier of any mode has handled a significant amount of the involved traffic for at least one year preceding the filing of the proposed rates;

(3) Where other carriers of any mode have handled a significant amount of traffic but there is no evidence of actual price competition in the past three years;

(4) Where the rate in issue exceeds the rate(s) charged by other carriers offering the same or interchangeable service between the involved points by 25 percent or more;

(5) Where the rate in issue exceeds the fully allocated cost of providing the service by 50 percent or more;

(6) Where the distance between the origin and destination exceeds 1,500 miles, except that when the involved movement occurs as a single-line movement, market dominance may be presumed where the distance exceeds 1,200 miles, providing, however, in either instance that when a rate is subject to a minimum weight, such minimum weight shall equal or exceed twenty net tons;

(7) Where the commodity moving under the rate in issue customarily moves in bulk shipments.

No presumptions were formulated for identifying those cases in which market dominance does *not* exist.

The proposed rules were generally supported by the shipper interests, but they were severely criticized by the railroads and the participating governmental parties. The critical comments alleged that the proposed presumptions either were inconsistent with Congress' recognition of intermodal competition, or were analytically faulty, or were unsupported by evidence in the record. In addition to pointing out the unsoundness of the ICC's proposals, the railroads and the government parties also suggested that, in order to comply with its statutory mandate, the ICC should seek to identify those cases in which market dominance is not likely to exist, as well as those cases in which it may be presumed to exist. Since all parties generally agreed that "market share" would be the most reliable indicator of market power, the railroads, the Department of Justice (DOJ) and the Department of Transportation (DOT) all urged the ICC to adopt a counterpresumption that effective competition exists when the market share of the proponent railroad(s) is insubstantial.

On August 23, 1976, the ICC issued an interim report which scrapped four of the original seven presumptions, modified the other three, and added one altogether new presumption. Although in certain respects the interim version of the rules represented a substantial improvement, serious deficiencies remained. First, although the ICC made its presumption based on market share more concrete by providing that market dominance would be presumed when the proponent railroad(s) controlled 70 percent of the "involved traffic," the agency defined the relevant market so as to preclude consideration, even on rebuttal, of traffic moving on alternative routes ("geographic competition") as well as movements of commodities readily substitutable for the commodity to which the rate at issue applies ("product competition"). The ICC flatly refused to consider these types of competition despite its own admission that they "could have an impact upon the ability of rail carriers to raise their rates." Second, the ICC lowered the rate/cost ratio at which its presumption of excess profits was triggered to 180 percent of variable costs without offering any explanation of how it derived that figure or why it would be a valid indicator of market dominance. Third, the commission adopted a new presumption of market dominance based on "substantial" investment by a shipper in rail-related equipment, but failed to reconcile that presumption with a capital investment provision adopted by Congress; moreover, the commission cast the presumption in terms so vague as to provide virtually no indication of what types of investments should be considered "substantial." Finally, the ICC failed to adopt any counterpresumptions of effective competition and, in fact, failed even to respond to the arguments in favor of such a presumption advanced by the railroads, DOJ, and DOT.

Further comments were received and on October 1, 1976, the ICC issued a final report which formally adopted market dominance rules.[10] Under the rules as adopted, a presumption of rail market dominance arises in the following three situations:

(1) Where the proponent carrier has handled 70 percent or more of the involved traffic or movement during the preceding year (the "market share presumption").[11]

(2) Where the rate in issue exceeds the variable costs of providing the service by 60 percent or more (the "variable costs presumption").

(3) Where affected shippers or consignees have made a substantial investment in rail-related equipment or facilities which prevents or makes impractical the use of another carrier or mode (the "equipment investment presumption").

---

[10] The rules are codified at 49 C.F.R., part 1109.
[11] The market share of the proponent carrier will be deemed to include the share of any affiliates and of any carrier participating in the rate or with whom the proponent carrier has discussed, considered, or approved the rate in issue.

With respect to the market share presumption, the final report reflects a continued refusal by the ICC to allow any consideration whatever of geographic and product competition. With respect to the variable costs presumption, the ICC further reduced the rate/cost "trigger" to 160 percent of variable costs—again without articulating a rational basis for adopting that figure. The equipment investment presumption remained unchanged, as the ICC failed to supply any concrete test for determining when an investment is substantial. Finally, the commission again failed to respond to the contentions of the railroads and the government parties that a counterpresumption of lack of market dominance based on insubstantial market share should be adopted.

Summary of Argument

The market dominance rules are the product of a legislative-type proceeding in the conduct of which the ICC admittedly exercised broad discretion. In at least four critical respects, the ICC's decision regarding these rules is so completely at odds with the available evidence and the commission's own findings as to be arbitrary and capricious, so lacking in reasoned explanation as to hinder seriously meaningful review, or so unnecessarily vague as to undermine the intent of Congress that railroads be free to adjust their rates without extensive litigation where effective competition exists.

While the difficulties inherent in consideration of geographic and product competition justified the ICC's decision not to consider those factors as part of the market share presumption, those difficulties provide no rational justification for prohibiting consideration of geographic and product competition even on rebuttal. Although alternative routes and products do not always provide effective competition, their impact undisputedly is sufficient to require that they be considered at least on rebuttal. The ICC's total exclusion of geographic and product competition renders the market share presumption analytically unsound.

The ICC's failure even to consider the merits of a counterpresumption of effective competition based on insubstantial market share violates the established duty of an agency engaged in rule making to address all significant proposals submitted to it. The obligation to respond is more pronounced where, as is the case here, the proposal is repeatedly advanced by other government agencies and would further the purposes of the underlying legislation.

It was arbitrary and capricious for the ICC to adopt a presumption based upon variable costs when the present ICC accounting system for railroads admittedly does not provide reliable cost data and is in the process of being revised. Moreover, the ICC failed to explain adequately its decision to set that presumption at 160 percent of variable costs.

Finally, the ICC's equipment investment presumption, which would consider future investments in excess of $1 million, encroaches upon an area preempted by Congress in enacting section 206 of the 4R Act. In any event, the ICC's equipment investment presumption is so vague as to be arbitrary and capricious. It fails to provide intelligible standards for determining when an investment may be deemed "substantial," and it fails to exclude investments which are readily marketable.

Taken as a whole, the ICC's market dominance rules will promote extensive litigation, will trigger a presumption of rail market dominance with respect to most rates likely to be disputed, and will afford the railroads virtually no greater rate flexibility than they enjoyed in the past—all in contradiction of the express intent of Congress in enacting the 4R Act.

Geographic and Product Competition. The ICC's market share presumption is invalid insofar as it precludes consideration, even on rebuttal, of geographic and product competition.

The commission's rules create a rebuttable presumption of market dominance where the proponent railroad has handled "70 percent or more of the involved traffic or movement during the preceding year." For purposes of this presumption, the proponent railroad's market share is deemed to include the share of any affiliates and of any other carriers participating in the rate or with whom the proponent carrier discussed approval of the rate.

Market share is, of course, the starting point for a traditional antitrust inquiry into suspected monopolization.[12] Monopoly power is imputed to a seller who has a statistically predominant share of the market.[13] Although Congress did not require the ICC "to strictly conform with the standards of the antitrust laws" in implementing the market dominance provision, it did intend that the commission "recognize the absence of forces which normally govern competitive markets."[14] In addition, Congress directed the ICC to "solicit and consider" the views of the Department of Justice and the Federal

---

[12] See United States v. Aluminum Company of America, 148 F.2d 416 (2d Cir. 1945).

[13] See United States v. Grinnell Corp., 384 U.S. 563 (1966).

[14] U.S. Congress, H. Rept. 781, p. 148.

Trade Commission (FTC) in view of their familiarity with competitive markets.[15] In relying on market share analysis as a test for market dominance, the ICC adopted a methodology widely used in antitrust analysis.

All parties before the commission agreed that market share is a valid indicator of market power. In addition, there was general agreement that a carrier controlling 70 percent of the relevant market could be presumed to exercise market dominance.[16] The disagreement with respect to the market share presumption centered around the proper definition of the market against which the proponent railroad's share was to be measured.

Section 202 defines market dominance as "an absence of effective competition from other carriers or modes of transportation, for the traffic or movement to which a rate applies." Thus, it was clear that, for purposes of an analysis of market share, the relevant market must include, at a minimum, all movements by railroad or other modes of transportation of the product(s) covered by the rate in issue between the points covered by that rate. For example, a competing railroad transporting the subject commodity between the involved points would presumably compete for the proponent railroad's share of the market. Likewise, movements of the subject commodity between the involved points by motor and water carriers would also constitute a portion of the relevant market, since those carriers would presumably compete for the proponent railroad's traffic.

The railroads and the governmental parties contended, however, that the analysis of market share should take into account four additional types of competition: (1) potential competition; (2) private competition; (3) geographic competition; and (4) product competition. The ICC's final decision provides that evidence of potential and private competition will not be considered as part of the market share presumption, but such evidence may be introduced to rebut a presumption of market dominance based on market share. The ICC ruled, however, that evidence of geographic and product competition may not be considered even on rebuttal.

---

[15] 4R Act, section 202(b).
[16] In their response to the rules proposed by the ICC on March 10, 1976, the railroads argued that a presumption of market dominance should not arise unless the proponent carrier controlled 80 percent of the market. However, the railroads have abandoned any objection to the ICC's selection of 70 percent as the proper standard. In a brief filed before the U.S. Court of Appeals for the District of Columbia Circuit as amicus curiae ("friend of the court"), the Federal Trade Commission argues that no presumptions should have been adopted but, assuming that presumtions are appropriate, does not quarrel with the ICC's choice of 70 percent.

The railroads' petitioners argue that the commission erred in its treatment of all four types of competition because it did not provide for them to be considered as part of the initial determination of whether a sufficiently high market share exists to engender a presumption of market dominance. For the reasons set forth below, we believe that the commission acted within its discretion in adopting a market share rule which leaves the rebuttal evidence of potential and private competition. We further believe that a rule which allows consideration of geographic and product competition only on rebuttal would be supported by a rational basis. However, the ICC's refusal to allow consideration of geographic and product competition *even* on rebuttal constitutes arbitrary and capricious action in that it renders unsound an otherwise valid analytical tool for determining whether market dominance exists.

Potential competition. Potential competition exists where carriers, or would-be carriers, are prepared to enter the market. The threat of entry by such potential competitors serves as a check on the level of rates charged by existing competitors and, in certain circumstances, may constitute a form of "effective competition" for railroad traffic within the meaning of the 4R Act. The commission recognized this when it stated in its interim report: "We do not wish to preclude carriers from presenting evidence of potential competition to rebut the presumption of market dominance under the market share test." The commission went on to indicate that general allegations of potential competition would not suffice to rebut a presumption of market dominance and that concrete evidence establishing the preparedness of potential competitors to enter the market would have to be presented.

The railroads argue that the commission erred in restricting consideration of potential competition to rebuttal, but we find it difficult to envision how potential competition could otherwise be considered under a rule based on market share. Since, by definition, a potential competitor controls no present share of the market, tonnage figures reflecting the traffic of a potential competitor could not be added to the market share calculation. Thus, the only practical role for evidence of potential competition is to establish, on rebuttal, that the market shares of existing competitors do not present an accurate picture of the level of competition. Indeed, this is the traditional role for evidence of potential competition when market share analysis is employed under the antitrust laws.[17]

---

[17] See United States v. Citizens & Southern National Bank, 422 U.S. 86, 120 (1975).

Moreover, the decision to consider potential competition only on rebuttal represents a reasonable method of streamlining the administrative proceedings. Since potential competition would not become relevant unless a 70 percent market share is possessed, there is no need for the ICC to consider evidence of potential competition until the relevance of such evidence is demonstrated.

The ICC indicated that it would consider evidence of potential competition on rebuttal, and we believe its treatment of the issue has a rational basis. If in some particular case the commission should refuse to consider, or should accord insufficient weight to, evidence of potential competition, a reviewing court could correct the error.[18]

Private competition. Under the Interstate Commerce Act, any shipper may transport its own freight in interstate commerce without obtaining a certificate or permit from the ICC.[19] Evidence introduced before the ICC established that many shippers transport significant amounts of their own traffic by means of privately owned trucks and barges, and that the ability of shippers to divert traffic from regulated carriers to their own trucks and barges constitutes a form of effective competition which constrains the ability of railroads to raise their rates. While noting that private carriage is a viable alternative only for shippers that are large and diverse enough to be able to afford it, the commission properly recognized that in certain circumstances competition from private carriage may constitute effective competition within the meaning of the 4R Act. Accordingly, the commission

---

[18] DOJ and DOT expressed concern before the commission that a "market dominant" position might be attributed to a railroad through no fault of the railroad where the ICC elected to limit competition by administering the entry-control provisions of the Interstate Commerce Act in an overly restrictive fashion. Accordingly, both DOJ and DOT recommended that the ICC's market share rule explicitly state that a presumption of market dominance is overcome upon demonstration that other carriers would enter the market but for the lack of commission certification. The commission responded that it is required by law to certificate motor carriers according to a standard of public convenience and necessity and rejected as "totally without merit" the suggestion that it consider competition from carriers who would enter the market but for regulation. We view the commission's response as rejecting the suggestion that its denial of a motor carrier application as not required by the public convenience and necessity should *automatically* establish that the railroad faces effective competition and, so construed, we do not challenge it here. However, where the commission denies the application of a prospective carrier on the ground that the market is already characterized by an adequate level of competition, we would expect the commission to give substantial weight to that finding in a subsequent market dominance proceeding involving the same market.

[19] A certificate is required only when transportation is undertaken "for compensation." 49 U.S.C., sections 303(14) and (15), 902(d) and (e).

stated that it would consider evidence of private competition in rebuttal of a presumption of market dominance based on market share.

The railroads contend that the ICC's refusal to consider private competition as part of the initial inquiry under the presumption rather than as rebuttal constitutes reversible error. We believe, however, that the ICC articulated a rational basis for its decision to relegate evidence of private competition to rebuttal.

First, assuming that private competition could at times have a significant impact even though no shipper presently moves any portion of its own traffic, such private competition could not rationally be considered as part of a market share presumption for the same reason the potential competition generally may not be so considered—it accounts for no present share of the market. Instead, evidence that the involved shippers have the present capacity to enter the market should properly be used to rebut a prima facie case of market dominance based on the market shares of existing competitors.

Second, to the extent that shippers subject to the proposed rate increase now transport a percentage of their own traffic, there are additional reasons for not including such private traffic in the market for purposes of the market share presumption. As the commission noted in both its interim and its final reports, the competition generated by a shipper that has a "share" of the market is different from that generated by a common carrier. Whereas the common carrier presumably competes for the entire market, each shipper competes (if at all) only for that portion of its own traffic that it is not now moving. Moreover, the effectiveness of competition from private carriage may vary from shipper to shipper, depending upon each shipper's size and resources. For these reasons, routine inclusion in the market share computation of a shipper's "share" of its own traffic would unduly complicate the presumption and could result in a distorted picture of the market's structure.[20]

---

[20] For example, assume that we are including the traffic moving in private carriage in the market share computation and that the railroad controls 60 percent of the market, of which 10 percent is traffic of shipper X. Assume also that shipper X controls the remaining 40 percent of the market (its own traffic) and that no other shipper moves any of its own traffic. Since the railroad controls only 60 percent of the market, it would not be presumed to have market dominance. However, shipper X can compete only for the remainder of its own traffic, or an additional 10 percent of the market. Shipper X cannot actively compete for the remaining 50 percent of the market, and the other shippers may not have the resources to resort to private carriage. Moreover, the prospect of losing the remaining 10 percent of shipper X's traffic may not prevent the railroad from taking an excessive increase on the remaining 50 percent of the market.

Of course, although a shipper may not compete for the general public's traffic, each shipper may nevertheless compete for the balance of its own traffic. Considered collectively, such private competition could on occasions preclude a finding that the railroad has market dominance. In addition, since railroads are generally required to charge the same rate to all shippers within a particular market,[21] the threat that even one substantial shipper would turn to private carriage could at times constitute the kind of "effective competition" that eliminates the need for regulation of maximum rates by the ICC. However, the commission has promised that it will consider this type of evidence in rebuttal of a presumption of market dominance based on market share, and this represents a rational approach to the issue of private competition.

Geographic and product competition. Unfortunately, the ICC did not follow the same rational approach in its treatment of geographic and product competition. Instead, the agency ruled that neither type of competition would be considered, even on rebuttal.[22]

A railroad faces geographic competition when a shipper-consignor may direct its product to a different destination or a shipper-consignee may secure the same product from a different origin. For example, a shipper receiving coal by rail from point A might also be able to secure coal from points B and C via different railroads or different modes of transportation. A railroad faces product competition when a shipper may substitute another product for the product subject to the rate in issue. Thus, if the rates on coal are increased, a shipper might be able to substitute alternative fuels with a minimum of expense and difficulty. A combination of geographic and product competition might be present in a particular case, as where substitutable products could be obtained from alternative origins.

The ICC's refusal to allow consideration of geographic and product competition even on rebuttal was not based upon a belief that such competition could not act as a constraint on the ability of a railroad to raise its rates, for the agency expressly acknowledged

---

[21] Section 2 of the Interstate Commerce Act makes it unlawful for a railroad to charge different rates to different shippers when providing them "a like and contemporaneous service in the transportation of a like kind of traffic under substantially similar circumstances and conditions."

[22] The market share rule as adopted contains no explicit reference to geographic or product competition, but simply defines the relevant market in terms of the "involved traffic or movement." 49 C.F.R., section 1109.1(g)(1). However, the commission discussed the issues of geographic and product competition at length in its interim report and left no doubt that these types of competition would not be considered. Although the railroads, DOJ, DOT, and the FTC urged the ICC to reconsider its position in their comments on the interim report, the agency's final report contains no further discussion of the issue.

in its interim report that such competition "could have an impact upon the ability of rail carriers to raise their rates."[23] Instead, the commission's decision was based upon its interpretation of section 202 of the 4R Act as precluding consideration of geographic and product competition and its concern that consideration of such factors would be difficult. As we will demonstrate, neither the wording of section 202 nor the complexity of the analysis required justified the total exclusion of evidence of geographic and product competition.

Section 202 defines market dominance as an absence of effective competition for "the traffic or movement to which a rate applies." The ICC observed that the words "movement" and "traffic" have a special meaning in the transportation industry,[24] and the commission reasoned that Congress' use of those words was meant to foreclose consideration of substitute routes or commodities. However, even accepting as accurate the ICC's interpretation of the words "movement" and "traffic," it simply does not follow that alternative routes and commodities become irrelevant. If a shipper faced with an increase in rail rates diverts its traffic to an alternative route or substitutes an alternative commodity, the proponent railroad will have lost the "traffic or movement to which [the] rate applies." It is therefore clear that, within the meaning of section 202, alternative routes and products may provide "effective competition" for the "traffic or movement to which [the] rate applies." The construction of section 202 adopted by the ICC is patently erroneous and represents the kind

---

[23] In the past, the ICC has frequently recognized the competitive force of alternative routes and commodities. See, for example, Increased Freight Rates and Charges, 1975, Nationwide, 349 I.C.C. 555, 613 (1975) (raw cane sugar and sugar beets are competitive commodities); grain to, from and within Southern Territory, 340 I.C.C. 846, 852 (1972) competition from wheat flour originating in one territory compelled reduction in rail rates on wheat flour originating in another territory); grain by Rent-a-Train, 339 I.C.C. 579, 590 (1971) (rail versus water competition on grain moving from different origins to the same ports); and Pennsylvania R.R. Co.—merger—New York Central R.R. Co., 327 I.C.C. 475, 515 (1966) (substitutability of oil for coal resulting in reduced rail rates on coal).

In its interim report, the commission sought to distinguish its prior decisions on the ground that, while geographic competition might be relevant where a merger is involved, its impact is generally not immediate enough to warrant consideration in a rate case. However, of the above-cited ICC decisions, only Pennsylvania R.R. involved a merger; each of the remaining cases involved a rate change.

[24] The commission stated in its interim report: "When used in this context in the transportation industry, the word 'movement' refers to transportation from a single origin point to a single destination point, while the word 'traffic' commonly denotes transportation services from a named set of points to another point or set of points; from specific origin points or areas to rate groups or blanket areas; or between stated mileage brackets on particular commodities in a given territory."

of "narrow [and] protectionist attitude" in interpreting the 4R Act which Congress warned against.

Likewise, the commission's fear that consideration of the substitutability of routes and products might at times become complex does not justify refusing to consider those factors even on rebuttal. Cases decided under the antitrust laws establish that proper definition of the relevant market is a prerequisite to meaningful analysis based on market shares, and that such a definition entails issues of substitutability of products and/or services as well as of the geographic area of competition.[25] Once the ICC decided to utilize market share analysis as a test for market dominance, it was obligated to use the analytical tool in a rational manner. As it happens, transportation is an industry in which the presence or absence of effective competition will at times depend not only upon the availability of alternative carriers or modes between two given points but also upon the availability of transportation to or from other points and the substitutability of alternative products. Although consideration of these factors may be difficult in some cases, the refusal to consider them in *any* case renders analytically unsound and patently irrational a test based on market share. Yet, this is precisely what the commission has done in prohibiting consideration, even on rebuttal, of product and geographic competition.

In any event, we believe that the ICC overstates the case when it suggests in its interim report that determining the impact of geographic and product competition in a typical market dominance proceeding "would require lengthy anti-trust type litigation." In many cases the significance or insignificance of alternative routes and products will be readily discernible. Even in the more difficult cases, a level of analysis that falls considerably short of "anti-trust type litigation" would be consistent with the intent of the 4R Act that the market dominance determination be made "without administrative delay."[26]

Finally, our disagreement with the ICC's refusal to consider geographic and product competition in *any* case should not be construed as suggesting that the relevant market should always include arguably substitutable routes and products. In particular cases, evidence offered by the proponent railroad(s) to rebut a presumption of market dominance based on market share may fail to establish that

---

[25] See, for example, United States v. Continental Can Co., 378 U.S. 441, 456–57 (1964); Brown Shoe Co. v. United States, 370 U.S. 294, 324 (1961); United States v. Dupont & Co., 351 U.S. 377, 395–400 (1956).
[26] 4R Act, section 202(b).

alternate routes and/or products provide effective competition. The ICC's error lies in arbitrarily refusing even to consider such evidence.

Insubstantial Market Share. The ICC erred in failing to adopt a rebuttable presumption that market dominance does *not* exist when the proponent railroad's market share is insubstantial.

Pursuant to the direction of Congress to develop standards and procedures for determining "whether and when" market dominance exists, the ICC formulated three major presumptions—each of which is a presumption that market dominance exists. Before the commission, the railroads and the government parties repeatedly recommended adoption of a counterpresumption that effective competition exists where the market share of the proponent railroad(s) is below a certain level. The ICC's unexplained refusal to adopt such a presumption constitutes a significant error warranting reversal by the court.[27]

There are a number of sound reasons why a counterpresumption based on market share should have been adopted. First, the very considerations that justify the use of market share analysis to identify those cases in which market dominance is likely to exist—namely, the need for a prompt resolution of the issue without extensive litigation—support the use of the same technique for identifying those cases in which market dominance is *not* likely to exist. Conversely, no public policy consideration militates against utilizing a reliable analytical tool such as market share to the fullest extent possible. There is nothing in the 4R Act that mandates adoption of only presumptions that market dominance exists. On the contrary, section 202 directs the commission to formulate rules for determining "whether and when" a railroad possesses market dominance in order to avoid unnecessary administrative hearings. The adoption of a presumption that market dominance does not exist where the railroad possesses less than a specified market share would foster that congressional goal. Moreover, adoption of such a counterpresumption was especially appropriate in light of the substantial evidence introduced before the commission by DOJ and DOT indicating that effective competition characterizes most modern transportation markets.[28] Finally, a counterpresumption of effective competition based on the

[27] On its face, the ICC's failure to adopt *any* presumptions designed to identify situations in which market dominance is unlikely to exist raises serious questions about the evenhandedness of the agency's approach.
[28] See, for example, the paper by Norman H. Jones, Jr., which is included in this volume as Chapter 13. Jones's verified statement was included in the evidence submitted before the ICC by the Department of Transportation.

railroad's insubstantial market share would not operate to the detriment of shippers because, like the 70 percent presumption adopted by the commission, the counterpresumption could be rebutted in appropriate cases.

Although an administrative agency is not generally required to adopt every measure which the logic of its policy would dictate, an agency's failure to adopt certain measures may be arbitrary and capricious when that failure is inconsistent with either the logic of the agency's policy or the intent of the underlying statute. Here, the ICC's failure to adopt some form of counterpresumption based on market share is inconsistent with both the intent of the 4R Act and the ICC's own reasoning in adopting the 70 percent market share presumption.[29]

At the very least, the ICC had an obligation to explain why a counterpresumption based upon an insubstantial market share should not be adopted. Throughout the administrative proceeding, the railroads and the government parties vigorously asserted the need for some kind of market share presumption that market dominance did not exist. At no time, however, did the commission confront the issue and explain why a counterpresumption was unwarranted or unnecessary. Moreover, the commission made statements which tacitly acknowledged the validity of a counterpresumption where the share of the proponent railroad(s) falls somewhere below 70 percent.[30] The obligation of an agency to explain the basis for its decision and to address the substantial issues raised by the parties is well established.[31] The need for a counterpresumption based on insubstantial market share represents the kind of "significant point" to which an

---

[29] The precise level at which such a counterpresumption should be established is an issue the court need not confront, but which the ICC should consider on remand. The railroads assert that, whenever the proponent railroad(s) controls less than 70 percent of the market, a presumption of effective competition should result. On the other hand, the FTC properly observes that, although rail market dominance may not *necessarily* exist at levels below 70 percent, it nevertheless could exist.

[30] Thus, in the interim report the ICC conceded that "if competitors [of the railroad(s)] are already handling 30 percent or more of the traffic, the competitive service is very likely to be a commercially possible alternative." In the same report, the ICC stated: "Where existing for-hire carriers [other than the proponent railroad(s)] already handle 30 percent of the traffic, we assume they would ordinarily be in a position to handle more should the traffic be diverted by higher rail rates."

[31] See Citizens to Preserve Overton Park v. Volpe, 401 U.S. 402, 416 (1971); Home Box Office, Inc. v. Federal Communications Commission, No. 75-1280 et al., U.S. Court of Appeals for the District of Columbia Circuit, March 25, 1977; Portland Cement Ass'n. v. Ruckelshaus, 486 F.2d 375, 393–94 (D.C. Cir. 1973).

agency is obligated to respond.[32] This is especially true where the point is advanced by another government agency whose views the ICC was directed by section 202 of the 4R Act to "solicit and consider." Thus, the ICC's complete failure to address this point is an error of law warranting remand.

Cost Presumption. The ICC's cost presumption is invalid both because it is based on a concededly unreliable accounting system and because the commission failed to articulate a reasoned basis for the choice it made.

The ability to earn supernormal profits is generally a valid indicator of market power. With this principle in mind, the ICC, after first using a figure of 195 percent and then 180 percent, ultimately adopted a presumption that market dominance exists whenever a railroad's rate equals 160 percent of the variable costs of providing the service. However, the variable costs presumption formulated by the commission is seriously defective in several important respects and will not succeed in identifying those situations where a rail carrier is earning supernormal profits.

First, the presumption is premised on a grossly distorted system of accounting which will not yield the accurate cost data that are absolutely essential for any reasoned presumption based on costs. Congress recognized that the ICC's antiquated accounting system underestimates actual costs[33] and consequently directed the commission in section 307 of the 4R Act to revise its uniform system of accounts before June 30, 1977. The commission itself acknowledged in the interim report that the present accounting system is "imperfect." Until the commission has completed the congressionally mandated revision of its accounting system, there can be no rationally supported presumption based on variable costs.

---

[32] Home Box Office, Inc. v. Federal Communications Commission, slip opinion, p. 50.
[33] The House Committee on Interstate and Foreign Commerce described the ICC's present accounting system for railroads in the following terms: "The rail uniform system of accounts was originally prescribed by the Commission in 1907. It has undergone no comprehensive revision since its inception. Although there have been many changes in the intervening years in the state of the art of accounting, including modern computer techniques, and in the rail industry operations and requirements, the Commission's accounting requirements have been changed only in detail and not in substance, technique or purpose. Consequently, they are outmoded and inadequate. The Commission's system of accounts is structurally deficient; it does not yield relevant cost information for evaluation whether rates are just and reasonable. The operating expense accounts do not yield adequate cost information for evaluating cost of service." U.S. Congress, House, Committee on Interstate and Foreign Commerce, H. Rept. 725, p. 63.

Even assuming, for the sake of argument, that a rational cost presumption could be established in the absence of reliable cost data, the commission failed to offer data, calculations, or analyses to justify its selection of the 160 percent level at which the presumption is triggered.[34] The full extent of the ICC's explanation is contained in a supplemental order issued on February 22, 1977, nearly five months after the agency's final report was released:

> *It further appearing,* That railroad fully allocated costs generally approximate 129 percent of variable cost, that a rate which exceeds 160 percent of variable cost generally will not only cover fully allocated cost, but will also cover non-cost items (such as Federal income tax), as well as a reasonable rate of return (as determined by the Coordinator in *Ex Parte 271, Net Investment—Railroad Rate Base and Rate of Return,* 345 I.C.C. 1494, 1605 (1976)), and that such rate will additionally provide a premium not related to or caused by the above factors; that such a premium above costs, expenditures, and a reasonable rate of return is indicative of a market dominant position in most instances; and that evidence may be presented in any case to show that market dominance does not exist, including a showing that special circumstances pertaining to the traffic or movement in issue exist such that the rate level does not include a premium attributable to a market dominant position.

It is not the court's function to determine whether 160 percent or some other figure would provide the most accurate approximation of when a presumption of market dominance is justified. That is the ICC's function. However, if judicial review of this type of rule making is to have any meaning, the court has every right to insist upon some reasonable explanation of why the agency concluded as it did. In this proceeding, the commission reached three different conclusions—195 percent, 180 percent, and finally 160 percent—as the number indicating market dominance. Yet, not only has the commission failed to give the court any information which would enable it to assess the reasonableness of each of the agency's conclusions, but it has also failed to explain why it repeatedly changed its conclusions. In failing to do so, it failed in its obligation to provide "a concise general statement of [the] basis" for its rule.[35]

---

[34] Neither was an adequate explanation provided for the commission's selection of higher trigger levels in its initial report (195 percent of variable costs) and its interim report (180 percent of variable costs). The ICC twice reduced the threshold level of its cost presumption without explanation.

[35] See 5 U.S.C., sections 553(b) and (c); Portland Cement Ass'n. v. Ruckelshaus, pp. 393–94; Kennecott Copper Corp. v. Environmental Protection Agency, 462 F.2d 846, 849 (1972).

Equipment Investment Presumption. The equipment investment presumption is inconsistent with section 206 of the 4R Act and, in any event, is impermissively vague.

The third major provision of the ICC's rules provides that a presumption of market dominance will arise "where affected shippers or consignees have made a substantial investment in rail-related equipment or facilities which prevents or makes impractical the use of another carrier or mode." It is true that railroads, in certain narrow circumstances, could exercise short-term market dominance where shippers transporting a preponderance of the freight moving in a particular market have made substantial investments in equipment and facilities that may not be easily liquidated. However, as with the presumptions about market share and excess profits, the ICC has seized upon a factor which concededly has some relevance to the issue of market dominance and transformed it into a presumption which will not be a reliable indicator of market dominance and will frustrate the purposes of the 4R Act.

The problems with the equipment investment presumption are essentially twofold. First, insofar as it applies to future investments of $1 million or more, it injects the ICC's regulation of maximum rates into an area where Congress has already provided shippers with a different form of protection. Second, the equipment investment presumption, as a whole, is without a rational basis because it is so needlessly vague as to encompass cases where no presumption of market dominance is warranted.

Section 206 of the 4R Act adds a new section to the Interstate Commerce Act designed to encourage future investments in rail-related equipment of $1 million or more and to protect any shipper making such an investment.[36] Where a proposed service will require a total capital investment of $1 million or more, the shipper and railroad making the investment may agree upon a rate schedule applicable for a five-year period and may file the negotiated schedule with the commission on 180 days' notice. Once it becomes effective, the agreed-upon rate may not be set aside as unlawful under sections 1, 2, 3, or 4 of the Interstate Commerce Act for the duration of the five-year period. The commission may, however, adjust the rate if it should at any time be exceeded by the variable costs of the movement.[37]

---

[36] 49 U.S.C., section 15(19).

[37] As originally enacted as part of the 4R Act, the new section 15(19) referred only to sections 2, 3, and 4 of the Interstate Commerce Act; reference to section 1 was apparently omitted inadvertently. The reference to section 1 was added to section 15(19) by a technical amendment contained in P.L. 94-555.

In enacting section 206 Congress provided a means whereby shippers that propose to make substantial investments in rail equipment may protect themselves from excessively high rate increases by entering into long-term rate agreements with rail carriers. The clear intent of that section is that carriers and shippers will negotiate a rate through arm's-length bargaining, that they will enter into a long-term agreement with respect to that rate, and that the agreement will protect both parties. If the rail carrier and the shipper fail to reach agreement on a rate schedule and the market is competitive, the shipper can elect not to make the investment and turn to other rail carriers or modes of transport. If the market is not competitive and no other transport alternatives are available, then market dominance would be attributed to the rail carrier under the market share presumption and the rate would continue to be subject to regulation. For these reasons, application of the ICC's equipment investment presumption to future investments of $1 million or more is unnecessary and will only serve to upset the competitive balance struck by Congress under section 206.

In any event, the ICC's investment presumption is so vague as to be irrational. Although in certain narrow circumstances shippers that have invested heavily in rail-related equipment might not be in a position to utilize the available services of other modes of transportation, the presumption as formulated by the commission needlessly fails to focus on those narrow circumstances.

For example, the commission refused to exclude depreciated, marketable, and convertible equipment from consideration at the presumption stage, even though such investments do not limit a shipper's ability to switch modes. The railroads, DOJ, and DOT argued that railcars owned by shippers should not be included under the presumption because such equipment is readily marketable. The ICC acknowledged the validity of that argument in its final report, stating: "Certainly the marketability of the equipment or facilities is an important factor in determining whether use of the services of another mode would be impossible or highly impractical." Nevertheless, the commission expressly stated in that same report that the presumption "would include . . . railcars."

Additionally, the commission's decision gives no intelligible meaning to the term "substantial investment," as used in the presumption. Thus, the ICC *apparently* recognized that the absolute size of an investment is not controlling and that an investment should only be considered substantial if it represents a large portion of the total rail cost incurred by the shipper at the time of the investment; however, the presumption as adopted does not so provide. Similarly, the commission *apparently* recognized that shippers which have made investments can be threatened by an excessive rail rate increase only if those shippers are moving a preponderance of the traffic;[38] however, the agency stated in both its interim and its final reports that a showing that the investments relate to a preponderance of the traffic is *not* a necessary element of the presumption and left it to the railroads to show the contrary.

In short, the ICC's equipment investment presumption will enable shippers to "establish" the existence of market dominance through reliance on virtually any type of investment. The presumption will place upon the railroads the burden of showing that individual investments are not truly substantial and have no bearing on the issue of market dominance. The commission's investment presumption does not provide the kind of intelligible standards essential to avoid arbitrary results in particular cases,[39] and will invite protests from shippers that should have little or no chance of ultimately prevailing on the merits. Congress directed the commission to design rules which would "provide for a practical determination without administrative delay."[40] This presumption fails to meet that standard.

Discussion of a Rate by Rate Bureau Members. The ICC properly ruled that discussion of a rate by railroad members of a rate bureau, standing alone, provides no basis for presuming that market dominance exists.

The very first presumption proposed by the ICC in its notice of proposed rule making provided that market dominance would be presumed to exist whenever the rate in issue had been discussed or considered before a rail carrier rate bureau. That proposal was severely criticized by the railroads and the government parties on the ground that it failed to take into account "effective competition from other . . . modes of transportation" and therefore was patently in conflict with the dictates of section 202. The ICC recognized its error and wisely revised its rules to provide that rate bureau discussions provide a basis for presuming only that the participating railroads do not compete with each other. The ICC put it quite clearly

---

[38] This is so because section 2 of the Interstate Commerce Act makes it unlawful for a railroad to apply selective increases to the traffic of particular shippers in the same market. Thus, if only one small shipper in a particular market has made a "substantial" investment, that shipper is nevertheless protected by the ability of the remaining shippers to divert their traffic to other modes of transportation.
[39] See Amalgamated Meat Cutters v. Connally, 377 F. Supp. 737 (D.D.C. 1971).
[40] 4R Act, section 202(b).

in its final report: "We state emphatically that rate bureau activity does not lead to a presumption of market dominance, per se."

Petitioners in *Commonwealth Edison* v. *Interstate Commerce Commission* now claim that the ICC erred in so limiting the rate bureau presumption, but that contention is wholly lacking in merit. The thrust of their presentation is that, when two or more railroads conspire to fix a rate, the rate is not set by the "forces of competition." Although this is quite true, it provides no reliable indication whether "effective competition" for the traffic subject to that rail rate is presented by other . . . modes of transportation."[41]

Congress clearly intended to relieve the railroads of ICC regulation of maximum rates in *all* cases where "effective competition" from other modes exist, notwithstanding the fact that in certain of those cases the railroads may not effectively compete with each other. Moreover, the evidence introduced before the commission confirmed Congress' belief that other modes of transportation effectively compete with railroads in most cases. Accordingly, a presumption of market dominance based solely on rate bureau activity would plainly be inconsistent with both the statute and the evidence. The ICC's limited presumption about rate bureaus should therefore be affirmed.

Conclusion

For the above reasons, the ICC's presumptions about market share, variable costs, and equipment investment should be reversed and remanded. The commission should be directed either to adopt a counterpresumption based on market share or to explain its refusal to adopt such a presumption. The ICC's limited rate bureau presumption about rate bureau activity should be affirmed.

---

[41]Ibid., section 202.

Cover and book design: Pat Taylor